D0077145

WILLIAM CAVENDISH
FOURTH DUKE OF DEVONSHIRE
MEMORANDA ON STATE
OF AFFAIRS
1759–1762

THE DEVONSHIRE DIARY

WILLAM CAVENDISH
FOURTH DUKE OF DEVONSHIRE
MEMORANDA ON STATE
OF AFFAIRS
1759–1762

edited by

PETER D. BROWN and KARL W. SCHWEIZER.

CAMDEN FOURTH SERIES
VOLUME 27

LONDON
OFFICES OF THE ROYAL HISTORICAL SOCIETY
UNIVERSITY COLLEGE LONDON,
GOWER STREET, WC1
1982

© Royal Historical Society

ISBN: 0 86193 097 5

Printed in Great Britain by Butler & Tanner Ltd
Frome and London

CONTENTS

PREFACE

Our first obligation is towards His Grace the Duke of Devonshire P.C. and the Trustees of the Chatsworth Settlement for permission to publish the text of the political diaries of the 4th Duke of Devonshire.

We have been greatly assisted by the most willing help and interest from the late Lieut-Col. T. S. 'Tom' Wragg M.B.E., as Keeper of the Chatsworth Collections. Our great regret is that he did not live to see this publication. We also thank Mr. Peter Day, the present Keeper of the Chatsworth Collections, for his unfailingly kind co-operation.

Our thanks are due to H.R.H. the Duke of Brunswick-Lüneburg, the Duke of Bedford and the Marquis of Bute for permission to study their archives.

We are grateful to Mr. John Brooke, Professor Ian Christie and the late Sir Herbert Butterfield for encouragement and advice.

We have been greatly assisted by Miss C. Draper, the Librarian at Woburn Abbey, Miss Catherine Armet, the Librarian at Mount Stuart, Professor W. Mediger of the University of Hanover, and Miss S. P. Anderson, Assistant Keeper, Royal Commission on Hist. MSS.

Our obligations are also due to the Inter-University Centre of European studies, Montreal, the Canada Council and Bishop's University, Lennoxville, in respect of financial assistance for research.

We are also obliged to the staff of the MSS. room and Reading room of the British Library, the Public Record Office, the Central Library of Cardiff, the Institute of Historical Research, London, Clements Library, Ann Arbor, Michigan, the Huntington Library, California, the Hampshire Record Office, Deutsches Zentral-Archiv, Merseburg, and the Libraries of Balliol College, Oxford and Peterhouse, Cambridge.

Finally in many ways our greatest debt is to Mrs. Margaret Harrison, who has patiently typed and indeed retyped the MSS., and for her intelligent hints and suggestions.

PETER BROWN
KARL SCHWEIZER.

ABBREVIATIONS

Place of publication London unless otherwise stated

Add. MSS.	Additional Manuscripts in the British Library
Bedford	*Correspondence of John, fourth Duke of Bedford*, ed. Lord John Russell, 3 Vols. (1842–6)
Bedford MSS.	Bedford Estate Office, London
Bute MSS.	Bute Manuscripts, Mount Stuart, Isle of Bute
Bute MSS. (Cardiff)	Bute Manuscripts, Cardiff Public Library
Chatham	*Correspondence of William Pitt, Earl of Chatham*, ed. W. S. Taylor and J. H. Pringle, 4 Vols. (1834–40)
Chatsworth MSS.	Papers of the Duke of Devonshire at Chatsworth, Derbyshire
D.Z.A.	Deutsches Zentral-Archiv, Merseburg, Germany
Eg. MSS.	Egerton Manscripts, British Library
Elliot	G. F. S. Elliot, *The Border Elliots* (Edinburgh, 1897)
E.H.R.	*English Historical Review*
Grenville	*The Grenville Papers; being the Correspondence of Richard Grenville Earl Temple ...*, ed. W. J. Smith, 4 Vols. (1852–3)
Namier	L. B. Namier, *England in the Age of the American Revolution* (1930)
Namier and Brooke	L. B. Namier and J. Brooke, *The History of Parliament. The House of Commons, 1754–1790*, 3 Vols. (1964)
P.R.O.	Public Record Office (Gifts and Deposits)
Sedgwick	*Letters from George III to Lord Bute, 1756–1766*, ed. R. Sedgwick (1939)
Shelburne MSS.	Shelburne Manuscripts, Clements Library, Ann Arbor, Michigan
S.P.	State Papers, Public Record Office
S.P.F.	State Papers Foreign, Public Record Office
Stanley MSS.	Stanley Manuscripts, Hampshire Record Office
Stowe MSS.	Stowe Manuscripts, Huntington Library, San Marino, California
Thackeray	F. Thackeray, *A History of the Right Honorable William Pitt Earl of Chatham*, 2 Vols. (1827)

T.S.   Treasury Solicitor, Public Record Office
Yorke   P. C. Yorke, *The Life and Correspondence of Philip Yorke, Earl of Hardwicke* ..., 3 Vols. (Cambridge, 1913)

INTRODUCTION

William Cavendish 4th Duke of Devonshire entered this world with the certainty, subject to his living to come of age, of every appurtenance of greatness. Exalted station and great wealth apart, his family was a principal buttress of the Whig establishment of the early Georges because they had helped place 'the present family', the House of Hanover, upon the throne of Great Britain. Fortunately, the chronicle of this Devonshire is not merely that of a great nobleman, moving with an unconscious ease between his country mansions, and thence to his town house, from where he might intrigue about the Court or sit idly in the House of Lords. A natural balance of judgement, prudence, patriotism, and above all a sense of service without self-seeking, were by common acclaim his characteristics. These qualities led Devonshire to appear briefly as Prime Minister from November 1756 until July 1757, to which he in no way aspired but undertook in the course of a crisis in time of war.

Devonshire was born *c.* 1720: it is remarkable that the year of his birth should be uncertain. His father, at that time Marquis of Hartington, was destined to succeed as 3rd Duke on June 4 1729. His mother was not of a great house. She was Catherine, daughter and heir of John Hoskins of Oxted, Surrey, steward to the Duke of Bedford. Hartington's mother, wife of the 2nd Duke of Devonshire, was Rachel, daughter of the Lord Russell who was beheaded in 1683, and granddaughter of the 1st Duke of Bedford. Evidently Hartington, on some visit to his mother's family, fell in love with Catherine Hoskins and made up his mind to marry her. The match must have occasioned surprise though there is no evidence of family opposition.

Like many a noble family down the ages, the Cavendishes owed their emergence from yeoman obscurity to the powerful ambition of a clever lawyer. Sir John Cavendish was Chief Justice of the King's Bench in 1366, 1373 and 1377 during the final years of Edward III. The proceeds of his career were devoted to the purchase of land at Cavendish Overhall in Suffolk, the small wool town from which no doubt the family derived their surname. He became associated with the enforcement of the Statute of Labourers in East Anglia. In the course of the Peasants' Revolt Cavendish, together with the Prior of Bury St. Edmunds, was beheaded by the mob. Thereafter the family lived quietly on their Suffolk estates for over a century.

Under the very different conditions of the early Tudors the brothers George and William Cavendish found opportunity for advancement. George was a chief secretary to Wolsey and because of the influence of his *Life* of the Cardinal, definitively published in 1814, became a founder of modern biography. The brother William, born *c.* 1505, was far more business man than scholar. A career on the administrative side of the court of Henry VIII led him to the Treasurership of the Chamber. He was a principal assistant to Thomas Cromwell in the destruction of the monasteries, and received a handsome share of the spoils in the south-eastern counties. Cavendish's near and more distinguished contemporary John Russell 1st Earl of Bedford, in the course of activities more martial than courtly, also accumulated vast estates from the monastic dissolutions.

William Cavendish continued as Treasurer of the Chamber to Edward VI. In 1549, having no children by his first two marriages, Cavendish espoused a great heiress much younger than he, Elizabeth, daughter of John Hardwick, of Hardwick co. Derby. Already she had been satisfactorily widowed by the wealthy Derbyshire squire Robert Barlow, of Barlow. She persuaded Cavendish to concentrate his interests in Derbyshire, and also in Nottinghamshire where he acquired Welbeck Abbey. With the accession of Mary I Cavendish conformed to the Roman Communion and remained Treasurer of the Chamber, though like others of similar recantation he retained his former church lands. By the time of his death in 1557 Cavendish had begun the Elizabethan version of Chatsworth. This his widow completed, built a new house at Hardwick, and at Oldcotes, besides several other houses. A third marriage to Sir William St. Loe yielded 'Bess of Hardwick' still greater riches by widowhood.

Her fourth espousal, to the 6th Earl of Shrewsbury in 1568, introduced the Cavendish family into the ancient aristocracy. Queen Elizabeth I gave her approval to the extraordinary arrangement, by which, on the day of her contract with Shrewsbury, her son Henry Cavendish married Shrewbury's daughter Lady Grace Talbot, whilst her third daughter Mary married Shrewsbury's heir, later the 7th Earl. Henry did not live to found a family but Mary's daughter in time would marry the Earl of Arundel and become ancestress to the present line of the Dukes of Norfolk. 'Bess of Hardwick's' eldest daughter Frances married Sir Henry Pierrepont and was ancestress to the Earls and Dukes of Kingston, whilst her next sister Elizabeth married the 5th Earl of Lennox, younger brother to the foolish Lord Darnley, and was mother to the unhappy Arabella Stuart.

Shrewsbury was for a time custodian of Mary Queen of Scots, who spent some years at Chatsworth. His relations with his wife ran into the disagreements of the utmost rancour accompanied by financial disputes. At her death on February 13 1607 'Bess of Hardwick', who had no children by her other husbands, bequeathed all her property to her two surviving sons, William and Charles. Through them she became the direct ancestress of two ducal houses, of Newcastle and Devonshire.

William Cavendish inherited Chatsworth and Hardwick. He was created Baron Cavendish of Hardwick in 1605, Earl of Devonshire in 1618. The family neither then nor subsequently has owned one acre of land in Devon: the county designation was of no importance and the title the consideration. Devonshire's son and successor the 2nd Earl was notable merely for his extravagant way of life. His son the 3rd Earl of Devonshire (1617–84), a zealous supporter of Charles I, was forced into exile and on his return in 1646 compounded for his estates. At the Restoration he was appointed Lord Lieutenant of Derbyshire and spent the remainder of his life in favour at Court. His real importance lay in his patronage of Thomas Hobbes.

The line of the younger of 'Bess of Hardwick's' sons, Charles Cavendish, was for a time the more important. He inherited Welbeck and married the heiress of the Barons Ogle of Bothal Castle, Northumberland. Their son William (1592–1676), a great magnifico in every way, one of the most generous and gallant supporters of Charles I in the Civil War, was created successively Earl, Marquis, and after the Restoration, Duke of Newcastle. His son the 2nd Duke of Newcastle died in 1691 without a male heir. Through a series of female descents the estates passed to Thomas Pelham-Holles, the great eighteenth-century Duke of Newcastle, and William Henry Cavendish-Bentinck, 3rd Duke of Portland.

It was William the 4th Earl of Devonshire who founded the political greatness of his branch of the Cavendish family. Unlike his predecessors, he was no courtier and as M.P. for Derby strongly advocated the exclusion of the Roman Catholic Duke of York from the throne. Shortly after his accession James II had him fined £30,000, with his ruin the object. Devonshire from his exile at Chatsworth watched the King make one mistake after another, and in 1688 was one of the Seven who signed the invitation to William of Orange to come and take the Crown. He was therefore rewarded with the Lord Lieutenancy of Derbyshire. In 1694 he was promoted as Duke of Devonshire and Marquis of Hartington in the creation which included the dukedom of Bedford. He was associated with the Act of Settlement of 1701, which entailed the throne upon the House of Hanover. He employed Talman to build a new house at Chatsworth, the home known to his great-grandson the 4th Duke.

The 2nd Duke of Devonshire, who succeeded in 1707, continued his father's espousal of Whig causes. With the Tory victory at the general election of 1710 he was dismissed from the Lord Stewardship of the Household and the Lord Lieutenancy of Derbyshire. The peaceful succession of George I saw him restored to both offices.

Subsequently he became the Lord President of the Council in the administration of Sir Robert Walpole. The Cavendish family was established with the new dynasty and from 1714 until 1764 the Lord Lieutenancy of Derbyshire was held by the Dukes of Devonshire without a break.

His son the 3rd Duke was regarded by Walpole as one of his most loyal adherents, and here was an administration Devonshire could never have been tempted to abandon. His kinsman Newcastle was a Secretary of State, and that nobleman's younger brother, Henry Pelham, Walpole's lieutenant in the management of the House of Commons. Devonshire served as Lord Privy Seal, 1731–3, Lord Steward of the Household, 1733–7, and Lord Lieutenant of Ireland from 1737, a position he retained for the exceptionally long period of seven years. It was in 1737 that Philip Yorke, the Dover attorney's son, became Lord Chancellor as Lord Hardwicke, and soon he was a mainstay of the ministry and closest confidant of Newcastle.

Shortly after his coming of age, Hartington, the future 4th Duke, entered the House of Commons in 1741 under auspices beyond cavil as a knight for the shire for Derbyshire. Horace Walpole somewhat ungenerously remarked: 'Lord Hartington and his father before him were the fashionable models of goodness, though their chief merit was a habit of ·caution. The Duke outside was unpolished; his inside was unpolishable.' Hartington did his best to rally support for Walpole, whose resignation in February 1742 under the impact of failure in the War of the Austrian Succession he could not have done anything to prevent. That November at the opening of Parliament Hartington, on Pelham's suggestion, moved the loyal Address of the House of Commons. After some confusion it was Pelham who emerged in 1743 as Walpole's ultimate successor as First Lord of the Treasury. George II would have preferred a complaisant administration and it was Hardwicke who in 1746 made a reluctant King recognize that no Prime Minister other than Pelham could lead the House of Commons. One of the conditions was that William Pitt become Paymaster-General. Hartington had had dealings with Pitt and judged him 'difficult' and 'impractical'. Hartington's kinsman, the Duke of Bedford, very much an aspiring politician, resented the promotion of 'the Orator and his junto'.

On March 27 1748 Hartington married Lady Charlotte Elizabeth Boyle, daughter and heir of the 3rd Earl of Burlington, the great exponent of palladian architecture. She had been born on November 24 1731 and this alliance had been arranged during her childhood. Lady Charlotte was, in her own right, Baroness de Clifford, 6th in line, a peerage created in 1628 by a writ issued in error to her ancestor Henry de Clifford, subsequently 5th Earl of Cumberland. In 1664 his

only child had married the 1st Earl of Burlington. Hartington's
mother, whose marriage had been much of the romantic order, was so
upset by her son's espousal that she separated from the Duke for some
years. However Lady Mary Montagu wrote of Hartington: 'I do not
know any man so fitted to make a wife happy: with so great a vocation
for matrimony, that I verily believe if it had not been established
before his time, he would have had the glory of the invention.'

The political importance of the Devonshire family was immeasurably enhanced. Hitherto, though by far the largest landowners in
Derbyshire, their estates had been confined to the Midlands. The
Burlington marriage brought Bolton Abbey and Londesborough with
a very great Yorkshire landholding, including the right to return two
members of the House of Commons for Knaresborough. There was
also property in London and Chiswick House in Middlesex. In Ireland
Lismore Castle, co. Waterford, with the right to return one member
to the Dublin House of Commons for Lismore town, and one of the
largest acreages in that kingdom, also passed to the Cavendishes.

Because of the acrimonious disputes between Pelham and Newcastle
over foreign policy, Devonshire withdrew from Court in 1749. But this
in no way constituted a check upon Hartington's progress. In 1751
Pelham had him appointed Master of the Horse, a very marked
distinction for the heir to a peerage, which necessitated his being
summoned to the House of Lords in his father's barony of Cavendish
on June 13. He was sworn a Privy Councillor on July 12. As knight of
the shire for Derbyshire, he was succeeded by this third brother Lord
Frederick Cavendish, whilst at the same time his second brother Lord
George Augustus entered the House of Commons as member for
Weymouth and Melcombe Regis.

The general expectation was that in the course of time Pelham's
successor would be Henry Fox, Secretary of War, one of Hartington's
closest friends. Fox rather than Pitt appeared to be the man of the
future. In addition to his intimate associations with the great aristo-
cratic houses, Fox enjoyed the approval of the Duke of Cumberland,
George II's favoured son and Commander-in-Chief. Though the in-
tegrity and abilities of Pitt were widely respected, he was vehemently
disliked by the King and the ambitions of his family connections,
notably the 2nd Earl Temple and George Grenville, were suspect. It
came as a great surprise that Fox should choose to incur the enmity of
the Lord Chancellor by his personally insulting opposition to Hardwicke's Marriage Act, one of the great reforms of an age disinclined to
change. When therefore Pelham died on March 6 1754, Fox had lost
all chance of Hardwicke pressing his claims.

The king looked for a disparate ministry which would turn to himself
for direction. Newcastle succeeded his brother at the Treasury, whilst

a career diplomat, Sir Thomas Robinson, became Secretary of State and was to lead the House of Commons. Pitt and Fox were left as they were to cool their heels, but that brilliant lawyer William Murray was promoted Attorney-General. The general election that summer was a triumph for Newcastle. Devonshire had the satisfaction of seeing his youngest brother John become a member of Parliament. The united opposition of Pitt and Fox prevented the inexperienced Robinson from leading the House of Commons effectively. Newcastle cajoled Fox with a seat in the Cabinet into giving his whole-hearted support, leaving Pitt in the lurch. Hartington, who had much disliked Fox ranging himself against administration, thought his capitulation prudent and proper.

On Christmas Eve 1754 Hartington suffered the tragedy of his life by the death of his wife, who was therefore never Duchess of Devonshire. She was buried with other members of the Cavendish family at All Saints, Derby. Hartington was left with the duty of bringing up their four children, William, born December 14 1748, who succeeded to his mother's barony of de Clifford, Dorothy, born August 27 1750, Richard, born June 19 1752, and George Augustus Henry, born March 21 1754.

In March 1755 Newcastle had Hartington appointed Lord Lieutenant of Ireland, again remarkable in that his father had been a fairly recent predecessor and that exalted position was not usually bestowed upon large Irish landowners. The circumstances were unprecedented in this period. The tranquility of Ireland over many years was resulting in prosperity and a hitherto unknown surplus on the Irish revenues. Consequently the Protestant legislators of Ireland began to show yearnings towards independence of Westminster. Hartington's Irish connections were expected to give a respectability to his putting the notables to order, whilst his unassailable position at home would leave no doubt as to a firmness of intention. A further aspect of Hartington's appointment was the imminence of war with France, which necessitated a united Irish administration. That April he became one of the Lord Justices of the realm during the King's annual absence in Hanover. The purpose on this occasion was not just a pleasurable sojourn but the negotiation of alliances with the German princes and Russia, against the expected alliance between Louis XV and Frederick II of Prussia.

The only opposition Newcastle had to fear in the House of Commons was from Pitt, who must be expected to speak out against a 'Hanover' policy based upon Continental subsidies. Pitt had recently offset his sense of isolation by reaching an understanding with the Earl of Bute, the mentor to the young Prince of Wales. They were glad to enlist the services of a clever, discontented politician who might one day help in their design of ousting Newcastle, of whose long influence over affairs they were jealous. None were surprised when on November 14 1755 Pitt divided the House of Commons over the issue of the subsidy treaties. He was defeated 311-105 and six days later he together with some placemen who had voted with him were dismissed.

The 3rd Duke of Devonshire died at the age of 57 on December 5 1755. All the loyalties of the new duke were towards Newcastle, his kinsman, 27 years older than himself and very much his political 'uncle'. No doubt he considered Pitt a good riddance and expected Newcastle to carry on perfectly well with the support of Fox and Murray. Devonshire's term in Ireland went off very well. By a series of new appointments, promotions and peerage creations he both intimidated and cajoled the dissidents, ending with the general satisfaction.

In May Devonshire returned home and found Newcastle in despair over Murray's decision to leave the House of Commons in order to become Lord Chief Justice of England as Lord Mansfield. On the Continent events took a completely unexpected turn with the coalition between the Empress Maria Theresa, Louis XV and Russia against Prussia, the object being the recovery of Silesia. When Frederick II took the offensive in Bohemia, he forced an unwilling George II into an alliance. The popular estimate of Newcastle's ability to wage war was shattered by the loss of Minorca on June 27 1756. When on October 15 Fox resigned rather than face a hostile Parliament, Newcastle had no alternative but to attempt to come to terms with Pitt.

To most men of sense the situation demanded that both Pitt and Fox serve in a composite ministry. But at this stage Pitt refused any accommodation with Newcastle or to enter a ministry which included Fox. It was however Pitt who suggested that Devonshire might prove a head of administration acceptable to himself and to the many members of both Houses jealous of their old loyalty to Newcastle. At the end of October Devonshire, 'sent for from Derbyshire', agreed with the King to take the Treasury but only until the end of the Session. Newcastle resigned on November 5 and Hardwicke decided to go with him.

Devonshire was appointed First Lord of the Treasury on November 6. By the middle of the month he and Pitt had their list of ministers ready, with Pitt Secretary of State for the South. On November 18 Devonshire was nominated a Knight of the Garter, always regarded as a mark of the Sovereign's favour. Parliament assembled on December 2 to hear the King's Speech and on the day following all the ministers kissed hands at Kensington. The Pitt and Devonshire ministry was never intended to form a lasting system. Devonshire was prompted by his duty to the King, which required that Parliament be confronted by a ministry capable of securing the services essential for the prosecution of the war, including the raising of loans in the City. He was appalled at Pitt's demands for places for his Grenville brothers-in-law and much disliked an arrangement which he always subsequently referred to as 'forcing the King's hand'.

Without the least malice towards Devonshire, the King early in March engaged in an intrigue with Fox, who set about drawing up lists of ministers. On March 23 Devonshire was installed K.G. at Windsor. Cumberland insisted upon the removal of Pitt and Temple as a condition of his taking up his command in Hanover, which was done in the first week of April. The King's design for a Fox ministry was however frustrated by the 'rain of gold boxes' for Pitt. On June 11 the ministers selected by Fox came to Kensington, only to be sent empty away when Mansfield told George II that a Fox ministry would never do. Between June 16 and 19 Hardwicke arranged the great ministry headed by Pitt as Secretary of State for the South, with Newcastle First Lord of the Treasury. Devonshire, who had no desire for effective office, became Lord Chamberlain but with a seat in the inner Cabinet.

During the autumn of 1757 the war continued to go badly. The expedition intended to take Louisbourg, the French fortress on Cape Breton Island at the mouth of the St. Lawrence, achieved nothing. Cumberland, defeated by the French, entered the Convention of Closterseven on September 8 1757, which left Hanover in enemy hands. There shortly followed the fiasco of the large and expensive expedition Pitt had sent against Rochefort. Pitt's only solace was that Cumberland was succeeded by Prince Ferdinand of Brunswick, in whom he had great confidence.

In the course of 1758 the political situation underwent an important shift in the coolness that arose in the minds of Bute and the Prince of Wales towards Pitt. He had sent a British reinforcement to Prince Ferdinand's army without consulting Bute's wishes. Their inability to comprehend the reasons behind Pitt's change of policy did not however in any way diminish their hostility to Newcastle. News of the capture of Louisbourg meant that at long last the war was going Pitt's way. That September Temple requested that he be made a Knight of the Garter. Newcastle, knowing how deeply George II disliked 'that fellow', pointed out that the next election was reserved for Prince Ferdinand of Brunswick. Temple talked of absenting himself from Court but a long letter from Pitt dissuaded him from so public a demonstration.

The *Annus Mirabilis* established Pitt as the darling of the nation. The object of Versailles was to end the war by an invasion of England:

a temporary occupation of even a southern county must cause a financial panic and bring down any administration. Then in June came news of the capture of Guadeloupe. On August 1 Prince Ferdinand beat the French army at Minden, a triumph marred by the disloyalty of Lord George Sackville. Later that month Admiral Edward Boscawen defeated the French Mediterranean fleet off Lagos in Portugal. News of Wolfe's expedition against Quebec was eagerly awaited.

Devonshire's Diary, in the meaning of a continuous record of events, begins in September 1759 with the renewal of Temple's application to be made a Knight of the Garter. News of the fall of Quebec, which reached London on October 16, enhanced immeasurably Pitt's position in the House of Commons and 'out-doors'. Devonshire grasped that no ministry without Pitt could be viable. When therefore Pitt on October 26 talked of resignation if Temple were not given the Garter, Devonshire decided that the King must be persuaded to get the thing done. The matter dragged through the autumn, with Temple staging a dramatic resignation, which however he soon retracted. At the end of January the King at last gave way and Temple, together with the Marquis of Rockingham and Prince Ferdinand, received the Garter on February 9.

The vindication of Pitt's policies did not restore a cordial relationship between him and Bute. To the contrary, the attempt by Bute and the Prince of Wales to champion the cause of Sackville deepened the rift. Devonshire recorded a talk he had on November 17 with an old crony of Newcastle, Count Viry, the Sardinian minister in London. Viry claimed that Bute had attempted to employ his services in seeking a reconcilation with Pitt. Viry declined and therefore Bute sent Gilbert Elliot, an old friend of him and Pitt, upon that errand but without success. Here Devonshire records an attempt at a rapprochement not previously known to historians.

The fall of Quebec opened the possibility of a satisfactory peace which Pitt talked of negotiating that winter. The King was bent upon 'Dédommagement', which was territorial compensation for the devastation of Hanover by the retreating French army in the spring of 1758. After Minden the French were in no condition to invade Hanover with a view to an exchange for Canada: delay left the chance that they might win a battle in the course of 1760. On November 22 the last danger of a French invasion of England was removed by the destruction of the French fleet in Quiberon Bay. Yet a complication was appearing from the views of the newly ascended King of Spain, Charles III, alarmed at the progress of British arms in North America.

One of the most important aspects of the Diaries lies in Devonshire's descriptions of Council meetings.[1] In law any Privy Councillor could be summoned but Devonshire's appearance as Lord Chamberlain was unusual and by no means the sole peculiarity. Hardwicke, holding no office at all, was regularly present. After his resignation in 1756 the Great Seal had been placed in commission with Sir Robert Henley as Lord Keeper, but although raised to the Privy Council he was not invited. Henley became Lord Chancellor as Lord Henley in January 1761, yet Devonshire does not record his appearance at a Council meeting until that of April 23. Thereafter both Hardwicke and Henley attended while the ministry remained in being.

The attendance of Ligonier, the Commander-in-Chief, and of Anson, First Lord of the Admiralty, was not constitutionally imperative but only to be expected in time of war. That Mansfield, the Lord Chief Justice, should be summoned was not customary and probably arranged by Newcastle to help counterbalance Pitt. The presence of Lord Granville, Lord President, and of Temple, Lord Privy Seal, was required. Newcastle the First Lord of the Treasury, was inevitably eclipsed by Pitt, the true man of war, whom however Devonshire always disliked. Indeed on one occasion he went so far as to inform George II of his resolve never to engage in a private conversation with Pitt.

The first Cabinet meeting recorded by Devonshire was that of December 10 1759, held either at the office or the house of the Earl of Holderness, Secretary of State for the North, to discuss the Memorial from M. d'Abreu, the Spanish Ambassador, expressing the desire of Charles III to mediate. Pitt's draft reply assuring the King of Spain of the British desire for peace, but on terms which would put it beyond the power of France to insult Britain again, was unanimously approved. Madrid was far from satisfied and an unsatisfactory series of talks resulted only in the formulation of 'the Spanish grievances'. The objection to the British exercise of a right of search on the high seas in time of war was of long standing. A claim to participate in the Newfoundland Fisheries was without prescriptive foundation. The objection to the cutting of logwood on the coast of Honduras further than the allowance by treaty had substance. Devonshire was always at a loss as to how these issues could possibly constitute a *casus belli*.

Devonshire's entries for 1760 until the death of the King in October were sparse. He did not record that in April Elliot once more approached Pitt on behalf of Bute. This time far more than a rapprochement was intended. The suggestion was that Pitt might support the

---

[1] Z. E. Rashed, *The Peace of Paris, 1763* (Liverpool, 1951), provides a full account of the evolution of British peace policy, 1759-62, but without benefit of various private manuscript collections not then available. The Diaries furnish interesting additional information about ministerial discussions.

appointment of Bute as First Lord of the Treasury in place of New-castle on the death of the present King. Much to the annoyance of the future George III, Pitt refused to consider the matter. Unlike the earlier episode, this has long been known to historians.

Devonshire was out of town when on the morning of Saturday October 25 George II was found dead by his *valet de chambre*. He was not present at the first Privy Council of the new reign held that afternoon. Bute had already told Newcastle of the King's wish that he continue at the Treasury. At seven o'clock that evening Bute saw Pitt and assured him that he had abandoned all thought of office. Pitt brusquely welcomed Bute's decision to remain 'a private man' and made clear that he would tolerate no interference in the management of the war.

Devonshire's account of events between October 1760 and May 1762 occupies the bulk of the Diaries and constitutes their main interest. The story falls into three distinct phases. The first covering the initial five months of the new reign, was of how Bute wriggled his way into becoming a Secretary of State. The second described the events leading up to Pitt's resignation of October 1761. The third was of Bute ousting Newcastle and attaining his ambition to become Premier.

Devonshire arrived in London on October 27. He first called on Cumberland and then attended the Privy Council at which Bute was sworn in. Newcastle had thought of retirement but Devonshire insisted that he had an absolute obligation to the country and the Whig party to carry on. From the outset the question of Bute's position was a prime difficulty. Devonshire felt certain he meant to be 'minister over them all', though incapable in point of intellect or temperament. Clearly Bute was to attend all Cabinet meetings, though merely Groom of the Stole. Devonshire, Newcastle and Hardwicke suspected that, on the eve of the King's accession, Pitt had struck a deal with Bute to help him oust Newcastle and take the Treasury. This tale may well have originated in the fertile imagination of Viry, who set himself the congenial task of acting as go-between. In the event Pitt advised Newcastle to carry on at the head of affairs and never showed the least inclination to favour the advancement of Bute.

Devonshire was bent upon holding the ministry together. He saw the necessity of keeping in combination Pitt, with his universal popu-larity, and Newcastle, with his hold upon the Whig party and the City. Devonshire grasped better than anyone that the King's emo-tional dependence upon Bute, though indeed tiresome, required sym-pathetic handling. Two issues were left over on the death of George II, a proposed expedition to take Belleisle and the establishment of a permanent militia, both dear to the heart of Pitt, and Bute was not disposed to thwart him. Pitt was gravely displeased at the reception awarded by the new Court to Sackville. The intrigue by the long discredited Earl of Bath to displace the highly respectable Earl of Powis as Lord Lieutenant of Shropshire was upsetting to Newcastle and Devonshire. Newcastle was disconcerted when on November 12 Viry told Devonshire of Bute's desire for a peerage of Great Britain, which was contrary to constitutional convention. Devonshire was not present at the Cabinet of November 13 which decided that the expedition against Belleisle might go ahead. Though Pitt constantly complained at being left out of things, Bute met his wishes over the appointment of Tories as Lords of the Bedchamber, of which Newcastle was not even informed. Devonshire was most anxious that Newcastle and Bute should come to an understanding so as to prevent Pitt and his friends 'putting a dagger to the King's throat; that they had done it several times in the late reign and would do it again whenever their ambition prompted them to it or made it necessary.'

On January 12 1761 Viry saw Devonshire and told him that the King was dissatisfied with Holderness and wanted Bute to take his place as Secretary of State for the North. Devonshire, anxious that Newcastle give no offence to Pitt, advised him to let the proposal of Bute as minister come from the King, though he should not show any opposition. Somehow a hint of what was afoot reached Pitt's ear and on January 20 he told Newcastle he could never give any support to the idea of the Favourite becoming minister. On the last day of the month Viry confided to Devonshire that Bute's real object was to be 'sole minister'.

The opportunity for Bute's advancement came when Pitt underwent a prolonged attack of gout between the third week of January and the third week of March. On February 12 Bute, with a skill by no means evident in most of his transactions, endeavoured to square Pitt by offering Temple the Lord Lieutenancy of Ireland, a move highly approved by Devonshire. Temple kept them waiting until February 25, when he finally declined. Newcastle made up his mind to meet the wishes of the King, whom he saw on March 6 and proposed Bute as a Secretary of State. The appointment followed shortly, on the understanding that Bute should leave foreign affairs and the running of the war to Pitt, except whenever Newcastle, Devonshire and Hardwicke 'shall think he goes too far'.

On April 9 Pitt in a momentous interview with Newcastle laid down his views about a peace with France. Already he had prescribed the principle of *uti possidetis*:[2] mutual conquests were to be the basis of negotiation. Pitt, confident that Britain was in a position to dictate,

---

[2] The principle of negotiation whereby belligerents retain possession of their acquisitions as standing upon a certain date.

demanded that the Cabinet settle the terms to be offered before the
appointment of envoys. Most important of all, Pitt declared his intention to keep 'all North America and the Fishery on the Banks of
Newfoundland'. As Newcastle at once pointed out, Pitt's expectation
of all the Fishery was bound to prove an insurmountable obstacle. To
insist on an exclusive right for Britain could drive Spain and other
powers into joining France. Pitt brushed aside all objections: if overruled by the Cabinet he would retire.

On April 22 Devonshire told Pitt that he could not consent that
terms should be laid down by the Cabinet before the views of the
French Court were known. At the Council five days later he won
Mansfield's support for the middle course of indicating a willingness
to treat, which was immediately approved. Devonshire then suggested
to Pitt that passports be arranged for the respective envoys, François
de Bussy for France and Hans Stanley, a great favourite with Pitt, for
Britain. In their opposition to Pitt's thrusting policies, Devonshire and
Newcastle found a forceful ally in Bedford, who took the view that a
further extension of British conquests was not only unnecessary but
must retard rather than secure a peace. On the French side the
negotiations were conducted by Louis XV's great Foreign Minister,
the Duke of Choiseul.

When on May 13 the Instructions to be given Stanley were debated
in Council, Pitt and Newcastle argued over whether or not Versailles
should be compelled to enter a declaration of intent for a peace
separate from her allies. Bute favoured that Britain announce her
willingness to treat independently, without demanding a parallel declaration, and when Devonshire agreed, Pitt came round. Pitt then
asked for Cabinet directions in the matter of *uti possidetis*, and all but
Temple were decided that Bussy must first be asked to put forward
the position of his government.

Devonshire was absent from Council through illness during the
latter part of May and the whole of June. On July 11 he talked to
Bute of the disrupted condition of the national counsels: Bedford had
taken such umbrage at Pitt's highhandedness that he no longer attended meetings; Newcastle was flustered and apprehensive. Bute
more than hinted that Newcastle's resignation would not be refused
but at the same time went a long way towards meeting Bedford's views
on the peace. On July 15 Newcastle, Bute, Hardwicke and Devonshire
reached agreement on the *sine qua non* of a compromise peace, by
which France was to be allowed to participate in the Fisheries on the
principles of the Treaty of Utrecht.

Devonshire was not present at the Council of July 24 of which
Newcastle sent him an account. That unity in the Cabinet was maintained was owing to Choiseul, who had forwarded with his *Memoire*

a separate Memorial detailing the Spanish grievances and asking that these be resolved within the framework of the negotiation with France. This Pitt rejected with unanimous approval. Devonshire was however at the Council of August 13, which proved decisive both in respect of the negotiations and the harmony of the ministry. Devonshire was convinced that Choiseul would never have allowed the grievances of Spain to stand in the way of a satisfactory peace. He recorded: 'The sole cause of the failure of this negotiation is the refusal of the entire Fishery.'

On August 14 Devonshire made clear to Bute that the time was approaching when he would have to choose between Newcastle and Pitt. Later that day the Council was continued, with Pitt absolutely refusing to alter his reply to Choiseul. Devonshire withdrew, pointing out that Pitt's attitude removed the letter from the Council's deliberations. On September 10 Pitt talked to Devonshire and Bute of his desire to retire. Bute was alarmed for himself but Newcastle discounted Pitt's threats: he might for ever talk of resignation as an easy means of getting his way.

The Councils of September 15, 18 and 21 were really one. At the first meeting, the Spanish grievances were briefly dismissed. Then the articles of Choiseul's final Ultimatum were gone through one by one. Three days later the Council discussed the consequences of a breach with Spain. Pitt was for warlike measures without procrastination. Granville and Hardwicke stressed that war with Spain always called for special consideration, because the Iberian peninsula was the best customer for English lamb and wool: the first casualty would be the British mercantile establishments. When Pitt's demand for the recall of the British Ambassador, the Earl of Bristol, was rejected, he read out a Paper which he intended giving to the King.

Devonshire's son William was one of the six eldest sons of peers chosen to support His Majesty's train at the Coronation of September 22. That morning soon after eight Devonshire met the King and urged him not to give in to Pitt, serious though the loss of his services in running the war might be. The following day, Lord Chancellor Henley, Newcastle, Bute, Anson and Mansfield met at Devonshire House to discuss 'what was to be done to justify our dissent from Mr. Pitt'. A first proposal to present a joint minute to the King was dropped in favour of a decision that each minister should see the King personally to explain his reasons. On September 24 Bute, Devonshire and Newcastle discussed the reconstruction of the ministry in view of the impending resignations of Pitt and Temple. Bute's first suggestion as to Pitt's successor was Fox, which however on talking to people he found would not prove acceptable. His next candidate was George Grenville, which Newcastle said 'was impossible ...'. Devonshire proposed that Bedford become Secretary of State, which, in view of his contribution to ousting Pitt, was not surprising.

Devonshire was present at the Council of October 2, the last attended by Pitt as the architect of war. Pitt made his final stand in terms which challenged them all: 'I will not be responsible for measures I do not direct.' The day after Pitt's resignation of October 5, Devonshire, Newcastle and Bute quickly settled that George Grenville should succeed Pitt as Leader of the House of Commons, whilst carrying on as Treasurer of the Navy. It was at Mansfield's suggestion that Bute proposed the Earl of Egremont as Secretary of State. When Devonshire pointed to Bedford's claims, Bute retorted that his known pacifism would make him an unpopular successor to Pitt. Egremont was appointed Secretary of State for the South.

Devonshire's hope was that Bute, Grenville and Egremont would with Newcastle form 'a council of four'. Shortly Newcastle was complaining to Devonshire that the three were edging him out. When on November 1 Devonshire returned to London after an absence of ten days, he urged the necessity of a united ministry. Devonshire cannot have considered Newcastle in any real danger, or he would hardly have got him to secure from Bute the appointment of his brother Lord George Augustus Cavendish as Comptroller of the Household. Devonshire thought little of Pitt's speech in the debate on the Address on the opening of Parliament, as he told the King when, five days later, he 'waited on him to thank him for his goodness to my brother'. And provided Bute and Newcastle worked together, Pitt 'would be of no consequence, but if they differed, he would get the better of them and take possession of H.M., as he had done of his the King's grand-father, which I should be very sorry to see'. Devonshire provided a full and interesting account of the debate in the House of Commons of December 11 1761, on the motion of Pitt's friends George Cooke and Alderman William Beckford for the production of the papers relating to Spain, which was negatived without a division.

After Christmas Devonshire returned to town on New Year's Day 1762. Spain had declared war on December 19 and war was declared in London on January 4. The extension of the maritime conflict must bring into question the maintenance of a British contingent in Germany, which Bute had always disapproved. Further, the second Treaty of Westminster guaranteeing Frederick of Prussia an annual subsidy of £670,000 was at the point of expiry. On January 6 Devonshire and Newcastle were summoned by Bute to his office, where were assembled Egremont, George Grenville, Anson and Ligonier. The decision was taken to send an expedition against Havana. Then Bute 'threw out' the idea of recalling the British troops from Germany. Devonshire spoke at length against the betrayal of Prussia, which must damage the reputation of Britain and leave Europe at the mercy of France. The following day Devonshire enlisted Cumberland's strong opinion that this treachery could not be contemplated.

When on January 8 Devonshire next saw Bute, his intention was merely to convey Cumberland's views. Bute however took the initiative completely, when he told Devonshire of a negotiation with France, known only to the King, which he had since November been conducting through the medium of Viry and the Bailli de Solar, the Sardinian Minister in Paris. Devonshire must have felt his expectations of any loyal accord between the Court and Newcastle completely dispelled. During the ensuing three weeks Devonshire was ill and could see no one. He did not meet Bute again until February 1, when he was confronted with the most bitter complaints. Bedford was attempting to force the hand of the ministry by moving in the House of Lords for the withdrawal of British troops from Germany. Devonshire told Bute that the fault was his for having raised the question in the first place. Newcastle left the debate of February 5 to Bute, who carried the previous question 105–16.

The entire Cabinet was agreed that a condition of the renewal of the Prussian subsidy must be that Frederick give evidence of an intention to bring his war with Maria Theresa to an early conclusion. But Frederick in a brief letter to George III of January 22 urged an intensification of conflict: Britain had her opportunity for aggrandisement with the Spanish declaration of war; he himself contemplated not only retaining Silesia but also depriving Maria Theresa of Bohemia. Even Newcastle felt impelled to make clear that a renewal of the subsidy must depend upon the overtures for peace.

The negotiations with Choiseul through the Sardinian ministers did not go smoothly and by the end of February Bute was considering breaking off. Then on March 21 came news of the capture of Martinique, which must compel Bute to raise the British terms. By this time Newcastle had become aware that Samuel Martin, the secretary to the Treasury, was betraying him by supplying Bute with financial information. On March 18 Martin wrote to Bute of Newcastle's suspicions. Devonshire attended at an informal gathering of ministers at Bute's office on March 26, when he urged that though this might not be a time to make concessions, the negotiation with France should not be dropped altogether. At a Council on March 29, at which Devonshire was present, Bute proposed the renewal of a direct negotiation with Versailles on the basis of *uti possidetis* by an exchange of ministers. When on April 8, with Devonshire there, Newcastle raised the question of presenting to Parliament the bill for the wars in Germany and Portugal, which together must call for a vote of £2 million, Grenville roundly asserted that £1 million would be sufficient.

The Council meetings of April 27 and 30 appear to have been the last Devonshire attended before Newcastle resigned. The whole question of peace was gone through point by point. The Council saw no trouble about granting France the use of the Fisheries on the basis of the Treaty of Utrecht, with St. Pierre and Miquelon as *abris*. South of Canada the river Mississippi was taken to be the boundary between the two nations, which kept France out of the Ohio valley. When three days later the Council reconvened, Newcastle, Devonshire and Hardwicke reiterated their opposition to a complete cessation of the Prussian subsidy.

Devonshire did not write about Newcastle's resignation, although he himself was more than an onlooker. It was on May 7 that Newcastle informed Bute that recent events made his resignation imperative. He then went to the King and announced this intention, recounting the scene in a letter he addressed to Devonshire 'at night': 'The King seem'd good natured and affected. Said, he hoped I would think better of it; that I had time to reconsider.' Three days later Newcastle again saw the King and the suggestion that he might 'reconsider' was not repeated. Devonshire and Mansfield went protesting to Bute, who treated the matter as a thing decided. When on May 14 Newcastle was once more at Court, the King was barely civil: 'C. *Viry* told the Duke of Devonshire that the resolution was taken not to *ask* me to stay.' Newcastle's audience of May 25 went off pleasantly enough: the King used Devonshire as go-between with the offer of a pension. The next day, May 26, Newcastle formally took his leave, and refused the suggestion of an emolument: 'The King was pleased, at parting, to say that he would depend upon my support, to which I made a bow, and said nothing.' The next day Bute was appointed First Lord of the Treasury. Grenville succeeded him as Secretary of State for the North.[3] Devonshire had always refused to enter any commitment as to his course of action should Newcastle resign and did not choose to make the downfall of his kinsman and ancient ally the occasion to step down altogether. Though he continued as Lord Chamberlain he absented himself from Council.

Devonshire wrongly expected a withdrawal from Germany followed by an immediate peace. In fact neither Bute nor Bedford would yield the French any substantial advantage other than the restitution of St. Lucia. On July 28 Devonshire gave the King his assurance that he would not only support peace on such terms but also endeavour to persuade others to do the same. The King was particularly concerned that Newcastle should not oppose a peace on terms which the inclusion of the Mississippi as the boundary made better than the propositions

[3] This account is based substantially upon Namier, *England in the Age of the American Revolution*, 318–25.

put before Pitt. Devonshire pointed out Newcastle's just resentment at finding himself a minister no longer.

The concluding episodes of the Diary show Newcastle and Devonshire at a loss to comprehend their lack of importance. Devonshire made the mistake of assuming that without either of them or Pitt, Bute must feel vulnerable and apprehensive of the meeting of Parliament, and here his old friend Fox rather fed his hopes. None the less on July 31 Devonshire strongly advised Newcastle against responding to an approach from Temple. Devonshire, back on his old theme, was certain that Pitt and his friends must be for a strong opposition: 'nothing would satisfy them but forcing the King as they had done his grand-father ...'

When on September 24 Devonshire dined with Cumberland at Windsor Lodge, the talk was of inducing Bute to retire before public hostility towards him became too open. They agreed that Cumberland should see Fox which he did on September 28, and commissioned him to find out whether Bute had any intention of entering a coalition with either Newcastle or Pitt. On the afternoon of September 29 Fox saw Bute, who made very clear that he had no intention whatsoever of uniting with either Newcastle or Pitt. The Diaries end with the same lack of direction as they displayed at the beginning, with a lengthy account of Cumberland's audience of the King of September 30 1762, when the peace terms were discussed.

Devonshire's long-expected resignation took place on November 28 1762. Then the King with his own hand struck his name from the list of Privy Councillors and he never held office again. In February 1764 Devonshire was dismissed from his Lord Lieutenancy of Derbyshire, which had been in his family without interruption since 1714. That October Devonshire suffered a stroke and proceeded to Spa in Germany, where he died on November 2 1764. He was buried with his wife in All Saints, Derby. His death at the age of 44 may have been hastened by grief over the ingratitude of the young Sovereign whose family had owed so much to the House of Cavendish.

Shortly before his death Devonshire had commissioned the delightful Zoffany portrait of his children playing in the grounds of Chiswick. William, the eldest son, succeeded as 5th Duke. Dorothy on November 8 1766, when she was only sixteen, was married to William Cavendish-Bentinck, 3rd Duke of Portland. Since 1755 Portland had used the additional surname of Cavendish, because he was the heir to Welbeck Abbey as the lineal descendant of the seventeenth-century Cavendish Duke of Newcastle. This marriage was of the utmost importance, for Portland was among those in a direct political succession to Devonshire himself. From April to December 1783 Dorothy saw her husband Prime Minister of the ill-fated Fox and North coalition.

They had a large family and then, as so frequently occurred, tragedy came and Dorothy died on June 14 1794. In that year Portland took office as Home Secretary with the younger Pitt Prime Minister, and from 1806–9 himself served a second term as Prime Minister.

The second son, Richard, was member for Lancaster, 1773–80, and for Derbyshire, 1780–1, at which point he died. The third son, George Augustus Henry, inherited the Bolton Abbey estate in Yorkshire. Though he represented the family pocket borough of Knaresborough, 1775–80, and the borough of Derby, 1780–96 and 1797–1831, he was always a dull backwoodsman. When in 1831 the earldom of Burlington was revived in his favour, this was a recognition of his great wealth rather than his political importance.

The Devonshire Diaries give no clear answer to the reader's enquiry as to the motives of the diarist—'author' would be too strong a word because the one certainty is the complete absence of any intention to publish to the world. The character of the Diaries is exclusively political. Devonshire never mentions his children, and his own or other people's house very occasionally, and then only in connection with meeting other politicians. The sole family reference is to Devonshire's brother Lord George Augustus and that too in a political context.

Yet the Diaries, far from being impersonal, abound in detail and revelation of character in the Kings and the politicians and, albeit unconsciously, Devonshire himself. He comes down to us with his complete self-assurance as to his place in the order of the world. He sits in Council as naturally as at his dining-room table. Devonshire's assumption was that Great Britain should be governed by an aristocracy, with himself a principal. So far as concerned Ireland, he took the conventional point of view of a great English nobleman who was also a grandee in the other kingdom: the dependence of the Dublin legislature upon the Westminster Privy Council was a desirable safeguard of the English ascendancy. Though never a Secretary of State and completely innocent of diplomatic experience, Devonshire discussed issues of peace and war as a personage entitled to command a hearing. No maker or unmaker of ministries, he advised Kings about ministers, though his main concern was always to preserve harmony amongst His Majesty's servants. One of Devonshire's most self-revealing moments was when Bute suggested Egremont as Secretary of State for the South in succession to Pitt. Though Devonshire's recommendation was Bedford, he had to observe of Egremont: 'a very good and proper man'. Egremont had no experience of foreign affairs, had indeed never before held office, but his acreages in Sussex, Yorkshire and Cumberland made him one of the richest men in England.

Because of Devonshire's responsibilities as Lord Chamberlain, matters which may appear trifles come to us curiously intermingled with grave issues. With the accession of George III Devonshire was given the task of finding the late King's Will and confides to paper his suspicion of duplicity in Baron von Münchhausen, the Hanoverian Minister in London, who was concealing his possession of the document in question. There was a humorous side to the episode, until it is recalled that George II had obtained and destroyed the Wills of George I. Again, Devonshire seems guilty of unconscious bathos when he passes immediately from the future of the Newfoundland Fisheries, the nub of the 1761 peace negotiations, to the squabble over precedence between the Earl of Huntingdon, Groom of the Stole, and the Lords of the Bedchamber. But to Devonshire the Household Lords were an integral part of the loyal majority in the House of Lords.

Devonshire was too much an onlooker to be called gregarious. He had no intimate friends in politics, not even Newcastle, as was proved by his decision not to resign in May 1762. This detachment was natural to him and inevitably confirmed by exalted station. Here however lay the key to Devonshire's usefulness, recognized by everyone. He was the supremely objective man, never led away by passion, completely reliable and so the ideal receiver of confidences. He made no pretensions to brilliance. The Diaries are evidence of a devotion to work and to duty rather than quickness of intellect, so that everything he undertook Devonshire did rather well.

Though Devonshire was aloof the Diaries are never stuffy. Devonshire never described physical characteristics or attempted the direct delineation of character. Yet he had a keen eye for the dramatic encounter, as when George II gave vent to his contempt for Temple and Pitt refused to be crossed by anyone. We have perhaps intentionally amusing descriptions of Bute, feigning puzzlement or disclaiming ambition, so that we instantly detect insincerity in his smile. They all come to life in Devonshire's pages, George II and Cumberland soldierly and forthright, Temple with his vulgar blustering, Newcastle a mixture of craft and cowardice. Here is nothing startlingly new and the enjoyment lies in encountering them as the people we had always suspected them to be.

The experience of the Devonshire Diaries deepens rather than changes our understanding of the watershed implicit in the accession of George III, who gloried 'in the name of Britain'. So Tories ceased to be Jacobites and found reconciliation with the throne. Pitt is the great man and his resignation the climax of Devonshire's story. We see him confronted by Newcastle, Bedford and Devonshire: 'Lords great in themselves and in their influence in the House of Commons, ...'. The 'proud' dukes as George III termed them, having goaded Pitt into resignation, themselves fell from power and, dismissed from their Lord Lieutenancies, were no longer *primus* even in their own counties. Yet keenly though Devonshire and Newcastle felt their unaccustomed isolation, the 'revolution' was merely one of persons. There were others dukes to carry on and Rutland happily accepted the Lord Lieutenancy of Derbyshire.

With any diary or correspondence the hero must be the writer. Here we get back to the mystery of Devonshire's motive in keeping his account, which both begins and ends in a state of uncertainty. Here is no effort at self-justification from a disappointed politician. Devonshire never regretted leaving the Treasury and found the business of waiting as Lord Chamberlain tedious. He seldom discusses himself, and then only as an aside, but for the most part keeps to describing what he and others said and did. Devonshire's purpose in writing can only have been for his own interest and just possibly the edification of his sons.

EDITORIAL NOTE

The text has been transcribed from the original manuscript in the Devonshire collection at Chatsworth, Derbyshire. As it survives the manuscript does not have the appearance of a diary, consisting as it does of loose, folded sheets, mostly uniform in size, without covers. The outer page, however, carries the author's note, 'Memoranda on State of Affairs', and following the first 15 pages, which comprise scattered notes on political events, 1754-9, and thumb-nail sketches of Devonshire's contemporaries in the public world, the manuscript assumes its diary form with the entry for September 1759, the point at which the text printed below begins. At some stage the 'Memoranda', although many pages contain the first person singular, had become mixed up with the 4th Duke of Devonshire's political correspondence. We and other scholars on visits to Chatsworth have therefore found sections of the manuscript which have been pieced together after a dispersal the nature of which is not now discoverable. There is reason to believe that Sir Lewis Namier and Romney Sedgwick knew of the existence of some sort of personal account but not of the present diary to anything like its full extent.

In general our policy has been to make the text as readable as possible with a minimum of alteration. Devonshire's original spelling has been retained, particularly of proper names; the correct or modern version has been given in a footnote. He was not consistent, even over the name of Lord Chancellor the Earl of Hardwicke, one of his closest friends, to whom he indiscriminately referred with or without the terminal 'e'. Abbreviations, however, usual in eighteenth-century documents, have been expanded; where Devonshire wrote 'D. of N.' we have printed 'Duke of Newcastle'. Capitalization, punctuation, and paragraphing has followed modern practice rather than the author's. Throughout Devonshire employed the ampersand which we have replaced by the conjunction.

A far greater problem has been set by Devonshire's frequent use of the masculine pronoun, in circumstances when the subject of the preceding sentence or clause cannot possibly be intended. Here we have explained the reference by adding in square brackets the name of the person he had in mind. All other insertions in square brackets are the editors'. Small slips made by the author have been silently corrected.

For the most part Devonshire used a facing page system, which allowed him to make additions on the left-hand page without disturbing the main text on the right. All such additions have been placed in the text between asterisks, thus: *...*. Where he records events out of sequence we have restored the chronology; where he is wrong about a day of the week, the correct date is given and the fact noted. Underlining in the manuscript has been represented by italics in the text.

care of, the King would rejoyce to see the aggrandissement of Spain at the expence of France. And that he, Mr. Pitt, hoped the King of Spain would reason in the same manner in regard to the advantages gained by us in America.

Prince Sanseverino seemed much embarrassed but recommended moderation. Mr. Pitt said moderation upon the situation of the affairs belonging to the party. That as Providence had decided for us and given us great advantages, it could not be expected, at least by a friend, that we would afterwards put it in the power of our enemies to encroach upon us and insult us hereafter.

Oct 26: George Grenville[13] well disposed to Duke of Newcastle. Mr. Pitt disposed to quit unless Lord Temple has the Garter.[14] Pitt full of acknowledgements for H.M.'s[15] communication by Munichhausen[16] of Mr. Steinberg at Copenhagen his letters;[17] he owned he thought them captious and insiduous both as to the matter and manner. Munichhausen says the King of the same opinion.[18]

Pitt disapproved of the King's way of talking of keepeing what we had got and getting back what we had lost; some were for another campaign, he against it; he did not think we should be in a better or even so good a condition as we were in now; that he feared the King would at a peace talk of Dedommagement;[19] that he could never be for it and desired the King might know it; that it would be destruction to him both as King and as Elector.

He [Pitt] seemed really desirous of peace this winter; saw the difficulties of carrying on the war in Germany for want of them [i.e. financial resources]; was desirous to keep Senegal and Goree, indifferent about Guardaloupe, supposed we must have Minorca again, talked of keeping possession of Niagara, the Lakes, Crown Point and a proper security for our own colonies, the Bay of Fundi, etc. As to Quebeck, Montreal[20] and Louisbourgh they were points to be treated of and not given up for nothing.

Philip, younger brother to Charles III of Spain, in 1748, on condition of a reversion to Sardinia on Don Philip's death without issue or on the succession of the King of Naples to the throne of Spain.

[13] George Grenville, brother to Temple, Treasurer of the Navy.

[14] News of the fall of Quebec, which reached London on 16 Oct. had greatly strengthened Pitt's position.

[15] George II.

[16] There were two Münchhausen brothers, the elder Gerlach, Minister of State in Hanover, the younger Philip Adolph, Hanoverian Minister in London.

[17] Georg Friedrich von Steinberg, Hanoverian envoy to Denmark.

[18] The letters relayed vaguely worded peace proposals from France and an offer by Denmark to mediate. Newcastle to Hardwicke, 31 Oct. 1759, Add. MSS. 32897, f. 513.

[19] Compensation for the devastation of Hanover by the retreating French army in 1758, in the form of the Bishoprics of Hildesheim, Paderborn and Osnabrück.

[20] Montreal was not taken until Sept. 1760.

Nov 11 1759: I was alone with Lady Yarmouth and told her that I could not help lamenting the unfortunate resolution the King had taken with regard to Lord Temple, that I had good reason to think he would resign his employment and that then H.M.'s affairs would go into confusion, for that Mr. Pitt would either quit or would show his ill humour by obstructing the measures and distressing the King's affairs. She said she saw it very plainly, but what could she do; she had said everything that was possible to say and the King had been so much out of humour that she had told him she would never trouble him again on the subject. I owned I had no patience to see him confound his own affairs when he had so fine an opportunity of fixing them on a firm and lasting footing.

Pitt complained that he was very ill at Leicester House[21] for not sending them intelligence, that he had wished to communicate all dispatches to them but as the King did not approve, he thought it his duty to obey, whereas Lord Holdernesse[22] ingratiated himself by shewing all the letters.

[That] Mr. Pitt[23] was most probably detached from Leicester House[24] and therefore if the King would be civil to him and shew him his countenance, might attach him to himself;[25] whereas if he would not grant him the only personal favour he had asked he would lose him. And in confidence I could tell her by a correspondence I had seen that had passed between the Duke of Newcastle and Lord Hardwick,[26] that if Pitt went out the Duke would not stay in and indeed, if he was to ask my opinion, I should tell him that he would endanger his head if he attempted to stay in. For the success we had had this last year had made Mr. Pitt so popular throughout the kingdom, that no ministry could be formed without him and therefore, if Lord Temple resigns now the consequences will be, that in a very little time, the King will find that nobody will venture to undertake his affairs; that he will be forced to take Mr. Pitt again, give him carte blanche and submit entirely to his will. In so doing H.M. will have made a very bad figure, and will lose all those people from about him that he likes best and has most confidence in; and concluded with saying that never

[21] The residence of the Prince of Wales and the name given to his political adherents.

[22] Robert D'Arcy, 4th Earl of Holderness, Secretary of State for the North.

[23] Here Devonshire resumed his account of his conversation with Lady Yarmouth.

[24] Devonshire was right. Tension between Pitt and Leicester House had originated in the year preceding, over his not properly consulting the Prince of Wales and Bute over the despatch of British regiments to Germany.

[25] As Hardwicke observed in his letter to Newcastle of 6 Oct.: 'I should think if by this means the King could gain Mr. Pitt from Leicester House it ought to be a strong reason with him to do it.' Add. MSS. 32896, f. 322.

[26] Philip Yorke, 1st Earl of Hardwicke, Lord Chancellor, 1737–56. Newcastle to Hardwicke, 11 Sept. 1759, Add. MSS. 32895, f. 326; Hardwicke to Newcastle, 12, 20 Sept. 1759; Add. MSS. 32895, ff. 326, 361–4; 32896, ff. 1–3.

man threw away so fine a game. She asked me whether I would speak to the King, or what I would have done.

I replied that I had once taken the liberty to give him my opinion unasked,[27] upon this subject but as I had not the good fortune to persuade him, I should not presume to trouble him any more.

She then said: 'Will you give me leave to tell him what you have said to me?'

'I have no objection, I have no motive but the King's service.'

Nov 12: She [Lady Yarmouth] told me she had given the King an account of our conversation; that he had heard her with great patience and coolness, and added: 'I wish he would send for Pitt tomorrow and tell him that he would give his brother[-in-law] the Garter.'

Nov 13: King very civil and seemed to have a mind to speak to me; asked whether I was going away. I told him I was obliged to go to the House of Lords to attend the Prince of Wales[28] when he took his seat.

Nov 14: Met Lord Temple in the outward room who told me he was going to resign.[29] I attempted to get in before him to give the King notice, but Lord Rochford[30] had already acquainted the King who sent for him in, where he stayed some time.

The King sent for me, told me that he had been very civil to Lord Temple and twice desired him to keep the Seal; that he had told him what he had taken ill of him; that he had in great measure explained and excused himself; that if he had not promised him the Garter that was no reason to resign for there were many in the same situation. Lord Temple put it upon repeated marks of dislike shewn by H.M. and in such a light his post became no more than a pension which was not honourable for him to keep; wished the King a continuation of success and that the close of his reign might be as glorious as the present time was. The King wished I would acquaint Mr. Pitt with what had passed and of his desire that his Lordship would continue. I answered I had in my own mind resolved never to have a private conversation with Mr. Pitt but if H.M. commanded I should certainly obey him.

He said: 'What do you think will be the consequence?'

'That, Sir, will depend upon the part Mr. Pitt shall take.'

'Oh, I will be very civil to him.'

'I hear he spoke very well yesterday.[31] I must do him the justice to say that it was impossible for man to do better or more judiciously than he did in the first place; doing justice to your Majesty by saying

[27] See p. 24.
[28] The future George III.
[29] The Privy Seal.
[30] 4th Earl of Rochford, Lord of the Bedchamber and Groom of the Stole to George II, 1755–60.
[31] *Parliamentary History*, xv. 947–50. Newcastle to Pitt, 14 Nov. 1759, Add. MSS. 32898, ff. 245–6.

that you had outrun him in promoting the popular part of the war;[32] that in America [that], if there had been extraordinary success, the merit was equally due to all the ministry and he made no doubt if in former times other people had had the same means they would have done as well; laid in for 10,000 men more for Prince Ferdinand;[33] said he had formerly notions that this country could stand by itself and ought not to meddle with the Continent; he saw his error it was a narrow and erroneous way of thinking; and concluded with the subject of the peace with great art and dexterity by not committing himself and yet saying a great deal upon the subject.'

Nov. 11 to 15 1759: Saw Mr. Pitt in the evening, acquainted him with what the King had said. Very civil, very cool, and decent, pleased with the King's condescention: it was a great deal to say that he admitted of Lord Temple's justification. I then assured him I had no authority but asked him if he thought it could not be made up by the King's being brought to be civil to him and promising the Garter at the end of the Session. After much talk he owned he wished it and was of opinion for it, but that the subject was of so delicate a nature considering the part he had had in it that he could not speak to Lord Temple. At last he agreed to tell him that I should be glad to speak to him before he went out of town. He complained of his situation at Court, that he had no favours shewn him or done for him; that the Duke of Newcastle, though they quarrelled some times, yet behaved decently to him but he knew that all his Grace's friends etc. railed at him and upon any ill success would have been ready to have torn him to pieces.

[Pitt] mentioned the Duke of Newcastle's and York's correspondence,[34] and the affair of Dedomagement for Hanover; these symptoms and the difficulties that would attend the making of the peace made him wish to retire, he had wished to be a minister, and now wished to be out of it. *Pitt said he knew nothing of Lord Temple's intention; he wished he had deferred it; that he had not had time to consider what to do, saw great difficulties either way; that though Lord Temple might desire him to continue he was not sure he could justify it to himself.* I told him that after the service he had done the

[32] i.e. the war in North America.

[33] Prince Ferdinand of Brunswick, Commander-in-Chief of the allied army in Germany.

[34] In late September Sir Joseph Yorke, Hardwicke's third son, who was British Minister at the Hague, had received several letters from the Princess of Anhalt-Zerbst under the pseudonym of Mdme. de Beaumer. Add. MSS. 35419, ff. 26-9. She was mother to Catherine, the wife of the Czarevitch Peter, Duke of Holstein-Gottorp, nephew to the Empress Elizabeth. The daughter was the future Catherine II the Great. Yorke relayed the letters to Newcastle who, without informing Pitt, disclosed them to the Prussian Minister Dodo von Knyphausen and Holderness. Holderness divulged the matter to Pitt who soundly rated Newcastle and Yorke.

public, and the justice they did him, ought to induce him to finish the work he had begun and secure the country by a good peace; that it must be the work of all the ministry and not a part of; that though no minister I should be very ready to give my sanction; upon the whole I think he does not intend to quit, at least not at present.

Nov 15 1759: Went to Lady Yarmouth, found that the King was alarmed and ready to do anything; told her all that had passed with Pitt. She seemed much out of humour with the Duke of Newcastle; she had asked the King what plan he had to carry on his affairs. He answered he did not think the Duke of Newcastle would leave him; he understood that he would not. She said the Duke of Devonshire is sure that if Mr. Pitt resigns this day, the Duke of Newcastle goes tomorrow. She said she had shewn the King my note and that he would be very civil to Lord Temple.

The levée was over, Lord Temple much pleased with his reception. Gave the King an account of my conversation with Mr. Pitt and told him that I was to see Lord Temple in the evening, and desired to know what powers:

'You may tell him I desire he will take the Privy Seal again.'

'That will not do alone; you must, Sir, allow me to give him hopes of the Garter at the end of the Session.'

'When I make a promotion.'

'But, Sir, that must be at the end of the Session.'

'Well I will, provided Mr. Pitt stays in to make the peace and they will support my affairs.'

Saw Lord Temple in the evening,[35] he agreed to take the Privy Seal; would not accept the Garter on terms but would be proud of it as a mark of the King's favour. He desired to be understood to come in devoted to the King's service and as much obliged as when the King made his mother a peeress;[36] that he was carte blanche with regard to everybody.

Nov 16: Acquainted the King that Lord Temple was ready to accept the Privy Seal as H.M. desired it. The King was in very ill humour, having pressed Mr. Pitt on the article of Dédommagement, who had absolutely refused to give him any hopes on that head.[37] I told him that all his ministers were equally of the same opinion with Mr. Pitt:

'Then I have a fine parcell of ministers indeed.'

I begged him not to make himself uneasy on a point which did not at present exist, and which acidents might alter before the time came

---

[35] See Devonshire to Newcastle, 15 Nov. 1759, Add. MSS. 32898, f. 261.

[36] As Countess Temple *suo jure* in 1749.

[37] At this time Britain and Prussia were preparing to issue a joint declaration calling for a Congress, from which George II hoped to win territorial gains for Hanover. For the Declaration presented at the Hague by Yorke on 25 Nov., see Thackeray, ii. 470-1.

and repeated my wishes that he would be civil when Lord Temple
came to take the Seal:

'Yes, he behaved very well to me when he was here last and I always
do justice.'

Duke of Newcastle spoke well to the King on the point of
Dédomagement from [for] Hanover;[38] told him that all his servants
were equally of the same opinion with Mr. Pitt; named Lord Hardwick, Lord Mansfield[39] and me and entered into whole state of the
Bishoprick of Hildesheim and endeavoured to show even the impossibility of his own plan.[40] The King very much out of humour but
however was very civil to Lord Temple.

Nov 17: Saw Viry:[41] approved much of Lord Temple's return; hoped
I would continue to interpose between them and the Duke of Newcastle in order to keep them together. I answered it was better for me
not to meddle, by which means I could be of more use when difficulties
arise; whereas if I was to interfere and decide on every trifling occasion
I could be of no service, as I must of course appear to lean more to one
side than another. He said Pitt and Lord Bute[42] were not well together
though outward appearances were preserved.[43] That Lord Bute had
made attempts to be reconciled; would have employed him [Viry]
which he refused and then sent Elliot[44] but to no purpose.[45] Mentioned
the treachery of Lord Holdernesse in communicating the most private
things to Lord Bute, which Pitt would not do. Mentioned the private
treaty made between the King of Spain and the Court of Vienna,[46]
and hoped we would take care of his master's[47] interests at the peace.

Nov 21: Saw Viry: came to ask my advice on a conference he had had
with Munichhausen, who desired him from the King to use his endeavours with the ministers about the Dèdomagement for the Electorate;
that he had seen Pitt yesterday and found the King had spoiled his

[38] See Newcastle to Hardwicke, 16 Nov. 1759, Add. MSS. 32898, ff. 284-9.

[39] William Murray, 1st Baron, later Earl of Mansfield, Lord Chief Justice of England
since 1756.

[40] See Memorandum 22 Nov. 1759, Add. MSS. 32899, ff. 35-6. '*Dédommagement*' came
to nothing: The King never secured the three bishoprics.

[41] Francesco Guiseppe, Count Viry, Sardinian Minister in London.

[42] John Stuart, 3rd Earl of Bute.

[43] See p. 26.

[44] Gilbert Elliot, M.P.

[45] This entry of 17 Nov. 1759 would seem to refer to a hitherto unknown attempt by
Bute at a reconciliation with Pitt. The first attempt of which record previously existed
was in May 1760, when Elliot tried to secure Pitt's agreement to Bute's taking the
Treasury whenever the Prince of Wales might succeed, to meet with a decided rebuff.
Elliot, 362-5.

[46] Whereby the Empress-Queen, in return for yielding to the Duchies of Parma and
Guastalla to Don Philip, Charles III's brother, was to receive the allodials of the House
of Medici in Tuscany and a portion of the Presidii.

[47] The King of Sardinia.

own business and therefore did not know what to say to Munichausen.[48] He then gave an account of his conversation with [Pitt], found him very reasonable, and very cool, and much pleased with the late transaction, but complained of the King, and his ill humour, but said he was determined to go on and do the best he could for the public and dropped something of difficulty to hold the balance between the foiblesse d'une viellard, and the humeure altiére d'une femme and l'ambition demeuseure d'un favourit.[49] He hoped honest men would assist him in it. Leicester House not pleased that Lord Temple resigned without communication but outrageous that he should accept it again in the same manner.[50] Pitt much softened as to Mr. Fox[51] and Duke of Cumberland; that Pitt was determined if the Duke of Newcastle would act openly and cordially with him, that he would do so too;[52] advised Viry to tell Munichausen that the King might be assured that he would do everything in his power; that he thought it was better to wait till the time came, as the situation of affairs might alter to recommend to the King to shew confidence and favour to Mr. Pitt, for by that means he might make him wholly his, as he was quite alienated from Leicester House; and that if Pitt saw he was well with the King, he would do more for him than any other person could.

Viry said the King's proposition could never do, but perhaps in making the peace, Russia might demand some amends to be made to the Elector of Saxony,[53] (some appanages that Saxony claims from the Elector of Cologne),[54] in that case the Elector of Hanover might be considered also.

Saw Lord Hardwick, very full of Mr. Yorke's affair[55] much pleased with Mr. Pitt who had told him that it should be entirely forgot and no slur thrown upon him and that the declaration for peace should pass through Mr. Yorke's hands,[56] and had insisted on it at a meeting and opposed Lord Holdernesse, (who told Lord Anson[57] that he was surprised their family would take it ill, that he meant no harm to them, but to the Duke of Newcastle).

Dec 10 1759: Was at a meeting at Lord Holdernesse['s] where Mr.

---

[48] See p. 26, n. 190.

[49] An allusion to Newcastle, the Princess of Wales and Bute.

[50] Prince George to Bute, 16 Nov. 1759. Sedgwick, No 34.

[51] Henry Fox, Paymaster General and friend of Cumberland, the King's third son.

[52] On 21 Nov. 1759 Newcastle wrote to Hardwicke: 'My real opinion is, that Mr. Pitt's present intention is to unite himself most cordially and confidentially with your Lordship and me and our friends.' Add. MSS. 32899, ff. 7–8.

[53] Augustus III, King of Poland and Elector of Saxony.

[54] Archbishop Prince Clement Augustus of Bavaria.

[55] See p. 29, n. 34.

[56] See p. 30, n. 27.

[57] Admiral 1st Baron Anson, First Lord of the Admiralty.

Pitt communicated to us a letter, or rather Memorial from M. d'Albreu[58] which he was directed by the King of Spain who was still at Sarragossa, to deliver to him.[59] It began with compliments and acquainting the King that he had been detained there by the illness of the Queen and his children who had had the measles; that he congratulated the King and saw with pleasure the success that had attended his Majesty's arms; that at the same time he was too much concerned in that part of the world to see with indifference one power gaining too great a superiority over the other, and therefore it was necessary for him to endeavour to preserve the equilibre settled by the Treaty of Utrecht, expressing his desire of mediation, and recommending moderation.

Mr. Pitt read to us his answer[60] which was highly approved on; civil with regard to Spain, taking notice how friendly we had been in regard to the settlement of Naples,[61] not admiring the idea of an equilibre in America, very strong and high respect of France, but declaring that we were not ready to make peace and had already taken steps towards it; that we should use moderation, but would certainly make use of the means God had put into our hands to secure ourselves for the future from the insults and infidelity of the French, and put it out of their power to molest us for the future.

Dec 13: Mr. Pitt told me that Prince Sanseverino had been with him by order of M. Wall,[62] to desire that we should point out what indemnification should be made to the King of Sardinia, for his *pretensions on Plaisentia*,[63] and making a sort of excuse of their not allowing them to be *droits* as *they* had not acceded to the Treaty of Aix;[64] he owned the communication of Squillaci's[65] Memorial, done without the knowledge of the Spanish ministers at Madrid who received a copy of it by the courier that passed through Madrid in his way hither.[66] Remarkable that Neopolitan ministers write to d'Abreu, and Wall to Sanseverino: probably Squillaci gained by France and by order of the Queen[67] took this step without concert

---

[58] Count Felix d'Abreu, Spanish Ambassador in London.

[59] Dated 5 Dec. 1759. See Pitt to Bristol, 1759 (secret), S.P.F. 94/160.

[60] Pitt to d'Abreu, 13 Dec. 1759, S.P.F. 94/160.

[61] Because his eldest son was mentally defective, Charles III had devised a settlement whereby his second son Charles would succeed as King of Spain and his third son Ferdinand to Naples and Sicily.

[62] General Richard Wall, Prime Minister of Spain.

[63] See p. 26, n. 12.

[64] Aix-la-Chapelle, 1748.

[65] Marquis de Squillaci, Neapolitan Foreign Minister.

[66] Evidently the Memorial had been drafted and despatched by Squillaci on orders from Charles III whilst he was travelling from Naples to Spain.

[67] The Queen of Spain, Maria Amelia of Saxony.

with the Spanish ministers, and after they had left Naples, consequently without Tanuci.[68]

Intelligence[69] that the King of Spain had ordered a very large fleet
to be immediately prepared; the marine remonstrated that it could
not be ready under six months; he answered he would have it in three
and would be obeyed.

Jan 1 1760: Lord Howe[70] waited on Duc d'Aiguillon[71] to demand
some prisoners that belonged to us. The Duke expressed a desire of
entering into a negotiation with him; shewed him the full powers he
had to conclude a peace the moment he set his foot on English ground[72]
and made no doubt but he should be authorised to do it equally there.
Lord Howe said he had no orders to treat. D'Aiguillon desired him to
apply to England for powers, and that he would do the same; that he
imagined they might settle matters very easily, without waiting for
Madame d'Hongrie.[73] [D'Aiguillon] intimated that he might have
been of the ministry but thought the times too difficult; that if he could
go in with *the olive* branch in his hand he would accept it; enquired
much after the English that had been his prisoners.

Pitt and Lord Harwick[74] against continuing any negotiation in that
manner; the Duke of Newcastle for,[75] myself so too; I was for sending
a civil answer and endeavour to find out on what terms they would
make peace. Pitt apprehensive that the Queen of Hungary would not
submit to the terms that France would accept for her[s], and that if
peace was made with France he should be under difficulties to support
the war on the Continent.[76] Lord Hardwick I imagine jealous[y] on
Mr. Yorke's account.[77]

Jan 8: France strongly disposed to treat without its allies. M. d'Affry[78]
dropped to Mr. Yorke that preliminarys were sent by them over here[79]
and that if his Court would give him orders they too might soon settle
matters at the Hague.

[68] Count Bernado Tanuci, Neapolitan Prime Minister.
[69] Bristol to Pitt, 4 and 19 Dec. 1759, S.P.F. 94/160.
[70] Admiral 4th Viscount Howe.
[71] Duke of Aiguillon, Governor of Brittany.
[72] Rather tactlessly, d'Aiguillon showed Howe the full powers given him by Choiseul
to treat for peace on English soil had the invasion succeeded. See Anson to Newcastle,
27 Dec. 1759, Add. MSS. 32900, ff. 351-3.
[73] The Empress Maria Theresa.
[74] See Hardwicke to Newcastle, 30 Dec. 1759, Add. MSS. 32900, ff. 423-4.
[75] See Newcastle to Hardwicke, 29 Dec. 1759, Add. MSS. 32900, ff. 399-401.
[76] Pitt realized too that once peace between Britain and France was in sight, parliamentary support for Frederick II's subsidy would be unobtainable. See Newcastle to
Hardwicke, 2 Jan. 1760, Add. MSS. 32901, f. 42.
[77] Joseph Yorke, see p. 29, n. 34.
[78] Count d'Affry, French representative at the Hague.
[79] Yorke to Newcastle, 1 Jan. 1760, Add. MSS. 32901, ff. 1-4.

The Court of Vienna strong (by intelligence from France)[80] against making peace. The Court of Petersberg the same, altered their language since the defeat of Finck.[81]

Jan 29: The Duke of Newcastle came to me full of complaints at the manner in which he was used by the King and also by Lady Yarmouth; that he had mentioned to him the giving the Garter away directly; that the King was very angry with him, said he had promised it at the end of the Session and would not do it sooner, and desired me to speak to both. He [Newcastle] then told me that Pitt had been applied to by Beckford[82] and Sir John Philips[83] in the name of the Tories, saying that they had supported the government and that they expected in return that something might be done for the country, and desired that the Qualification Oath[84] might be taken when the members took their seats as well as when they were elected. He [Pitt] told the Duke of Newcastle that he had promised to be for it and hoped there would be a concurrence of the King's servants.[85] The Duke had spoken to the King who was rather against it; he had consulted Lord Hardwick and Lord Mansfield and they agreed it could not be resisted. I said I was of the same opinion. He said Lord Legonier[86] had told the King that Lord George Sackville[87] had desired that Lord Cadogan[88] might be President of the Court Martial upon him[89] (which was in order to include St. Clair)[90] upon which the King replied: 'I will have Onslow'.[91]

A letter is wrote to Prince Ferdinand[92] to send such witnesses as he thinks proper. Lord George has asked for 10.

Jan 30: Being the first time I came to Court, the King sent for me and began the conversation by saying that the Duke of Newcastle he understood was with me the day before to inform me of the situation of affairs and added: 'Well, what do you think with regard to foreign affairs, Sir?'

[80] Intelligence (Versailles), 24 Dec. 1759, Add. MSS. 32900, ff. 270–3.
[81] Friedrich August von Finck, defeated by the Austrians at Maxen that October.
[82] William Beckford, M.P., Alderman of the City of London.
[83] Sir John Philipps, 6th Bart., M.P.
[84] To assure the requisite property qualification of £300 p.a. in land for knights of the shire.
[85] See Newcastle to Hardwicke, 26 Jan. 1760, Add. MSS. 32901, f. 479.
[86] 1st Viscount Ligonier, Field Marshal and Commander-in-Chief since Cumberland's resignation, 1757.
[87] Lord George Sackville, M.P., third son of the 1st Duke of Dorset, court-martialled after his disobedience at the battle of Minden.
[88] General the 2nd Baron Cadogan, Governor of Gravesend and Tilbury.
[89] The court martial was requested by Sackville himself.
[90] Lieut-General James St. Clair.
[91] General Richard Onslow, Governor of Plymouth.
[92] Holderness to Prince Ferdinand, 22 Jan. 1760, S.P. 87/37, ff. 8–9.

'I think them in a very bad situation.'

'Yes,' said he, 'the King of Prussia has ruined himself and me too.'[93]

'And Sir, with regard to the interior they seem likewise going into confusion and, since your Majesty asks me, I think it my duty to inform you of what I hear; the Duke of Newcastle is hurt to the last degree with the reception he meets from your Majesty; he vows and protests that he has no view in continuing in employment but your Majesty's service; that his views go no farther; that the predilection your Majesty has always shewn him made him undergo the difficulties attending his situation with chearfullness and that if he loses it, it will be impossible for him to serve.'

The King expressed a good deal of acrimony towards him, said that he was always considering how to strengthen himself, and had no regard for him: 'When Mr. Pelham[94] and you were in my service, you both told people that they were to support you in office, but were to belong to me.'

'Sir, he thinks that you are more angry with him than other of your servants about the business of the dédomagement;[95] now give[s] me leave to say, that your Majesty's pressing your ministers at the time you did was the most unfortunate step that you could have taken, for Sir, if they had been disposed or thought it practicable to do anything for Hanover, the very promising it would have rendered it impossible; whereas I am persuaded that if when the peace comes to be made, our affairs were in a situation to admit of it, that they would all be glad to do what they could to serve and assist your Majesty, and on the other hand an explicit promise could do you no good and would only tend to ruin and discredit them with all mankind it it was known.'

The King said: 'Though they would not promise, yet they might give me some hopes.'

He then mentioned my Lord Temple and expressed great wrath at the Duke of Newcastle's having meddled about the Garter. I told him I was very sorry that point had been agitated at a time when I could not have come out, but that since it had been started, and I knew Lord Temple had been informed of it, I hoped H.M. would give the Garters away immediately.

He said: 'You know I promised to do it at the end of the Session, I will keep my word; why am I to be plagued? I don't care to do it sooner.'

'Good God, Sir, what can it signify to your Majesty whether you do it now or three months hence; is it worth while to risque putting your

---

[93] Frederick II had been heavily defeated at Kunersdorf and Maxen.

[94] Henry Pelham, First Lord of the Treasury, 1743-54, when his brother Newcastle succeeded him.

[95] See p. 26, n. 19.

affairs into confusion for such a trifle? Lord Temple is highly pleased with the reception he has received from your Majesty since the last affair, and by the several conversations I have had with him [I] am very sure that he is totally free from all connections or attachments, and wishes to be well with your Majesty and I am very sure would be glad to do everything in his power to please and serve you, and you may depend upon it as a truth that Mr. Pitt and he can be of more service to you than any man or set of people whatsoever.'

'Do you think that their popularity still continues?'

'Yes, Sir, as great as ever, for all the success of the last year is attributed to Mr. Pitt.'

'But then,' said the King, 'he is giving in to popular measures; what do you say to the bill to oblige members to take Oaths when they take their seats?'[96]

'Why, Sir, I think there is no harm in it, and could not well be opposed. I hear Pitt talks reasonably upon it, that as there has been so great a unanimity in supporting your Majesty, he thinks something should be done to please the people, and by giving way in a point of no consequence he shall be the better able to resist in any essential point; in that, Sir, I think he argues wisely, he has entered more deeply into Continental measures than any minister ever did and seems disposed to support them to the utmost, but he has always felt his way beforehand and if by giving way in trifles he can carry those measures with unanimity he does your Majesty most essential service, and I must repeat that it is a most fortunate circumstance that your Majesty has a minister at this time of day that is in his situation and therefore I beg you will give him the Garters now as I am sure it will fix them in your service.'

I could not get a promise but we parted in very good humour.

Jan 30: Went downstairs,[97] related what had passed with the King and desired her [Lady Yarmouth] to enforce it; said it would be confusion if it was not done, and that it would put it out of my power to be of service to the King if there should be any fresh disagreement. I then delivered the Duke of Newcastle's message, or rather complaint.[98] She denied it totally, said he was a child and was jealous because he saw Lord Holdernesse there, who has been repeating that it will be impossible for him to continue in the service if he is not made first plenipotentiary.[99]

Jan 31: Went to Lady Yarmouth who told me that the King would do as I desired and that I should notify it to Lord Temple and Lord

[96] See p. 35.
[97] i.e. to Lady Yarmouth.
[98] About the King's alleged coolness.
[99] To the proposed Congress, which never met. See p. 35, n. 84.

Rockingham.[100] From thence went to attend the King to the Drawing Room; a letter sent in to me from Lord Temple[101] saying that after what had passed he must decline accepting the Garter; put it in my pocket and from Court went to Mr. Pitt, told what was done and complained to Lord Temple's manner, and that I thought I had reason to expect to be consulted before such a step was taken. He endeavoured to justify Lord Temple and was greatly pleased. I desired him to communicate it to his Lordship who sent me a letter assuring me that all difficulties were removed and that he accepted most thankfully.[102]

The King asked the Duke of Newcastle how he could be such a fool as to think him changed to him, which satisfied his Grace.[103] Feb 3: When Lord Temple came into the Chapelle, Lady Augusta[104] looked at me and with a smile turned her eyes towards him. I had heard that Leicester House was not pleased that Prince William[105] had not the Garter. So when we came into the Drawing Room I said to her I had nothing to do with the Garters more than notifying.

'Did you do it?'

'Yes, Madam, the King ordered me; I hope you approve of Lord Rockingham, which I own I am glad of.'

She shook her head and said: 'I love your little friend; it is not material for my brother William to have it now, but only for the appearance.'

'Why, Madam, is [he] of age for it; had Prince Edward it as soon?'

'Yes, he is 16 and Edward was only 13 when he had it.'[106]

I replied: 'I am sorry for it, I would always have appearances kept up. But I assure I had nothing to do in regard to the nomination, I only spoke to the King as to the point of time in giving it to Lord Temple.'

Feb 27 1760: Mitchell's letter[107] says that the King of Prussia thinks he shall not be able to bring into the field exclusive of his garrisons 90,000 men and some of them only fit to make a show; that the two

---

[100] 2nd Marquis of Rockingham, Lord of the Bedchamber since 1751, who was to receive the Garter at the same time as Temple and Prince Ferdinand.

[101] Temple to Devonshire, 31 Jan. 1760, Chatsworth MSS. 402/5.

[102] Temple to Devonshire, 31 Jan. 1760 (two letters), Chatsworth MSS. 402/6.

[103] Newcastle to Devonshire, 31 Jan. 1760, Chatsworth MSS. 182/136.

[104] Princess Augusta of Wales, sister to the Prince of Wales, the future George III.

[105] Prince William, third son of Frederick Prince of Wales and younger brother to George III, received the Garter in 1762 and was created Duke of Gloucester in 1764.

[106] Edward, Duke of York, second son of Frederick Prince of Wales and senior brother to George III, had been nominated K.G. on 13 Mar. 1752, the day before his fourteenth birthday, and was installed on 4 June following.

[107] Sir Andrew Mitchell, British Minister to Prussia, to Holderness, 12 Feb. 1760, S.P.F. 90/75.

Empresses[108] will have 230,000, begs we would try for peace. Sent a copy of a letter he has wrote to Abbé Froulay[109] to commence a separate negotiation with France; very able and ingenious.

Letter from Lord Bristol at Madrid.[110] There seems to be disagreement between France and the Court of Vienna, that the respective ministers[111] even show it. General Wal made a very strong declaration to him[Bristol] that while he was a minister, (which he should remain no longer than while he had credit with his court), we need not fear that they should be partial to France, and that if we would place confidence in them we should find our account in it with regard to the mediation.

April 3 1760: Duke of Newcastle showed me a letter from a Scotch judge[112] in answer to the Advocate who desired to know how he come to join in a petition for a militia; said that he had wrote to Lord Holdernesse in October for arms. In January, [he] received an answer that the King had ordered them and adds he hears there was a scheme for militia in Scotland which he sincerely wished success to.[113] Strong proof of his connection with Lord Bute.

May 23 1760: Prince Ferdinand wrote to Mr. Pitt to desire the King's orders for defensive or offensive campaign;[114] answered, offensive.[115]

Oct 20 1760: Some coolness still remaining between the Duke of Newcastle and Mr. Pitt in relation to the expedition, the latter still continuing to push it on.[116]

His Grace told me that Mr. Pitt had acquainted Lady Yarmouth, that the making the militia perpetual would be moved immediately after the opening of the Sessions; that he [Pitt] was engaged to be for it, and threw out some sort of threats if it did not pass, which had alarmed her, and consequently the King and his Grace likewise very

[108] Elizabeth of Russia and Maria Theresa.

[109] René François, Baillie de Froulay, Maltese representative in Paris, 1741–66. The letter was conveyed by a young Prussian nobleman, Georg Ludwig von Edelsheim. The overture proved abortive but Edelsheim was subsequently sent to London to submit the relevant correspondence. Newcastle sent copies to Devonshire on 18 Apr. 1760, Add. MSS. 32904, f. 260; Chatsworth MSS. 260/268.

[110] 2nd Earl of Bristol, Ambassador to Spain, to Pitt (secret), 11 Feb. 1760, S.P.F. 94/161.

[111] Marquis d'Ossun, Spanish Ambassador in Madrid, 1759–79. Count Rosenberg, Austrian Ambassador in Madrid, 1756–65.

[112] Alexander Boswell, Lord Auchinleck, Lord of the Court of Sessions, to Robert Dundas, Lord Arniston, Lord Advocate, 20 Mar. 1760, Add, MSS. 32903, ff. 400–3.

[113] Boswell to Holderness, 12 Oct. 1759, Eg. MSS. 3434, ff. 246–7. Holderness to Boswell, [Jan. 1760], Eg. MSS. 3434, ff. 280–1.

[114] Prince Ferdinand to Pitt, 23 May 1760 (copy), Add. MSS. 32906, ff. 229–30.

[115] Pitt to Newcastle, June 1 1760, Add. MSS. 32906, f. 410.

[116] Against Belleisle, which Pitt had planned but Newcastle opposed.

uneasy about it.[117] The King sent for me, told me the same story; asked me whether I thought it would pass both Houses; said he was very much against it.

I replied I was so too, and would do everything in my power to put an end to it.

He [the King] told the Duke of Newcastle that if it passed both Houses he would not give his consent, and that this country would grow too hot for him [Pitt] when a peace came. The Duke of Newcastle shewed me two letters on the subject from Lord Hardwicke[118] who was not so warm for opposing it as formerly [and] proposed a short term. The Duke says it is owing to Lord Royston[119] being afraid of his popularity. The Duke, Lord Mansfield and Mr. Stone[120] and I talked it over and were all of opinion that it was not adviseable to attempt to lay the militia quite aside at present; that it was better either to adjourn the consideration till next year, when the sense of the nation might be taken upon it in a new Parliament,[121] or else to continue it till the end of the war, and the result was that I should talk to Lord Temple and try by him to moderate Mr. Pitt.

His Lordship [Temple] came to me the next morning [Oct 21] and we entered upon the subject. I told him I was sorry that no Session could begin without some rub; that I found by Mr. Pitt's conversation with Lady Yarmouth he had alarmed the King and the Duke of Newcastle about the militia; that he knew my sentiments, how strongly I was against it, and that I wished the continuance of the present harmony so much that I would come into anything that was reasonable to accommodate this business and prevent any misunderstanding. He [Temple] expressed very strongly that he wished the same; that they were engaged, particularly Mr. Pitt, who had been obliged to declare as much in Parliament last year,[122] merely to prevent the country gentlemen from throwing up their commissions; that it was his opinion that when a peace came there would be an end of it, for he would own to me, that he found the generality of those who had engaged in it were tired, but yet made a point of honour not to give it

[117] The militia was a hobby-horse of Pitt but always disliked by Devonshire, Newcastle and Hardwicke, and by the King. Although the militia never captured the popular imagination in the way Pitt had hoped, he now proposed making the institution perpetual.

[118] Hardwicke to Newcastle, 12, 19 Oct. 1760, Add. MSS. 32913, ff. 67-71, 207-10.

[119] Philip Yorke, Viscount Royston, M.P., Hardwicke's eldest son, had as Lord Lieutenant of Cambridgeshire run up against popular opposition to the militia during the autumn of 1757.

[120] Andrew Stone, M.P., a commissioner of trade, formerly private secretary to Newcastle.

[121] A general election was due in 1761.

[122] 13 Nov. 1759, in the debate on the Address.

up now; that therefore he wished some method could be found out to adjust it amicably. I then proposed the two schemes, to the putting off the consideration till next year. He said that they could not come into [it], to the end of the war.[123] He [Temple] said he should have no objection but that he feared their friends would say: 'Why you allow us to remain while you have occasion for us and when the necessity is over you dismiss us with a kick of the britch?' He added that he thought the only thing that would do was a renewal of the term which he believed would satisfy their friends, as they would construe that to be an acknowledgement of their utility.

I answered I much doubted whether our people would agree to it; that if they did it must be for a very short term, and named 3 years from the present time. He pressed for five. I promised to endeavour to settle but recommended that in case we could not come to any agreement, that we should act with temper, every body go according to their own opinion and whatever was the result of it not to suffer it to create any ill humour or misunderstanding in the ministry, which would be very unfortunate at this juncture. This latter part I repeated to Mr. Pitt.

I told the Duke of Newcastle the purport of the conversation. He informed the King, who said he would not agree to a renewal, but was for continuing it to the end of the war. The Duke of Cumberland told me that the King had spoken to him; asked him how Fox and several other people would act upon the occasion. He answered, as to Mr. Fox, he believed he would be against it; that he did not imagine, when the ministers did not take it up warmly, that he would set himself at the head of the opposition to Mr. Pitt. His advice to the King was, as soon as the expedition[124] was over, that the King should send the militia to their homes with thanks, and then there would be an end of them and if it was moved to make them perpetual, that then you would be able to throw it out with a high hand.

Oct 27 1760: As soon as I came to town [I] waited on the Duke of Cumberland. [He] gave me an account of the gracious reception he had met with from the young King,[125] who said that he was very sorry for the misunderstandings that there had formerly been; that it should be his endeavour to introduce a new custom that all the family should live well together. The Duke replied it would make him very happy; that it was his interest as well as his inclination to support him, for

[123] Devonshire's meaning is obscure. Temple was trying to convey that Pitt and his following could not consent to a postponement, but that he personally would be ready to see the militia dropped once the war was over.

[124] To take Belleisle.

[125] George II died early in the morning of 25 Oct., to be succeeded by his grandson George III.

that the greater figure His Majesty made, the more honourable it was for the family, and that he might be assured that he would upon all occasions, if he consulted him, give him the best advice he was able.

In answer to the Duke's being well received, I reminded him of a conversation I had with Lord Bute when first I came into the Treasury, [126] in which he said that he looked upon His Royal Highness as one of the great props of the Royal Family, and something that he should always wish to see him at the head of the Army. The Duke said: 'I should not now choose it, but if the King, who seems to be very fond of it, would take the management himself, I should be very ready to give him my assistance,' and intimated that he should like to be in a situation to be consulted on great points.

He [Cumberland] mentioned to me a Will that the late King had given to Princess Amelia, and that he thought to speak to the King about it and take his pleasure, what he would have done with it. I could not help telling him that I thought it was a nice point for H.R.H. to meddle with, as he probably was interested in it, and that if it could be of any use, I had not the least difficulty in doing it. He thanked me but said he thought it would be proper in him to acquaint the King that there was such a thing. I reminded him of what I had often heard of the late King's secreting his father's Will. He said it was very true but then he got *them all into his own* possession: one in the possession of the Archbishop of Canterbury, another in some foreigner's hands which Lord Waldegrave, then Ambassador at Paris, got for him.[127]

From thence went to Savile House,[128] kissed the King's hand I thought coldly received. When the Council met [Oct. 27] the Duke of York was sworn in and afterwards Lord Bute: the King declared him of the Cabinet Council; great court paid to his Lordship by everybody.

The Duke of Newcastle told me he had had a long conference with him[Bute] the purport of which was that the King thought him [Newcastle] to be the properest person to be at the head of the Treasury, and wished that he would continue there, and he Lord Bute made great professions of supporting him and acting in concert with him. The Duke replied that he was much obliged to H.M. and to his Lordship; that he was now very old; that it was high time for him to retire from business and that he begged to be excused. And he said the same to the King, who replied: 'That must not be.'

[126] In Nov. 1756.

[127] Horatio Walpole was Ambassador to Paris, 1724-7. The 1st Earl Waldegrave was *chargé d'affaires* until Mar. 1738. George I deposited 3 copies of his Will, with Dr. Wake, Archbishop of Canterbury, the Imperial Chancellery at Vienna, and Augustus William, Duke of Brunswick-Wolfenbüttel. George II extracted all three, the second in return for a guarantee of the Pragmatic Sanction and the third in return for a subsidy.

[128] Alternately Leicester House.

He [Newcastle] asked my opinion. I said that as a friend merely to the Duke of Newcastle, I should advise him to adhere to that opinion: at the same time as a friend to the public, I should certainly advise him to continue; that I thought he owed it to his friends and the Whig Party who would be broke to pieces and turned adrift. That therefore upon the whole my advice was that if he was pressed again, (for his Grace was in some doubt whether after their strong expressions and offers they did not mean to take him at his word), that he should say, though it was his inclination to retire, yet considering the critical conjuncture, the great sums that were immediately to be raised and the Sessions of Parliament so near, he would if it was His Majesty's desire continue for this Session. But that it should be understood that he was at full liberty then to retire. By that means he would be able to judge how business was like to go on, and then would be the time for him to consider whether it was prudent or honourable for him to continue. By that time likewise, he would be able to judge what would become or what was to be done with Lord Bute, who by all that appears seems not only ignorant of business but visionary. For it was plain by every step that he meant to be the minister over them all and yet had no plan of administration, or even thought of the practicability of effecting it. It appeared plainly to be his intention to confine all the ministers to their separate departments, thinking by that means to direct them all; how far that ought or could be submitted to was a matter of future consideration; that the various incidents that would arise during the course of the Sessions, would afford materials to form a judgement of what was to be done at the close of it.

Lord Mansfield said that he was very glad to hear my opinion as it confirmed him in his own, which tallied exactly with that I had given; that he the Duke of Newcastle should take great care to have it clearly understood that he was at full liberty to retire at the end of the Session, without assigning any reason, and that then the consideration would be *alors comme alors*.

There was to have been a meeting on the expedition[129] at Lord Anson's. Lord Bute told Mr. Pitt that the King would have no meetings held at which he [Bute] was not present, and that for the future everything should be considered and debated in his presence, and then His Majesty would determine as he thought proper. Lord Temple told me that Lord Bute had said to him he would remain a Private Man. Oct 28 1760: Saw Lord Temple [who] made strong personal professions for himself and Mr. Pitt to me. I endeavoured to get him to open upon the situation of affairs, which at first he seemed more shy of doing than usual. He said in general that he thought the union that was necessary in the late King's time was become more so at present,

[129] To take Belleisle.

and that they should endeavour to preserve it. I told him that I thought it absolutely necessary for the preservation of this country; that if the present system was broke this country would again fall into confusion and in the present crisis would be in danger of being ruined; that Mr. Pitt might if he pleased, with taking very little pains, gain the Duke of Newcastle and make his party friends to him, which I wished to see and was surely his interest, as they were undoubtedly the most powerful and the most respectable body in this kingdom; and that if he would shew a little more regard to them and less to his Tories, (though I did not desire him to quarrel with them), it might easily be effected.

He [Temple] said it would be their desire; that it was their desire; that he believed the old outline of ministry would be kept; that he and Mr. Pitt had separately had much conversation with Lord Bute; that he had talked like a man upon the coolness that had subsisted among them for the last year, that it was removed and he flattered himself they should go on amicably and well; that Mr. Pitt had told Lord Bute, if there was any alteration of measures, he must beg to be excused from continuing in the service.[130] The purport of my discourse [was] to convince his Lordship that if they and the Duke of Newcastle were strongly united, they might easily get the better of a Favourite. Though he did not differ with me, yet he was tender upon the point and convinced me that Bute and them were better together and come more to an understanding than he would own to me.[131]

Waited on the Duke of Cumberland who said that the young King continued extremely civil to him; that he mentioned the Wills to him, one an English and the other a German,[132] that were in the hands of Princess Amelia, and she would be glad to know what His Majesty would have done with them. He [the King] answered that as to the Wills, he was but one, and as the whole family were concerned, he thought it would be right that they would meet as soon as the Princess

[130] On 30 Apr. 1760 Gilbert Elliot, a friend to both Pitt and Bute, had spoken to Pitt about the suggestion that Bute might assume the head of the ministry as First Lord of the Treasury whenever the new reign might come about. Much to the annoyance of the future George III, Pitt had refused even to consider the matter. At seven o'clock, following the first Privy Council of the new reign on Oct. 25, Bute saw Pitt and assured him that he had abandoned all thought of taking the Treasury. Elliot, 362–5; Sedgwick, 44–6. See p. 11.

[131] From the outset, Newcastle, Hardwicke and Devonshire wrongly convinced themselves that Pitt, so far from keeping Bute in his place, had struck a deal to back his taking the Treasury in place of Newcastle.

[132] The German Will was dated 3 Apr. 1751 (O.S.), the English Will 11 Apr. 1751 (O.S.). Copies of George II's Wills and Codicils are in the Niedersächscheisches staatsarchiv Hanover K.G. Cal. Or. Des 3 Abtl. I, No. 35. See also 'Opinion of King's Advocate Hay, Attorney-General Pratt and Solicitor-General Yorke on the bequest made by King George II of his Jewels.' 12 Feb. 1761, T.S. 18, 249, part 1. 08320.

was well enough to come out. The Duke then said that he did not know whether H.M. was apprised that the late King had made a very considerable cession to him the beginning of the year of Dettingen,[133] and that he had rather be put into possession of it by H.M. than to take it himself. The King replied he had so much business just at present and was so much hurried that he desired to postpone the consideration of it for a few days. I remarked that it was what he did to everybody, when anything was asked him that had not been concerted between him and Lord Bute; that he declined giving any answer till they could settle it.

The Duke then asked me how I thought he had behaved to Lord Bute. I answered that my errand to H.R.H. was to remonstrate on that head; that I hoped he would forgive me if I told him that he was not civil enough to him; that I did not wish that he should let down his dignity or do anything unbecoming his rank, and yet on the other hand as the young King had been very civil to H.R.H., it would be a proper return to show civility to one that was understood to be his Favourite and adviser, and consequently might be supposed to have influenced him in his behaviour to H.R.H. The Duke said he thanked me; that he took notice at the time [and] that I observed. [He] wanted to know and would *mind his conduct* the next time.[134] I told him that it was not only my opinion but it had been remarked by several other people.

Went to Court: found the Duke of Newcastle rather changed in his opinion and wavering whether he should stay in. Lord Hardwicke had advised him to the contrary, at least, not without stipulations for power.[135] The Duke of Bedford[136] had advised him to insist upon choosing the new Parliament. I could not help observing that it was very weak advice; that I would never mention the choosing Parliament as long as I could avoid it; that he should continue to settle the elections; that being at the head of the Treasury would at least make the country look upon him as minister, and enable him in great measure to form the new Parliament; that if nothing was said they might very possibly not think about it and if the new Parliament could be filled with good men, it would be a great point gained, and one very material piece of service he would do this country in staying in this Session.

I met one of his [Newcastle's] most intimate friends[137] and told him

---

[133] The Battle of Dettingen, 1743.

[134] The general purport is plain: Cumberland had made no attempt to conceal his contempt for Bute and Devonshire had been asked, certainly by the King, to remonstrate.

[135] Hardwicke to Newcastle, 29 Oct. 1760, Add. MSS. 32913, ff. 426–9.

[136] 4th Duke of Bedford, Lord Lieutenant of Ireland, had left Dublin having completed his term of residence, and began regularly to attend Cabinet meetings in London.

[137] The reference is unlikely to be to Hardwicke, because Devonshire has objected to his advice. Stone or Dupplin are very possible.

I was sorry to see the Duke rather changed from his opinion of yesterday and thinking of retiring. He replied: 'Indeed he is wise if he does; Leicester House, my Lord, will never forgive his usage of them four years ago; and I say to you they have great reason for not doing it; they find they cannot go on without him and therefore they conjole [cajole] him but believe me, they only make a catspaw of him and mean to sacrifice him the first moment they have it in their power.

Pitt came up to me and said the Duke of Newcastle has changed his mind and is doubtfull about coming in. I thought at first he [Pitt] had engaged; he seemed much alarmed and appeared to me chagrined as if it would thwart his measures. He [Pitt] then told me the purport of what had passed on his account, the reconciliation with Lord Bute, and then that unless the same system and the same method of conducting the war was continued, that it would be impossible for him to serve, and particularly the supporting of the Princes of the House of Bruns-wic,[138] who had acted so heroically and well, and intimated that he could not suffer countenance to be shewn to Lord George Sackville, which would deservedly give uneasiness to Prince Ferdinand.[139] He [Pitt] hinted that he had received satisfaction on that head and that he was ordered to prepare drafts of letters for the King to write in his own hand to Prince Ferdinand and the Hereditary Prince.[140]

Oct 29 1760: Saw Viry: he had been with the Duke of Newcastle and had advised to continue in provisionaly. He said that Lord Bute professed his design of remaining a Private Man; that he wished to keep the present ministry; that he advised the King to be civil and to endeavour to gain the great Lords such as the Duke of Bedford and myself. I told him my suspicions that Lord Bute was agreed with Pitt and Temple. He owned it was true, that immediately on the death of the King that Pitt humbled himself and was accepted; that he believes he begins to repent a little and thinks he submitted too much, abused Lord Temple, but spoke well of Pitt.

Went to Court: M. Pitt came up to me immediately, very anxious about the Duke of Newcastle's taking on, and said that if affairs remained in the confusion they were in ten days longer Europe might be lost. I told him I wished they were settled but that unless the Duke of Newcastle and he came to [a] right understanding and went hand in hand, it would not do nor I could not advise his Grace to continue in the Treasury. I found he had some difficulties and at the bottom was apprehensive that Lord Bute would be jealous if there was too

---

[138] Charles I, Duke of Brunswick, his brother Prince Ferdinand and his son Charles the Hereditary Prince.

[139] Sackville had been court-martialled in Mar. 1760 and declared 'unfit to serve His Majesty in any military capacity whatsoever.'

[140] George III to Prince Ferdinand, 19 Dec. 1760, S.P. 87/38.

close a union. I then endeavoured to soften it by proposing that they should give mutual assurances of goodwill and friendship and that they would go on upon the same footing they had done in the late King's time. At last he [Pitt] said he was not angry with the Duke of Newcastle; that he was ready to live friendly with him and: 'in short, My Lord, I will say or do whatever you would have me do.'

I thanked him and said it was too much for me to take upon me to advise him, but that I would talk to his Grace and endeavour to bring them together. I observed in his conversation that he had taken the hint from what I had said to Lord Temple, for he spoke several times with great respect of the Duke of Newcastle's friends and the Party, as the most considerable people of this country, and the regard he had for them and that ought to be shewn towards them.

Found the Duke of Newcastle more disposed to come in; told him the purport of Mr. Pitt's conversation and his desire of living well with him; found his Grace had the same apprehensions and difficulties about too close a union with Mr. Pitt. He said he would write a letter to the King, which he would first shew to Lord Bute, and desire him to deliver, offering his services for one year upon promise of such support from the King as would enable him to carry on his Majesty's business.

Oct 30 1760: Went to Newcastle House: the Duke shewed me Lord Hardwicke's account of his conversation with Pitt,[141] which was indeed very full and friendly. Pitt said: 'Lord Bute professes to be a Private Man, what does he mean? Lord Holdernesse and I go into the King with our Bags in our hands, but are no ministers, and I know no more than anyone in the outer room.'

Lord Hardwicke doubted rather of his sincerity. I told the Duke of Newcastle that I was very sure he [Pitt] was really alarmed when he found his Grace hesitated about coming in and rather out of humour and hurt. How far that might proceed from the apprehension of its defeating any plan settled with Lord Bute, I could not pretend to say. I asked his Grace whether he was determined to accept. He said some of his friends were for his hanging back; that then they would find the necessity of courting him and he might make better terms. I told him some of his friends loved indecision, which in my opinion was the worst policy in the world; that it was plain his Grace intended to come in, and therefore begged of him that he would act like a man and do it in a handsome manner, or else he would disgust them and lose the merit in offering his service, and pressed him to have his conference immediately with Lord Bute, and to say that he would put himself into the King's hands and trust to his Majesty's goodness to enable him to carry on the business. He promised to do it directly. At Court

[141] Hardwicke to Newcastle, 29 Oct. 1760, Add. MSS. 32913, ff. 426-9.

Mr. Pitt came up to me and said that the Duke of Newcastle's indecision would have very bad effects; that he found Lord Bute and the King began to grow uneasy; that it had the appearance as if his Grace wanted to fetter them, and that they desired to have his final answer that they might know what they had to depend upon. I said that I was sure it was not his [Newcastle's] intention [to retire] and that I believed he was coming to Court and would speak both to him and Lord Bute in a very proper manner.

Pitt and his Grace talked together and I was desired to hear their mutual assurances to each other which were very strong. The Duke of Newcastle talked with Lord Bute and agreed to go to him [Bute] tomorrow morning. They agreed, for he was in high spirits; said: 'Bute has already promised that I [Newcastle] should choose the new Parliament; I think there will be no occasion for me to send the Paper to the King.' I was very strong in my advice that the Paper should go to the King; conversations and assurances may be forgot, a letter would always appear.

Oct 30 1760: Saw Viry: told me that Pitt repented of having put himself too submissively into Lord Bute's hands, thinking there was not a proper return made, and probably jealous of the Duke of Newcastle. Lord Bute had complained to him that the Duke of Newcastle hung off. Viry told him [Bute] that he believed he [Newcastle] would come into the King's service, for that I had taken great pains to persuade him to it and to offer himself in a respectfull manner and to rely upon the King; that I had succeeded with him and that it would be declared presently.

'Good God,' said Bute, 'you surprise me; has the Duke of Devonshire given such advice?'

He [Bute] looked down upon the ground and with a sigh said:

'How have I been deceived by some people upon his account. I lament that I did not cultivate the intimacy that I had once begun with him.'

I told Viry that I begged that nothing that passed between us might bring on a *Pourparler* with Bute; that I could be sensible whether I was treated as I ought to be, but it was a first principle with me, that no personal considerations should have any weight with me where the good of the public was concerned. They were in a hurry for the Funeral.[142] I acquainted the King that we could soon be ready but that there was one thing to be considered, that the late King might perhaps have given some orders relative to his funeral, and that we might be acting counter to them; that I understood [from] Princess Amelia that there were in her possession an English Will, which was a very small one, and a German Will with another Paper which was

---

[142] George II's funeral.

endorsed, to be opened at the same time with 'my [George II's] Will before several persons.'

The King said that he chose to have all the Family present and that he did not know whether the Princess would be well enough to come; desired me to enquire of the Duke of Cumberland, and also whether there was any particular persons named to be present.

I waited on the Duke who sent word[143] that it was wrote upon *before several witnesses* and that the Princess would be ready to wait upon his Majesty the next day. In consequence they [and the] King fixed to meet at Carlton House[144] between six and seven the next evening.

Oct 31 1760: At Court Lord Bute said that he had heard how handsomely I had acted by the King in the good advice I had given the Duke of Newcastle, and how much obliged they were to me and thanked me. I said no thanks were due; that I had only done what I hoped I should do upon all occasions, to give that advice which I thought best for the King and for the country. He said it was acting with the same public spirit that my family always had done.

The King sent for me and said the same. I told H.M. I had only done my duty and that he would always find me zealous to do everything in my power for the service of his government. Upon the whole he was very gracious. He then gave me a key of Lady Yarmouth's bureau, (in which the King [George II] always kept some money, which he had often said he intended for her at his death), and desired I would take Munichausen[145] with me to Kensington, and open it, and that I would tell Lady Yarmouth that he desired she would accept it as the first mark of his regard for her, and to see if there was not a Will of 1757. For that those the Princess had were of 1751; that Munichausen had one of 1759 and that there was one of '57,[146] which the King had kept but had sent a copy of it to Hanover. Accordingly we went to Kensington but found no Will. There was in the drawer a pocket book with £9,000 in bank bills and 11 bags with a 100 gold sovereigns in each, 2 gold snuff boxes with Lady Yarmouth's picture in them, 2 miniatures of the King and one of Madam Olderhausen.[147] There were also two papers signed by the King, one that he gave all the bank bills in that drawer to Lady Yarmouth, upon which she refused to take the rest. The other paper [directed] that Lady Yarmouth should deliver to whoever was his successor his large diamond George, the Collars of the three Orders and the Garter. She

---

[143] Cumberland to Devonshire, 30 Oct. 1760, Chatsworth MSS. 332/10.

[144] The residence of Augusta Princess of Wales.

[145] Hanoverian Minister in London.

[146] A reference to the codicils to the English and German Wills, dated respectively 6 Oct. 1757 and 15 Sept. 1759; see p. 44, n. 132.

[147] Identity not known.

immediately gave me the George, which was set round with eight very large diamonds: the rest she said were in the King's custody.

I carried it to the King and acquainted him what she said about the money. He ordered me to insist upon her taking the whole and said he should have done the same if it had been double the whole sum. He then gave [me] the late King's keys, which were sealed up, [and] ordered me to go again to Kensington to examine his bureaus for the Will. Munichausen went with me, we could find none, and what is very extraordinary, scarse any papers. [I] mentioned this circumstance to Mr. Stone, who said the King never loved to keep papers.* (The Will of 1757 was all the while in Munichausen's custody.)* I then locked all the late King's keys up in his strong box and carried the key to the King. I took an opportunity of telling him how sensible the Duke of Cumberland was of his Majesty's civility and goodness to him.

He answered: 'My Lord, it is my wish to live well with all my Family, and it shall not be my fault if we do not.'

I could not help saying: 'Sir, it is very good as well as wise in your Majesty.'

In the chariot had much conversation with Munichausen. He said that in the Will of 1751 there was left to the Duke 1,300,000 crowns; that in 1757 it was taken away; that in 1759 the King took notice of having revoked that legacy, and said it was not owing to any dislike, for he was the best son that ever was, but that the war had run away with the money; that therefore he left him a third part of the 200,000 crowns that was to come among the daughters. He added that he had a great deal of conversation with the young King; that he told him he must act for himself; that if he suffered himself to be governed by a Favourite he would be undone and ruin his country. He cited the King of Poland[148] and that the history of all nations were full of examples.

The Duke of Newcastle in high spirits, the King most gracious to him, and his conversation with Lord Bute friendly and well: it looked much as if they now preferred him [Newcastle] to Pitt and Lord Temple.

Lord Bute sent Viry to him [Newcastle] to complain of Pitt's behaviour and ill humour on Lord George Sackville's reception at Court.[149]

Nov 1 1760: Called on Mr. Pitt, much out of humour on account of the reception Lord George Sackville had met with at Court. [He] complained that he had taken the precaution to speak to Lord Bute beforehand; that he apprehended the worst consequences; that Prince

---

[148] An allusion to Count Heinrich von Brühl, Prime Minister to Augustus III, Elector of Saxony and King of Poland.

[149] Sackville had presented himself at the King's first Levee, to be received graciously.

Ferdinand would justly be alarmed and must doubt their sincerity, when he should hear this at the same time that he should receive the letter from the King, *and feared he would resign the command of the Army which would at once break the whole system.* That to be sure there was the outward appearance of a desire of going on with good humour and cordiality and even confidence, but that there was every now and then some *excentric* motion than nobody saw the spring of. That mouths were to be stopped with *the King*;[150] that this was one instance, the declaration[151] the first day was another, and an extra-ordinary step to be taken without the previous advice or the knowledge of any of the ministers. That this last step did not particularly concern him, but that it was such a damp to the measures that it would be impossible to go on: in short, much agitated and very uneasy.

I endeavoured to quiet him; said that I heard Lord Bute had given assurances that there was not the least intention of taking Lord George by the hand; that his coming to Court was unknown to them and it was a surprise upon them. I added that I thought if a letter was wrote to the Army[152] to say that he came to Court among the crowd the first day, but that they might be assured nothing further was intended by it: that there could not be any serious uneasiness about it. I found that the coldness which had subsisted for some time between Mr. Pitt and Lord Bute had begun upon the latter desiring Pitt to take some steps tending to save Lord George when he first came from abroad, which the other absolutely refused.

Pitt was so full of this subject that there was no getting him to talk upon any other. I asked him what he intended about the expedition.[153] He said Sir Edward Hawke's letter[154] did not convince him that his scheme was impracticable; observed that instead of giving his opinion for or against the plan, he enters into reasonings and gives another plan; desired I would speak to the Duke of Newcastle, that there might be a meeting upon it and the thing determined one way or [the] other. That he thought it depended on two questions to be asked: one to

[150] Pitt seems to be suggesting that the King was to be used to protect Sackville.

[151] George III's Declaration to the Privy Council on the first day of the reign, composed by Bute, had ended with these words: '. . . as I mount the throne in the midst of a bloody war, I shall endeavour to prosecute it in a manner most likely to bring an honourable and lasting peace.' Pitt had insisted upon the substitution in the published verison of 'expensive but just and necessary' for 'bloody', and that the words 'in concert with our allies' be added.

[152] i.e. to Prince Ferdinand.

[153] To Belleisle.

[154] Admiral Hawke's reply to Anson's request for a report on the feasibility of the Belleisle expedition, in which he not only advised against the scheme but suggested the establishment of a permanent bridgehead on the French mainland. In Pitt's opinion Hawke went beyond his proper terms. Hawke to Anson, 17 Oct. 1760, Add. Mss. 32913, ff. 163–6.

Lord Anson whether the ships could get near enough to protect the landing, which he believed he would answer in the affirmative; the other to Lord Legonier, whether a siege could be carried on at this time of the year, which the experience of all wars had shewn might be done.

Saw Sir Edward Hawke's letter. I thought a very sensible one and strong against the plan.

Nov 2 1760: The King came privately through the garden to St. James's before chapelle to avoid ceremonial, as his Family[155] was not settled. During the whole service [he] did not speak one word nor take the least notice of anybody.

Told the Duke of Newcastle that I had seen Mr. Pitt; that I found him very uneasy about this affair of Lord George Sackville, so much so that I desired his Grace would have some management towards him and see it set right. Soon after passing through the waiting room, where the Duke of Newcastle and Lord Bute were conversing, his Grace called me up [and] said: 'I hear from everybody that Mr. Pitt is much out of humour about Lord George Sackville.'

I replied that I saw him yesterday and that it hurt him much. Lord Bute expressed his surprise; that he had assured him it was unknown to the King and nothing was meant, and that he ought to be satisfied; and intimated that he did not understand such behaviour. I could not help saying that I thought it very necessary to have some management for Mr. Pitt, that affairs were in such a situation that it would be impossible to do without him; that you could neither carry on the war nor make peace without his assistance.

Lord Bute replied: 'My Lord, I would not for the world [that] the King should hear such language; he would [not] bear it a moment.'

I answered: 'Not bear it! he must bear it, every King must make use of human means to attain human ends or his affairs will go to ruin.'

He was called for to the King, stayed some time in the Closet, and then the King came out to return to Carlton House. As we went down the back stairs Lord Bute said to me: 'I will go this afternoon and see Mr. Pitt.'

Nov 3 1760: Viry had seen Lord Bute who had been above an hour with Mr. Pitt the night before: mutual professions of friendship, not one word of Lord George Sackville mentioned on either side. Bute complained that he had been very civil to me, and had made the King thank me for the advice I had given the Duke of Newcastle, and yet I was the only one of the great people that had not made him professions or said something personally obliging to him. I insisted that he [Viry] should not commit me with Lord Bute; that I thought I had been very civil to his Lordship, such as was due to one that the King marked out for his Favourite, but that it was beneath me to be paying court or

[155] The Royal Household.

making professions to him on that account. If his Lordship did right he would find that I should support him, but I was determined to continue independent.

I observed to him [Viry] that Lord Bute had appeared cold this morning at Court to the Duke of Newcastle and likewise to me. He said that they, meaning Lord Temple and family, (always excluding Pitt), had been insinuating, (and somebody had even to the King), that by promising the Duke of Newcastle to choose the Parliament, they had thrown the King and this country absolutely into his [Newcastle's] hand; that these insinuations had made impression and raised great jealousy, and made Lord Bute incline more to Temple &c. These pressed to have the militia recommended in the Speech. The King had lately declared strong against it, but they have reminded him of a promise made to Mr. Pitt to support it; scheme to name numbers to the Duke of Newcastle to be chose in Parliament.

Nov 5 1760: Pitt and Duke of Newcastle well together; upon comparing notes found that they were treated alike and kept equally in the dark. Pitt said to me: 'My Lord, I can call it nothing but the shell of an administration, I like not the appearance, we can not go on in this manner.'

I recommended to him patience; allowances ought to be made for a young King who was entirely in the hands of a Favourite; that this situation made it more requisite for the Duke of Newcastle and him to unite and act in concert, and if they could to take Lord Bute along with them. He [Pitt] complained of particular treatment he had met with.

I shewed him it was the same with the Duke of Newcastle and instanced the King and Lord Bute telling the Duke of Bedford that Lord Gower[156] should be Great Master of the Wardrobe, without ever mentioning it to the Duke [of Newcastle] or desiring to know what his friend Sir Thomas Robinson[157] would say to it. They proposed that he [Robinson] should be taken care of.[158] We agreed that Bute meant to govern absolutely. However I recommended strongly that it should be borne with.

Lord Bute met me and resumed the conversation of Sunday. He said he had not meant that the King should not bear to hear advice or to be told what means were necessary for his service, but that he would not suffer to have his prerogative touched in so tender a point as to be told who he was to speak to. I endeavoured to convince him that the objection was that it would have an effect on public measures, in this instance; that otherways nobody was to pretend to dictate to the King

[156] 2nd Earl Gower, whose sister Gertrude was the Duchess of Bedford.

[157] The then Master of the Wardrobe.

[158] Gower became Master of the Wardrobe and Robinson was compensated with a peerage as Lord Grantham.

who he should speak to, or not speak to. I then recommended strongly for the King's sake and for the peace of this country, that he [Bute] should keep well both with Mr. Pitt and the Duke of Newcastle; that the former had to support his popularity and the cry both of Town and Country, and the successes which had attended his measures had almost raised an infatuation in the minds of the people, so that it would be impossible to do without him.

I desired him [Bute] to consider that our affairs in Germany seemed to be upon the decline;[159] that therefore if he [Pitt] quitted now, and our situation should grow worse, which is not improbable, he would have to say, that when first I came to be minister I found this country sunk to nothing and hastening to its ruin; that by proper measures and a proper exertion of its strength the honour and glory of it is restored; that now other measures are pursued that he could not agree to, and the consequence is that our affairs are going back again. This sort of language, which would undoubtedly be held, would raise such a flame as could not be withstood. On the other hand, the Duke of Newcastle had united with him the principle nobility, the moneyed men and that interest which had brought about the Revolution,[160] had set this Family on the throne and supported them in it, and were not only the most considerable party but the true solid strength that might be depended on for the support of government. That therefore his Grace was undoubtedly the most necessary person for the King to cultivate; that he would find him always disposed to please as well as serve him; that he had his jealousies and was easily to be managed and at any time set right by a kind word added to good usage.

This being the state of parties, I could not help recommending to [Bute], for the sake of the King, that he would endeavour to hold the ballance even between them; that the task was hard, but if he did not pursue that plan there would be confusion and he would be undone. He heard it patiently and seemed to allow the force of what I said.

Nov 6 1760: Duke of Newcastle sent to me to give me an account of what passed the night before: there met Lords Hardwicke, Bute, Mr. Pitt and himself. It was agreed that the first should draw up the Speech.[161] They went through all the different parts that were to compose it without any difference of opinion, till at the close Mr. Pitt said that the militia must be included in the Speech. Lord Bute agreed with him[162] and the other two opposed it: Pitt was very calm in what

[159] By the end of 1760 Prince Ferdinand had been driven out of Hesse.
[160] The Glorious Revolution of 1688.
[161] The King's Speech. To select Hardwicke was a change, for Pitt had insisted upon drawing up the Speech for the four previous Sessions.
[162] Bute called the militia 'this most constitutional idea'. Bute to George Townshend, 19 Nov. 1760, Bute MSS. 107.

he said but remained firm and they parted without coming to any agreement. I told the Duke of Newcastle that I thought it very ill-judged in anybody to desire it; that for my part everybody knew I was against the militia in my opinion, and therefore I should if I was called to Council when the King's Speech was read, enter my protest against it.

Mr. Pitt spoke to me afterwards: I told him it was very wrong to mention any subject in his [the King's] Speech that was a point of controversy; that it was even begging a debate upon a day that every man who wished well must desire should pass with unanimity and was putting those that were against the militia under a cruel dilemma; that I had taken as much pains and gone as far to keep things quiet as any man could do, but convinced as I was of the danger of perpetuating the militia, I could neither in honour or conscience come into a measure of this sort.

He [Pitt] said that though he differed with me upon the utility of the measure, yet he should be very desirous of accommodation; that he had proposed the inserting it in the Speech with a view to keep things quiet and as a means to prevent more being asked on the point than he thought those that were against it could be brought to consent to; that he had declared, that the expressions should be measured carefully; that surely I could not be against thanking the gentlemen that had served as I would not deny the utility they had been of.

I answered: 'No, but why take that day to do it and spoil the unanimity?' I added that probably as there was a new reign some notice must be taken of keeping it out; if so, let there be a message and then it might fairly be debated.

Nov 7 1760: Pitt spoke to me again, desiring I would give him some hopes that I would not be against the bare mention of the militia; threw out some hint as if I was influenced by the Duke of Newcastle. I told him that I could come to no resolution till such time as I saw the King's Speech; that upon this point I must judge for myself, and that though the Duke of Newcastle and I might think alike upon the militia, yet in this instance I should not be guided by him, and that when I had formed my resolution, I should desire him and not the Duke of Newcastle to explain my reasons to the King.[163]

Nov 9 1760: Lord Bute asked me whether anything was settled as to the naming the militia in the Speech, and added: 'I wish to God we had been five, that it might have been determined that night.'[164]

I answered I imagined not as yet; that I was very sorry it was ever thought; that I could not help being of opinion that it would be very

---

[163] A most remarkable departure for Devonshire.

[164] This must refer to a Council meeting made up of Bute, Pitt, Hardwicke and Devonshire. Over the militia Bute will have sided with Pitt.

bad advice to the King and cruel usage of those who were in opinion against it; that if some part of the ministry thought it necessary to shew that the King was of their opinion, let them take some other time of doing it, but not oblige us either to give up our opinions, or appear in the odious light of opposing the Address, and desired him [Bute] to consider what a bad effect a debate on that day must have abroad.

He [Bute] lamented the unsettled situation of affairs at home. I said that the King was to be pitied who came to the Crown at a time that, with the best intentions, it was hardly possible to avoid falling into the greatest difficulties; that they had a very nice part to act and that the only thing to be done was to keep ballance even between the two parties, which was almost impossible, and yet they would be thrown into the greatest confusion if they did not. I told him that I had had some of the most considerable men [of] the City with me, to desire to know whether I thought the ministry would continue, for if the Duke of Newcastle did not remain in the Treasury they should not care to lend their money. He did not like it and expressed his surprise that one man should have such influence: 'Why, what would they do if he was dead?' To which I gave him no answer.

I acquainted the King that Clavering[165] refused to set up.[166] The King said that he should resent any neglect shewn to the late King, just the same as done to himself. He ordered me to tell Lord Rochford[167] to send another Groom to Kensington to take his place immediately and to forbid him walking at the funeral. The King ordered him to be forbad the Court.

Nov 12 1760: Viry said that Lord Bute was in the hands of Pitt and Lord Temple; that he was afraid of the former in the House of Commons, and therefore came into all his measures; that by Lord Temple's ridiculing the Duke of Newcastle, they had made Bute despise him, and seemed to allow that they would try to lay the Duke aside as soon as they could after the money was raised. Bute had desired Viry to sound the Duke of Newcastle about making him an English peer; that his Grace and Lord Hardwicke could do it if they pleased and put it as a test of their friendship towards him. Viry said he had endeavoured to dissuade him [Bute] from it; that it would create great jealousy and envy against him, and that it would be looked upon as a bad precedent and contrary to the determination of the House of Lords.[168]

---

[165] John Clavering, Groom of the Bedchamber to George II.
[166] i.e. to sit the watch over the late King's body.
[167] As Lord of the Bedchamber.
[168] The House of Lords had in 1711 passed a resolution condemning the conferment of peerages of Great Britain upon Scots peers, who were deemed represented by the 16 peers allowed under the Act of Union of 1707. Bute entered Parliament in 1761 as a

He [Bute] answered that the King's good will towards him was known and that he thought the Lords might overrule their order and make him the compliment. Viry was in doubt whether he should speak of it to the Duke of Newcastle, and if he did whether he should do it as from himself or from Lord Bute. I advised the latter, for otherways the Duke of Newcastle might if he pleased not understand it as a direct proposition made to him, and take no notice, and then Lord Bute would think he had neglected a point that he had so much at heart. Viry lamented that our affairs went very ill, and that Bute would not do right.

The Duke of Newcastle's credit at Court appeared visibly to be sinking every day, and Lord Temple seemed to be in great favour. At the same time Pitt complained that he was nobody, that he knew nothing; that he was consulted on no occasion; that it was impossible it should go on long; that however he would wait. They had not so much as mentioned the Civil List[169] to him; that he understood they intended to make peers; that he wished for Sir Richard Grosvenor and Mr. Spencer,[170] who were undoubtedly the most proper people, but that they gave him no opportunity of recommending them. [Pitt] professed great desire of union with the Duke of Newcastle.

I told him that the only means to prevent confusion was for them two to unite; that it was visible Lord Bute meant to keep the power in himself; that the Duke of Newcastle was no more consulted than he was; that there ought to be an inclination to indulge a young King in regard to one he was so fond of. And that a King of England, if he attempted to govern by a Favourite, would be unhappy; for his affairs would always go ill, unless he placed his confidence in those whose abilities and situation rendered them the most considerable. *Pitt said he had told his mind very explicitly on that subject to a friend[171] of Lord Bute's that he was sure would tell him, and that it did not differ from mine.* Pitt observed, that Lord Bath[172] and Dodington having long audiences had a bad appearance. I said that it plainly shewed the intention of gaining individuals independent of the ministers. He seemed very jealous of it [and]* took notice that they plumed themselves on the Addresses from all parts and agreed with me they were

---

representative Scots peer but the objection was circumvented by the creation of the barony of Mountstuart of Wortley for Lady Bute, which must pass together with the earldom of Bute to their eldest son.

[169] Which had still to be arranged.

[170] Sir Richard Grosvenor, 7th Bart., became Baron Grosvenor and John Spencer Viscount Spencer in 1761.

[171] Probably Gilbert Elliot.

[172] 1st Earl of Bath.

nothing. I instanced Richard Cromwell,[173] who said he had the lives and fortunes of all the people of England in a box.* Stone[174] thought things looked very ill for the Duke of Newcastle, sorry he had ever accepted, said that they would either turn him out or force him to retire the moment they had got their Civil List and the money, and would chouse a Parliament of their own.

Lord Mansfield gave me an account of the meeting on the expedition:[175] Pitt with great art endeavoured to draw Lord Anson and Lord Legonier in to give their opinions for it, which they had not resolution not to give into. The Duke of Newcastle and Lord Hardwicke protested against, and Mr. Legge,[176] and everybody else for. Lord Mansfield said he was no judge of military operations but should acquiesce in Lord Legonier's and Lord Anson's opinion. The Duke of Newcastle very angry with him, said he did it to save his Chief Justice's place. Lord Temple in high spirits, thought it a victory; treated the minority with great contempt and wished I had been there; as a candid man I should have been convinced; that he himself went *undetermined* and had no *participation* with Mr. Pitt.

I replied that if I had been there I should certainly have been against the expedition, for that the season of the year was an unsurmountable difficulty with me, and that I thought them bold men. Lord Bute made a strange bombast speech for it and took an opportunity of declaring strongly for the militia, both which the King and he had declared against before the late King dyed: plain proof of giving in to Mr. Pitt's measures. Pitt told me that when he shewed the King the words in the Speech about the militia, he [Pitt][177] said he wished they had been stronger but saw the necessity of acquiesceing. Nov 14 1760: Viry spoke to the Duke of Newcastle from Lord Bute about his being made an English peer.[178] His Grace spoke out boldly that it was absolutely impossible; that was he to attempt it, he did not believe he could get ten people to be for it.

Temple said to Lord Bute: 'Promise the Duke of Newcastle everything; when he has raised the money you may dismiss him; don't mind deceiving him, for he would deceive you.' Bute refused.

James Greenville[179] said at the time that the Duke of Newcastle was in doubt whether he should come into the King's service: 'We must do

[173] Richard Cromwell, Lord Protector, 1658-9.
[174] Andrew Stone.
[175] Against Belleisle, on 13 Nov. Yorke, iii. 311.
[176] Henry Bilson Legge, M.P.
[177] Meaning unclear but Pitt was almost certainly referring to himself, not the King. Hardwicke to Newcastle, 7 Nov. 1760, Add. MSS. 32914, ff. 169-70.
[178] See p. 56, n. 168.
[179] James Grenville, a lord of the Treasury and younger brother to Earl Temple and George Grenville.

everything to make the old woman continue in the King's service till the money is got, and then turn him out.'

Nov 15: Lord Bute came to be sworn in Groom of the Stole. I told him that Lord Rochford ought to deliver up his Key.[180] He was sworn and desired that I would tell Lord Rochford to be at Court the next day to resign the Gold Key.

No discourse upon the interior,[181] but [Bute] said that it looked like war with Spain;[182] that they persisted for an answer in writing to their Memorial and particularly to that of the Fishery on the Banks of Newfoundland. I told him that the Spanish Ambassador was with me about a week ago, and that I thought he was well disposed and that the difference seemed to rest upon a punctilio; that as to the Fishery, he said they did not insist upon an answer to it; that they would agree to give us what logwood we wanted at a stated price, but the point he insisted on was that we should evacuate our possessions and demolish our fortifications on the Masqueto shore previous to any agreement about the logwood. I told him they ought to go hand in hand, but he seemed firm on that point.[183]

Lord Bute mentioned my appointment as Lord Chamberlain, immediately that the Bedchamber and Master of the Horse were to be done on Monday: I believe unknown to the Duke of Newcastle and Pitt.

Spanish Ambassador came to tell me that the dispatch to Lord Bristol had been received;[184] that his Court continued firm and insisted on an answer in writing to the Memorial,[185] and that they would enter into no treaty, till we had given orders for evacuating our possessions on the Masqueto shore. That it was an insult committed against them in time of peace and therefore demanded reparation; that he had told Mr. Pitt that the King of Spain would give us the logwood, and as to the Fishery he did not press for an answer; that we ought to be contented with an assurance from the King of Spain.

[180] He had been Groom of the Stole to George II.

[181] i.e. domestic politics.

[182] In June 1760, following the collapse of the Yorke–d'Affry talks, d'Affry was succeeded as Spanish Ambassador by Count Fuentes.

[183] The first mention of the 'Spanish grievances'. For years Spain had challenged the British 'right of search' on the high seas in time of war. On 9 Sept. Fuentes had presented Pitt with two Memorials, the one advocating Spanish claims to participate in the Newfoundland Fisheries, the other relating to the British right to cut logwood in Honduras, S.P.F. 94/162.

[184] Pitt to Bristol, 26 Sept. 1760, notifying him of the Cabinet decision to reject the Spanish claim to participate in the Newfoundland Fishery but offering to continue negotiating over logwood, S.P.F. 94/162.

[185] Pitt had given merely a verbal acknowledgement of the two Memorials, at which he expressed considerable surprise. Résponde verbale faite à M. le Comte de Fuentes par M. Pitt, 16 Sept. 1760, S.P.F. 94/162.

I told him that I thought we only differed upon a punctilio and that it would be an unheard of thing to go to war for such a trifle, which made me apprehensive that their Court was changed. He protested not, and [I said] that I could not advise Mr. Pitt to send orders for evacuating the coast without some satisfaction given at the same time to us. He seemed struck and concerned. His orders were positive. Nov 17: Lord Bute and Mr. Pitt had warm words at Court. Pitt attacked him very roughly upon the treatment he met with; that he was kept in ignorance; that the Speaker[186] had asked him the evening before what was to be done about the Civil List, and he, the minister for the House of Commons, did not know one word of it; that he could serve on though ill used but the world should know it. Pitt by his appearance very angry, the other yielding. Pitt called in to the King. Lord Bute called Lord Temple and was as warm to him. When Pitt returned they conversed for an hour, the King waiting near an hour for Lord Bute and sending several times, who did not stir; rather extraordinary treatment to a King, who his Lordship represents to be so tender and nice as to the manner of his being treated. He [Bute] told the Duke of Newcastle on this affair that the King would not bear his ministers should talk such language. Temple talked strongly to the Duke of Newcastle for union.

Nov 24 1760: Viry had seen Lord Bute, who complained of the ill treatment he had received from Pitt, and yet could not go on without him; mentioned his perpetual insinuations against the Duke of Newcastle's power; much hurt with it, the whole Cabinet Council being present and seeing the treatment he received from Mr. Pitt. I desired Viry to take this opportunity of shewing his Lordship the folly of throwing himself into Mr. Pitt's hands entirely; and to endeavour to remove the jealousies that they instilled into him against the Duke of Newcastle and his friends; for that they were infallibly the people that the King must trust to for the effectual support of his government. Temple and all the Greenvilles had been with Lord Bute to mollifie him and to apologise for Mr. Pitt's behaviour. The whole was a mortifying circumstance to Bute, and which he will not forgive.

Spanish Ambassador and Wall[187] not well together; when at Turin he was furious against the French,[188] but changed his notions on the death of the King of Spain and governed here by Sanseverino and those who are in the French interest. I desired Lord Bute to thank the King for the honour he intended me of continuing me about his person; that I should certainly accept it with a pleasure in order to

---

[186] Arthur Onslow, Speaker of the House of Commons since 1727.

[187] General Richard Wall, Prime Minister of Spain.

[188] Fuentes had been Spanish Minister at Turin, 1754-8, and a strong opponent of France.

shew my desire of supporting the King and contributing to the utmost of my power to make his reign easy and glorious to him. But that I had long wished to retire; that I had made it my request to the late King when I quitted the Treasury, but he would not suffer it; that he was a very indulgent master and permitted [me] to do as I pleased; that I was very fond of the country and therefore was apprehensive that my way of life which I could not alter would be inconsistent with the attendance that I was sensible I ought to pay to a young King. And therefore if I did accept, I must have it understood that I was at full liberty to retire without assigning any cause whenever I found it inconvenient. And I did assure him that the King would always find me equally zealous to serve him, in place or out of place.

The King and Lord Bute much more civil to the Duke of Newcastle. Duke of Newcastle, Mr. Pitt and Mr. Legge met to settle the method of granting the Civil List. Pitt and Legge were for giving £800,000 p.a.: certain the Duke [Cumberland] would not differ from them. The King certainly wished to have it as his grandfather had it, because if there was a deficiency, it was to be made up to him, and if there was an overplus it was his.[189]

Nov 26: Pitt told the Duke of Newcastle he saw the necessity of peace, it being impossible to continue the war, and wished that his Grace and Lord Hardwicke would consult upon the method of attaining it.[190]

[Newcastle] appeared to be in great humour; said that some of the zealous people for militia were for bringing in a bill for perpetuity or a long term; that he would use his utmost endeavours to stop them; said the same to me, that he thought it very unadvisable in them; that he had told the most reasonable people among them, that as a friend to militia he must go along with them but that it was very ill judged, as the term under the present Act proved to be longer than he imagined,[191] and that it would be more prudent to take the sense of a new Parliament than of the present, in which the majority would probably be against them.

I told him [Newcastle] that I heard they said that as they must have new commissions they would not accept them without they saw a prospect of stability, and that they could make the militia a disciplined force, as some of them undoubtedly meant in time to substitute it in lieu of the standing army, as an army of the People against that of the Crown. He [Newcastle] said the first did not appear to him as a good reason, and if the other was ever attempted, he would be against it and that he had always declared so.

Dec 2 1760: The Lords Justices of Ireland transmitted two common

---

189 In the late reign surplus was rare and at best negligible.
190 Memorandum, 26 Nov. 1760, Add. MSS. 32915, f. 78.
191 The Militia Act of 1757 was for five years.

bills over as reasons for calling a Parliament,[192] and omitted sending a money bill, which had been the constant custom, giving for reason that if they had proposed it in Council that it would have been rejected and have set the country in a flame. The Primate[193] added in his private letter,[194] that if it was done he should not wish to see the Duke of Bedford in Ireland again.[195] This very extraordinary letter was laid before the Cabinet Council, where everybody was of opinion that the two bills should be returned to Ireland, as not being a sufficient cause for calling a Parliament, except Mr. Pitt who leant to the popular side and thought it was not essentially necessary and would occasion a great flame at a time when any disturbance there would be of bad consequence in our critical situation.[196] Lord Bute strong of the other side. Temple did not open his lips. It was determined that a Letter should be laid before the King in Council for that purpose.

Dec 3 1760: Pitt much out of humour about the Letter to Ireland and did not come to the Council where the Letter was read and agreed to without the least objection, Lord Temple and George Greenville signing it.[197] Lord Bute spoke to me about it. I told him that I was strongly of opinion for insisting on the money bill; that it was one step towards throwing off their dependancy on England which it was visible they were aiming at very fast; and that this instance took its rise from an error that had crept into the administration of government in that country, of increasing the Privy Council there and making an Irish one instead of an English. For that the Council there was wisely made a part of the Legislature, to enable England to preserve its authority over them and therefore the Council used to be composed of the great officers of the State, the heads of the Church and the Law and perhaps two or three of the first nobility that could be depended upon. And as they were by this means under the power and influence of the Crown, they took care to prevent and check any attempt that the Irish Parliament might take to throw off their dependancy. It was plain by his [Bute's] manner of speaking of Pitt, that he had not forgiven him.

Lord Fitzmorris[198] made Aid de Camp with rank of Colonel. Lord

---

[192] Privy Council of Ireland, 26 Nov. 1760, S.P. 63/418, f. 344. Bedford MSS. XLII, No. 221 (Two bills enclosed).

[193] George Stone, Archbishop of Ireland and Primate of Armagh, 1747–64.

[194] This letter has not been traced.

[195] Bedford as Lord Lieutenant of Ireland was insistent that, after the usual principle, the Lords Justices be required to transmit the money bill. *Bedford*, ii. 421–3.

[196] Hardwicke to Newcastle, 2 Dec. 1760, Add. MSS. 32915, ff. 246–7.

[197] Newcastle to Hardwicke, 3 Dec. 1760, Add. MSS. 32915, ff. 268–71. Hardwicke had been absent from Council owing to a severe cold.

[198] Viscount Fitzmaurice was in 1761 to succeed as 2nd Earl of Shelburne and Lord Wycombe in the peerage of Great Britain. He had distinguished himself as an officer in the army of Prince Ferdinand, and had attached himself to Bute.

Legonier said that he had remonstrated as going over many Lieutenant-Colonels of great merit, and mentioned Lord George Lenox[199] and Fitzroy.[200] The King said that he had recommended him to be a Lieutenant-Colonel four years ago, which ought to have been done at that time, and then this step would not have been extraordinary, and he was determined to do it. Lord Fitzmorris a great friend and adviser of Lord Bute's.

They had had a consultation this day at Elliot's at the Admiralty. The Duke [Cumberland] told me that Lord Bute paid great court through him to Fox, a sure sign that he wants to keep so far fair with him as to be able to make use of him against Pitt, if he quarrels with him. Dec 4 1760: Duke of Newcastle wrote to me[201] to know if it was true that Lords Oxford[202] and Bruce[203] were to be Lords and George Pitt,[204] Norborne Berkeley[205] and Northey[206] Grooms of the Bedchamber; wrote him word that I understood so.[207]

Dec 5: Duke of Newcastle remonstrated strongly to Lord Bute against the addition to the Bedchamber, a measure not only done without his knowledge but totally against his opinion,[208] and that would render it impossible for him to serve the King.[209] Lord Bute defended it and Pitt coming from the King joined them and took it up strongly; owned himself the adviser and that it was the wisest step that could be taken to preserve the unanimity and make the King's reign quiet.

Pitt came to justify it to me; said he was surprised to find the Duke of Newcastle uneasy at this step; that he would be judged by any candid man whether his Grace ought or the Whigs could take umbrage at a few of the principal Tories being taken into the King's service as supernumeraries. Had anybody been turned out for them, he himself would have objected to it, but when people of such characters offered their services, they ought to be accepted. I hinted to him that they boasted they had not sollicited but had been offered their employment. He said he had advised the measure, not the men.

---

[199] Lord George Lennox, brother to the 3rd Duke of Richmond, Lord of the Bedchamber. Richmond resigned in protest, which effrontery George III never forgave. Devonshire to Bute, 9 Dec. 1760, Bute MSS.

[200] Charles Fitzroy, M.P., A.D.C. to Prince Ferdinand and younger brother to the 3rd Duke of Grafton.

[201] Newcastle to Devonshire, 4 Dec. 1760, Chatsworth MSS. 182/157.

[202] 4th Earl of Oxford.

[203] 2nd Baron Bruce, after 1776 Earl of Ailesbury.

[204] George Pitt, M.P.

[205] Norborne Berkeley, M.P.

[206] William Northey, M.P.

[207] Devonshire to Newcastle, 5 Dec. 1760, Add. MSS. 32915, f. 286.

[208] All these appointments were Tory.

[209] Newcastle to Joseph Yorke, 5 Dec. 1760, Add. MSS. 32915, f. 308.

I observed to him that the manner of doing a thing was often worse than the thing itself and certainly so in this instance, for if it had been calculated to give umbrage to the Whigs, it could not have been more strongly marked. In the first place it was using the Duke of Newcastle very ill to take such a step without condescending to inform him of it, for that he had sent to me the day before at 4 oClock when the town had known it 24 hours, to desire I would let him know whether it was true or not. And in the next place the manner of doing it by adding them a week after the Bedchamber had been settled. By which means it would have the appearance that the first was a ministerial arrangement, the latter a measure of the King's, and by that means give a signal to the world that those set of people had his predilection, which must of course give great uneasiness to the true friends of his [the King's] family, and that were the main support of it. He [Pitt] replied that it was certainly wrong in my Lord Bute not to have acquainted the Duke of Newcastle with it: that as to the other, it was a refinement.

I said I did not see it and I was sure he would find people very much alarmed and displeased; that if they had communicated their intentions and mixed them with the rest of the Bedchamber when it was first settled, nobody could have objected; and that the doing it in this manner was rather reviving party heats than allaying them. And I added that this manner of acting without previous concert with one another would never do, and we should soon be thrown into confusion.

Lord Bute talked very civilly to the Duke of Newcastle and professed his desire to act in concert with him; said that when he was displeased with anything, he shewed his dissatisfaction as a man ought to do, not with that violence that Mr. Pitt assumed on every occasion; that from the treatment he had received from him in a month, he could feel what his Grace had endured for two years. The Duke of Newcastle desired to know what he was to expect; that for his part it was ridiculous for one at his time of life to go on in this manner and be treated as a cypher; that he must know what he was to do in regard to the choosing a new Parliament; that treated as he was he did not [know] what to say to people or how he could engage with them. Lord Bute replied that the King desired to see a list of his own burroughs; that the King, he supposed, was to have the nomination to them; that His Majesty was against spending any money and so was Mr. Pitt,[210] who said the King ought to have a Parliament composed of all his people, as they were all unanimous for him.

The Duke of Newcastle asked my opinion on this conversation. I

---

[210] Devonshire inserted in the left margin: 'he [Newcastle] thought some might be necessary.'

told him I disliked it much; that Pitt's meaning was evidently to get a Tory Parliament or as many of those people as [he] could, which would be a strength to him. That I thought he [Newcastle] had nothing to do but to prepare a scheme for the Parliament and lay it before the King, with the expense that would attend it, to acquiesce in any reasonable alterations. But if they objected to it in general, to say that it was impossible for him to be of any service to the King and retire; that he might hint their promise to him[211] that this would be the touchstone to shew what was their real disposition towards him, which did not appear at present to be favourable. Lord Bute had told Pitt that the Duke of Newcastle wanted money for the elections, and Pitt protested against it to his Grace. The Duke apprehensive that Pitt was capable of laying hold of it in Parliament, and with reason.

Pitt talked to me of the King of Prussia's letter to him[212] and related to me his conversation with Kniphausen,[213] showing him the impossibility of carrying on the war and insinuating to him that if a general pacification could not be obtained, it would be even better for his master that we should make a separate peace with France.[214]

Dec 6 1760: Saw Viry: said that he had been with Pitt on Thursday, who pretended to be much out of humour; that he knew nothing; that every arrangement was taken without consulting him. [Pitt] did not say a word of the scheme of taking in the Tories to Viry, who found when he came to Court that it was public. And James Greenville came to him [Viry] that evening and told him that they [the Grenvilles] approved of the measure, though it was done without their privity: 'And to shew the perfidy of these people,' says he [Viry], 'Lord Bute owned to me he had never thought of the measure till Pitt proposed it to him, and that indeed he approved of it and recommended it to the King.'

[Viry] very angry with Pitt and his family; said that they acted unfairly and treacherously; that they were doing everything in their power to undermine and ruin the Duke of Newcastle, whilst they made the strongest professions to him; that they deceived Lord Bute and drew him in to assist them in getting the better of the Duke of Newcastle, and would then tyrannise over him; that the impression

---

[211] i.e. that he would have the choice of the new Parliament.

[212] Frederick II's letter of condolence to Pitt of 7 Nov. 1760, upon the death of George II, wherein he outlined his views on peace and expressed his confidence in Pitt. *Chatham*, ii. 77–9.

[213] Dodo Heinrich, Baron von Knyphausen, Prussian Minister in London.

[214] Knyphausen's report to Frederick II, 5 Dec. 1760. Talks were in progress between London and Berlin, with a view to a new agreement allowing Britain to make a separate peace, which article IV of the treaty of 1758 had forbidden. Conditions of a new treaty were to be that Prussia receive security guarantees together with an increased subsidy. D.Z.A., Rep. 36. 33. D, ff. 135–6.

they had made in him and the King, that the Duke of Newcastle would be absolute master, by the promise he had got of chusing the Parliament, was the grievance, and cause of jealousy against him; that he was to see Bute the next morning and would try to undeceive him. [Viry] said that Pitt talked of peace but he believed did not mean it.

I encouraged him [Viry] to talk to Bute, for that if they forced the Duke of Newcastle to retire, which as an honest man, I should soon be obliged to advise him to do, that these gentlemen would tyrannise over him and the King; that they had no difficulties in putting the dagger to the King's throat; that they had done it several times in the late reign and would do it again whenever their ambition prompted them to it or made it necessary.[215] [That] I was much concerned for the King and apprehensive that Lord Bute, through want of judgement and aiming at a power which it was impossible for him to attain, would throw his master into great difficulties. That not content with being the Favourite, he must be the minister over the other ministers, would inevitably bring on attempts to force him from the King, the thought of which I abhorred and the consequences I dreaded, as the impression it must naturally make on the mind of a young King would be such as will render his reign uneasy to him and throw the greatest confusion into his affairs. And that if Lord Bute went on in the way he proceeds at present, that stroke would inevitably come, an indecency to the King that I should see with sorrow, and a blow that would throw this country into the greatest confusion.

Dec 8 1760: Viry had been with Lord Bute [who] took notice of the Duke of Newcastle being out of humour at the addition to the Bedchamber; sorry he had not communicated it to him, said that he had done everything to oblige the Duke of Newcastle; that in filling up the Bedchamber he had refused nobody that he had recommended. That when Mr. Spencer applied for the peerage, he had sent him to the Duke of Newcastle as the proper channel:[216] 'And yet he makes no return to me, or has offered to do anything to oblige me.' [That] the temper of Pitt was not to be borne or submitted to, that the King was quite tired of him, but that they must keep him to make the peace and then they hoped to be in a situation to get rid of him;[217] that therefore in regard to choosing the Parliament, they meant to consult the Duke of Newcastle, for that if he did not do it, Mr. Pitt would get greater weight and become more formidable and more troublesome. Viry was

---

[215] A reference to the events of 1746 and 1754-7, when Pitt and his Grenville brothers-in-law were considered to have pressed their own interests further than decency allowed.

[216] John Spencer to Newcastle, 27 Nov. 1760, Add. MSS. 32915, ff. 115-16.

[217] George III to Bute, [mid-Nov.] 1760, Sedgwick, 49.

to acquaint the Duke of Newcastle with the purport of this conversation.[218]

The Duke of Newcastle desired me to come to him this evening where was Lord Kinnoul,[219] Lord Hardwicke and Mr. Stone. I gave my opinion that he should join with Lord Bute heartily, keeping fair with Mr. Pitt; that I was persuaded Lord Bute was desirous of it; that he should talk to him on the subject of choosing the Parliament, ask him what people the King and he wished to have in; that he would place them to their satisfaction, and after they were settled show him the general plan; that if Lord Bute was sincere they would accept of his list. If they objected I should then advise him to retire. Lord Hardwicke said the Duke of Newcastle must not go alone and several hints were given me to know what I would do in that case.

At last I told them, that as a friend to the Duke of Newcastle I gave him my advice what I thought best for him to do as a minister and the head of the most considerable party in this country. That with regard to myself, I was determined to remain my own master; that I had so often declared both in public and private, that I would be free and independant; that I could not act any other part; that therefore I could enter into no agreement to go out with his Grace; that whenever the time came, I should judge for myself and do what I thought most for my own honour, and that I believed neither his Grace nor those I had always acted with would have [no] reason to complain of him [me]. There was one thing I would declare, that if I went out it should be once for all; to retire and not enter into any engagement to force myself or others into power again. The conclusion was that he [Newcastle] should give intimation the next day to Viry that he was ready to talk confidentially with Lord Bute and to come to a thorough good understanding.

Dec 9 1760: Viry called after he had seen the Duke of Newcastle; said that everything passed very well, and that he wished I would talk to Lord Bute on the subject before he related his conversation with the Duke of Newcastle to him.

Meeting Lord Bute at Court, I told him that seeing the King's affairs in danger of running into confusion, I thought I owed it to the King to apprise his Lordship of it, but that I desired it might not be known I had talked with him. I informed him that this measure [the Bedchamber] had given great umbrage to the Whigs in general and repeated what had passed between Mr. Pitt and myself* *vide* Dec 5.*

Lord Bute replied that being apprehensive that the enlarging the number of places might give umbrage to the House of Commons, he

---

[218] Which he did next day. See Minute of Newcastle's conversation with Count de Viry, 9 Dec. 1760, Add. MSS. 32915, ff. 358-60.

[219] 9th Earl of Kinnoull, formerly Viscount Dupplin.

asked Mr. Pitt's opinion, who answered certainly not, and proposed to him adding some of the Tories; that he owned he approved the thought and mentioned it to the King, who liked it and agreed to it; that he was sorry it had been done in the manner it was and that it had not been communicated to us. That with regard to what Mr. Pitt said about the persons: '*My Lord, I desired my old friend Norborne Berkeley might be one: the rest I had nothing to do with.*'

I then told him [Bute] I had been the night before at Newcastle House, where was Lord Hardwicke, Lord Kinnoul and Mr. Stone. The Duke wanted to know our opinions [on] what he was to do, or whether it was possible for him to continue in the King's service; that some were of opinion that it was most advisable for him to retire; that I had given him mine to continue, provided he could come to a right understanding with his Lordship [Bute], and recommended that he should desire to have a full and explicit conversation with your Lordship [Bute] and particularly in relation to the choice of the Parliament; that if they two could agree that then I thought he might safely and with honour continue to serve the King, and that I had left him with the intention of following my advice.

Lord Bute answered that he would go more than half way; he had long wished for an entire union with his Grace; that he could not get him to an explanation. I laid great stress on its being done in such a manner as should not give umbrage to Mr. Pitt, who would grow jealous if he saw that they were agreed, and that it would be impossible to go on without him. He assented to it but shewed great dislike to that set of men. Went to Council [December 11][220] upon Mr. Pitt's Paper[221] that he had settled with Kniphausen relative to peace. He had complained of the gout in his hand and said he would not come; however he came seemingly not well pleased. He opened the subject with an account [of] how he came dipped in an affair which was not properly in his department,[222] (viz. by the King of Prussia's letter to him which flattered him to a great degree). He wrapped Lord Holdernesse related his consulting the Duke of Newcastle, without whose concurrence he was determined never to take any step; mentioned his communication to me, and to Lord Hardwicke and what had passed with Lord Bute; apologised that he had not had an opportunity of talking with the President[223] upon it; took no notice of the Duke of

[220] Hardwicke to Newcastle, 11 Dec. 1760, Add. MSS. 32915, ff. 399–400.

[221] A lengthy document entitled *Précis de la Dépêche*, sent to Frederick II on Dec. 12, in which he was asked to submit his financial requirements in the event of a separate peace between Britain and France.

[222] Holderness, Secretary of State for the North, had the right to conduct Prussian correspondence.

[223] John Carteret, 2nd Earl Granville, Lord President of the Council.

Bedford. The Council were unanimous in their opinion of approving the methods proposed to bring about the peace.[224]

Lord Temple very fond, asked what I thought of the late transaction.[225] I replied I was persuaded he knew my opinion. He said, yes, and that to be sure the Duke of Newcastle and I had great reason to be displeased; that it was done in the manner the most offensive to us that was possible; and in short made use almost of my words to Mr. Pitt on the occasion, *endeavouring to throw the whole blame on Lord Bute,* to which I made very little reply.

Dec. 11: Pitt told Viry that the Duke of Newcastle was the strangest man in the world; that he was outragious upon taking in of a few Tories, which every honest Englishman must approve of, and did not say word upon that shamefull promotion of Lord Fitzmorris, and that it was impossible to act with such a man, and was in very ill humour.

Lord Bute convinced of the double dealing of that set, but had a better opinion of Mr. Pitt than the rest.

Jan 1 1761: When I came to town, Lord Bute exscused himself from having any concern in the promise the King had made to Lord Bath of the Lieutenancy of Shropshire; that he did not know he was my friend and that he wished anything could be done to satisfy Lord Powis.[226] I said as to his being my friend, that was a private consideration, the removing of him a public one, and enlarged upon the arguments of my letter to the Duke of Newcastle,[227] and that Lord Powis had eight or ten members in the House of Commons, men of fortune that went with him. Whereas Lord Bath could not bring his own son into Parliament,[228] that he [Powis] and his friends were independent of all ministers and at all times ready to serve the King, and therefore the sort of people that the King ought naturally to wish to oblige. He [Bute] said he saw the force of what was said and was much concerned at it, but that he did not see how the King could get off; that Lord Bath was his friend. He should desire him to release the King from his promise but he feared he was not a man to comply with

---

[224] The Council discussed terms for a separate negotiation with France acceptable to Frederick II. Knyphausen was to be informed that as on the following day, 12 Dec. the Prussian subsidy was due for a final renewal before the treaty expired in May 1762, a statement of his master's intentions was necessary, especially with a view to his seeking an accommodation with Austria and Russia. Charles Jenkinson, Memorandum, Add. MSS. 38333, ff. 40–61. Knyphausen to Frederick II, 5 and 12 Dec. 1760, D.Z.A., Rep. 96. 33. D. Vol. XV, ff. 135–8, 157–8.

[225] The appointments to the Bedchamber.

[226] The 1st Earl of Powis, Lord Lieutenant of Salop. For Bath's successful intrigue to oust Powis see L. B. Namier, *The Structure of Politics at the Accession of George III* (1939), 325 et seq.

[227] Devonshire to Newcastle, 17 Dec. 1760, Add. MSS. 32916, f. 152.

[228] Bath's unsuccessful attempt to put up his son Viscount Pulteney as candidate for Shrewsbury.

such a request. I observed that Kings ought, (and especially a young one), to consider when anybody desired another's employment, the consequence of the person that was to [be] disobliged as well as of him that was to be gratified. He answered he hoped this would be a useful lesson. He concluded with desiring me to talk to Lord Powis and to see if no means could be found to make him easy. Lord Powis said no advantage to himself should make him give up his friends.[229]

Mr. Bridgeman,[230] Mr. Forrester[231] and General Whitmore[232] came to me. I represented to them[233] the King's promise which made it very difficult to know how to act, for that it was impossible to ask him to break his word; that therefore if H.M. could not be released and should find himself under the necessity of appointing Lord Bath Lieutenant of Shropshire, I desired them to consider whether it was not better to acquiesce, if by that means the power and authority of the Crown in the county should be continued in the present channel, and the other have only the name of it. They were unanimously of opinion not to submit in any shape to Lord Bath and they should look upon Lord Powis as the last [best] of men and that he gave them up if he listened to any accommodation of that sort. They said they had never given but one vote against government and that was when, with Lord Powis at their head, they voted for an additional allowance to the late Prince of Wales.[234]

After the King had made Lord Bath Lord Lieutenant,[235] they all came to me and said they were ready to do everything in their power to serve the King, but that nothing should make them concur with Lord Bath: on the contrary, they would oppose him to the utmost.

Jan 4 1761: [I] took an opportunity of asking Lord Bute how the Duke of Newcastle and he came not to meet, as was agreed before the Holydays; that they then on both sides seemed desirous to come to a good understanding and that I was sorry to see it in a manner gone off. He protested that he was sorry for what had passed; that he thought his Grace had not acted fairly by him, particularly when he desired that Hunter might have the government interest to be re-chose at Winchelsea.[236] He [Newcastle] told him [Bute] that he had

[229] Powis to Devonshire, 16 Dec. 1760, Chatsworth MSS. 320. 9A.

[230] Henry Bridgeman, M.P.

[231] Brooke Forester, M.P.

[232] Lieut-General William Whitmore, M.P.

[233] Old Whigs of the Powis connection.

[234] On 2 Feb. 1737, when Walpole defeated by a narrow margin the opposition motion to augment the Civil List provision for Frederick Prince of Wales.

[235] Powis accepted the Lord Lieutenancy of Montgomeryshire in lieu of Salop. However on Bath's death in 1764 Powis was reappointed to Salop.

[236] Thomas Orby Hunter, M.P., to Bute, 10 Dec. 1760: 'As to Winchelsea election. Desires the King's protection'; Register of Bute's correspondence, Add. MSS. 36796, f. 59.

promised Lord Egremont[237] to be against Hunter; that he Lord Bute sent to Lord Egremont, who denied it, said he had no engagements with Duke of Newcastle; was independent, but if any connection it was with Lord Granville.

This unfair proceeding put him [Bute] out of humour; that his Grace was warmer than ever he had seen him, and so they parted; that if I had been in town he believed it would not have happened.[238] That he did assure me his dispositions were still the same; that he imagined the Duke of Newcastle thought he wished him ill, and that he wanted his place. That so far from it, he wished him very well and desired that he should remain in the Treasury; that he was ready to talk with him upon a fair, open and friendly footing; that if he assisted the Duke of Newcastle's friends, he expected in return that his Grace should do the same by those that belonged to him; that there were some people he wished to serve, not many; that he should not find him unreasonable, but that his Grace must not expect *the whole Lyons Skin*. I told him if he was in that disposition, I found his Grace was the same way disposed; that what he offered was very fair, and that I would endeavour to make the other act the same part, and desired that when they met at Court they would talk confidentially to each other.

The Duke of Newcastle sent to desire I would come to him in the evening, told me that I had done wonders; that Lord Bute came up and spoke to him in the most friendly manner; that he spoke upon a supposition of a vacancy in the Admiralty by the death of Boscawen;[239] mentioned Sir Edmond Thomas,[240] but said that Mr. Thomas Pelham[241] might go to the Admiralty and then the Board of Trade would be open for *Lord Hardwicke's* youngest son.[242] *Lord Bute had asked who had most weight with the Duke of Newcastle, I told him Lord Hardwicke and who would not let affairs go well if his family were not taken care of. He said he fancied it was so.* [Bute] would give up his friend [Hunter] to shew his good disposition to his Grace and Lord Hardwicke. This made the Duke very happy.

I then related the substance of the conversation, told him of what had passed with Lord Egremont as to Hunter, not as to his own connections. He [Newcastle] gave me full proof that what he had done was at Lord Egremont's request and through the channell of Browne

237 The 2nd Earl of Egremont.
238 Devonshire had spent the Christmas holiday at Chatsworth.
239 Admiral Edward Boscawen, M.P., died on 10 Jan. 1761, after a short illness.
240 Sir Edmund Thomas, 3rd Bart., M.P.
241 First cousin to Newcastle, for whom he acted as agent in Sussex, and at present a Lord of Trade.
242 John Yorke, M.P., was appointed to the Board of Trade that March.

the surveyor.[243] He then declared that he would act fairly by Lord Bute and talk with him on all points without reserve; said there would be a difficulty about the Board of Trade, for Pitt had long wanted it for Lord Villiers.[244]

Jan. 12: Saw Viry: talked over Lord Powis's affair,[245] which I told him went very ill. [Viry] then told me in great confidence that the King was displeased with Lord Holdernesse and had pressed Lord Bute to be Secretary of State in his room; that as yet he had declined it, asked me what I thought of it.[246] My opinion was that no friend ought to advise him to it; that it was a very dangerous undertaking; that it was very material to know Mr. Pitt's opinion. He [Viry] answered he did not imagine he [Pitt] could have any objection to it, and that if Lord Bute was Secretary of State, they might act jointly to make a peace.

Jan. 16: Duke of Newcastle desired me to meet Lord Hardwicke and Kinnoul that evening at his house. He informed us that Viry had been with him, and threw out to him as an idea of his own, that his Grace should propose to the King the making Lord Bute Secretary of State in the room of Lord Holdernesse. It was debated whether Viry did it of his own head, or at the desire of Lord Bute; the latter opinion prevailed. *Lord Hardwicke* seemed to relish much his being Secretary of State, *partly out of pique to Lord Holdernesse, not having forgot the attempt to make Mr. Pitt angry last year with General Yorke.[247] The reason he gave was that Lord Bute would be more tractable and more dependent when he was in a responsible office.*

I told his Grace that I thought he should not make the least objection to it, on the contrary should seem to relish it. [But] that his proposing it directly to the King was a very different consideration. It would give jealousy to Pitt and perhaps umbrage to his own friends; that therefore he should tell Viry that, if Lord Bute liked it he should certainly approve and be ready to promote it; that he thought his Lordship should well consider the manner of doing it not to create any jealousy or uneasiness to Mr. Pitt, which he was apprehensive would be the case if he [Newcastle] was to propose, but however to leave that point for further consideration.

Saw Viry: mentioned again Lord Bute's being Secretary of State; agreed that it would be improper for the Duke of Newcastle to propose it. [Viry] asked me if I would. I said that I was not in a situation to propose ministerial alterations; that if the King thought fit to send me

[243] Identity not known.
[244] Viscount Villiers, M.P., who became a Lord of Admiralty.
[245] See pp. 69–70.
[246] The first mention that Bute might become Secretary of State for the North in place of Holderness.
[247] Over the Princess of Anhalt-Zerbst's letter, see p. 29, n. 34.

of a message I would certainly obey, but I still thought Lord Bute should go to Pitt himself. [I] mentioned the report of the lawyers on the late King's Will.[248] Viry said Lord Bute would advise the King to act generously by the Duke [Cumberland]; bad me advise him [Cumberland] to send to Lord Bute and speak to him upon it; said that if he took Secretary of State he depended on the assistance of the Duke [Cumberland], and the Duke of Bedford and me and Mr. Fox. I replied, and of the Duke of Newcastle, and if he was wise should give his Grace as much éclat in public as possible.

Jan 21 1761: Viry had seen the Duke of Newcastle, who told him that he relished his idea, but that great care was to be taken not to give umbrage to Mr. Pitt. I mentioned to him [Viry] that Lord Bute should break it himself to Pitt, and add that he would accept on no condition but that of acting in concert with him. He [Viry] said Lord Bute would never do that.

Duke of Newcastle saw Mr. Pitt the day before,[249] very cool and very calm. [Pitt] told him that he was unacquainted with what was doing and did not imagine his Grace was much more informed; that there had been often favourites but that the nation would never suffer them to be both favourites and ministers. [Pitt] instanced King William,[250] as great a prince as ever filled the throne, had favourites, the Duke of Portland[251] and Lord Albemarle,[252] but then they confined them selves within the circle of the Court and did not interfere as ministers. But in the present case, not to lay any stress on the country he belongs to,[253] it would never be borne and *he for one would never consent or lend a helping hand to make him one.* It was probable by this conversation that he had some intimation of Lord Bute's design, perhaps by his friend Elliot of the Admiralty.

Lord Hardwicke remarked that a few days after the death of the late King, Pitt had told Lord Bute that if he would take the Treasury he would support him in it.

Viry advised the Duke of Newcastle to settle the Parliament and

[248] A report prepared by the Crown lawyers at George III's request, dated 13 Jan. 1761, on the two Wills of George II, the English and the German. It was the unanimous opinion of the lawyers that by the terms of the German Will, jewels which George II had bought with his own money or had been left to him by his ancestors, were to pass to George III, whilst by the English Will all the other jewels were to go to Cumberland. T.S. 8/249, pt. 1; Chatsworth MSS. 622.2. Unfortunately the report followed the Wills in not making a clear distinction between the German and the English effects of the late King and to specify the jewels that might be deemed the property of Cumberland.

[249] Newcastle to Hardwicke, 20 Jan. 1761, Add. MSS. 32917, f. 435.

[250] William III.

[251] Pitt was in fact referring to William Bentinck, 1st Earl of Portland. It was his son the 2nd Earl who was given a dukedom by George I in 1716.

[252] 1st Earl of Albemarle.

[253] Bute's Scots and Stuart descent.

what changes were to be made with Lord Bute soon, for every day it was deferred it was the worse as people got promises from the King. This was said at Lord Bute's desire.

Jan 22 1761: Viry said he had sounded Lord Bute on speaking to Pitt but he did not choose it; could not the Duke of Newcastle break it to the King as a measure that would be for the service of his government? He might depend upon the King's secresy: that His Majesty might be trusted. That he did not even tell Lord Bute everything, for he had talked to him [Viry] on some points and bid him not mention them to Lord Bute; that he was afraid of too much appearance of confidence and for that reason went more rarely to Court.

I told him there would be great objections to the Duke of Newcastle's making such a proposition; he must first know from Lord Bute that it was his desire, and next in my own opinion it would not be honourable towards Mr. Pitt to take such a step without acquainting him first and having his concurrence. Viry acknowledged the force of those reasons. I asked him why he could not sound Pitt himself: he said he would consider it.

Jan 23: Viry came and said he had turned my proposition in his thoughts and did not think it adviseable in his situation to speak to Mr. Pitt on the subject; that as an honest man he could not advise the measure to Mr. Pitt, or if he was questioned say that Lord Bute means Pitt well and to act in confidence with him. He saw the objections to the Duke of Newcastle's proposing it, and did not know what method could be taken. I proposed to him that Lord Bute night very well do it by the means of Mr. George Greenville who was his [Bute's] friend[254] and *had reason to be in good humour*.

When Mr. Greenville went to the King to receive his consent for being Speaker, the King asked him if he could do anything to shew his regard for him. He asked to be a Cabinet Counsellor, which the King promised. I told Viry it was a very bad measure to make the Speaker of the House of Commons of the Cabinet Council and they would, I fear, soon find their error.*[255] That the method [of approaching Grenville] would be for Lord Bute to tell him [Grenville] that the King, not approving Lord Holdernesse and seeing that business did not go well, had pressed him, Lord Bute, to take the Seals, as thinking that there would be less difficulty when they came to make the peace, when he, Lord Bute, who was known to be so well with him, [the King], was to act in conjunction with Mr. Pitt. That *it was what he was much averse to himself, as he was much safer in a post where he was not*

---

[254] Recently George Grenville had been moving away from Pitt in Bute's direction, largely through the instrumentality of Charles Jenkinson.

[255] Grenville never became Speaker. He was admitted to the nominal Cabinet that February.

responsible, * the substance of what Viry had always declared whenever he entered on this conversation.* But as he [Bute] saw the King more eager on it every day, he wished he [Grenville] would in great confidence sound Mr. Pitt upon it, to see whether he would approve of it and that he [Pitt] might depend upon his [Bute's] acting confidentially with him, and that he would keep no secret in his office as Secretary from him [Pitt]. That if Lord Bute wished the thing, this seemed the most probable method of succeeding, for that the only way to make Pitt come into it, was to make him the first informed of it and a party to it.

Viry seemed to approve this method and said he would sound Lord Bute upon it, who might safely say to Mr. George Greenville that Pitt was the first of the King's ministers that he had entrusted with it. For when Viry spoke to the Duke of Newcastle, it was only as an idea of his own, and what he had said to me was not as a message from Lord Bute. But that he [Bute] had desired him [Viry] to tell me and to find out my opinion and that if the King hereafter should have a mind to part with Mr. Pitt, Lord Bute's engagement would not stand in the way, as it was only to act confidentially with him as Secretary of State. He [Viry] owned the King's aversion to Pitt grew stronger every day; they disliked his popular notions and his principles; he abused Lord Temple and the Greenvilles. [Viry] said that if this scheme did not take place, Lord Bute would withdraw himself from the meetings and would not in any shape meddle with business, but leave the peace to be made by Mr. Pitt with the approbation of the other ministers. It is very plain that Lord Bute wishes the thing very much and that Viry tells him everything, and takes likewise from him what he is to say. Jan 27 1761: Viry had sounded Lord Bute on the proposition of endeavouring to find out by George Greenville whether Mr. Pitt would come into the scheme of making him Secretary of State. He (Lord Bute) did not approve of it. Viry had been this morning to the Duke of Newcastle and had told him that he had dropped any further thoughts of pursuing his idea of Lord Bute's being made Secretary of State. He insisted strongly to me that it was absolutely contrary to Lord Bute's inclination, and that if he had taken it, his only inducement would have been to have complied with the King's inclinations and that there might have been some system of government established. He let fall that Lord Bute would withdraw himself from business, or perhaps that the King might entirely give up Germany and the Continent, and then make a ministry of his own, independent of the present ministers.

I could not help telling him the last scheme was a very idle one; that the popularity which would attend such a step would last a very little while, and would be much censured by all sober thinking people;

and that any ministry formed without the present ministers, or at least part of them, would not last a month. It was very clear that Lord Bute is very desirous of being a minister and much out of humour at seeing any difficulties in the way, and wants to have it pressed upon him, instead of his appearing to seek it.[256] The conversation finished with Viry promising to endeavour to persuade Lord Bute to go on with the Duke of Newcastle and Pitt.

Saw Mr. Pitt who talked of nothing but foreign affairs; said there were letters from Mr. Mitchell[257] which explained the King of Prussia's intentions much more plainly than what his ministers had done here. He [Frederick] made no difficulties in giving us leave to conclude a separate peace: his demands for troops and money afterwards, in case there was not a general peace, were large[258] and that Mitchell seemed to have given in to them rather too much;[259] that every letter he saw convinced him more amd more of the necessity of settling what we were to give the King of Prussia, in case of a separate peace with France previous to our entering into any negotiations; for he had strong suspicions that France and the King of Prussia were in a manner agreed.[260] It was not their interest to see the King of Prussia ruined and the House of Austria rendered more powerful at his expense; that therefore it would be very necessary to know not only the terms and the duration of our subsidy but the nature of it. He [Frederick II] might perhaps expect it to enable him to carry on an offensive [against Austria], which might be doing the business of France and could never be for the interest of England; that all the powers were weary of the war; that Denmark though a slave to France declared she would not see the King of Prussia ruined.

Jan 29 1761: Viry had been with Mr. Pitt who talked to him in very high and strong terms that there was no business done, no system, and though he had great patience, that he was tired and it could not last in this way. Viry took an opportunity to insinuate, that the getting Lord Bute into a ministerial office would be the means to make business go on, and that he thought he would be more easily managed

---

[256] Newcastle ascribed Bute's hesitancy 'to a jealousy that we have more management for Mr. Pitt than he wishes or designs we should have.' Secret Memorandum, 27 Jan. 1761, Add. MSS. 32918, ff. 82–6.

[257] Mitchell to Holderness, 3 Jan. 1761 (secret), S.P.F. 90/77.

[258] For Frederick's terms see ibid.; Frederick II to Knyphausen, 19, 21, 28 Dec.1760, 3 Jan. 1761; *Politische Correspondenz Friedrichs des Grossen*, ed. G.B. Volz et al., 46 Vols. (1879–1939), xx. 162–8, 175–7.

[259] Pitt had always suspected Mitchell of an unnecessary compliance towards Frederick II. In 1758 he had briefly contemplated Mitchell's recall but relented after a personal intervention by Frederick.

[260] Pitt was not accusing Frederick II of some conspiracy with Louis XV, but he perceived the unnatural element in the alliance between France and Austria.

if he was in a responsible office, whereas at present, he had the King's favour and could not be called upon. Pitt was startled and seemed displeased, but made no reply, grew cool, and then said for his part he should be glad to retire from business himself. If the King *would place him in some honourable post in the Cabinet he should like it or if not he could retire and live in the country.* [Pitt] said the same to the Duke of Newcastle. In returning from Lord Ashburnham's[261] Christning, the King called me into his Closet: said that the Duke of Cumberland had named Lord Albemarle[262] and that he desired I would on his part inspect the late King's *scrutores*[263] to see what jewels there were in order to separate them, for that they were to belong to H.R.H. I thanked His Majesty for the confidence he was pleased to repose in me, that I should always be ready to obey his commands. But I hoped he would forgive me if I had a little delicacy on this occasion, that the Duke had always been very kind to me and had permitted me to live in a great degree of intimacy with him, which was very well known in the world. For which reason, I could wish that some other person that had been longer about his [the King's] person might be added and named Lord Bute. And I told him that the Duke had mentioned, as he came from H.M. this morning, what had passed and his desire that Lord Bute and I might be the two persons appointed to inspect the late King's scrutores etc. The King would not hear of it, but gave me the key of the strong box in which I had locked everything up at Kensington.

I acquainted the Duke with the King's intentions. He seemed surprised, said that the King, he believed, did not put the same construction on the lawyers' report that he did, for he imagined those were excepted and belonged to the King. I told H.R.H. that I was of his opinion, that they certainly imagined nothing belonged to him but the jewels in the strong boxes and we agreed that I should go to Lord Bute and let him know for the King's information the construction the Duke put upon the report. The Duke said he had told the King that he would abide by the report and he understood the King would do so too. He thought they did not see it in the extent he did.

Jan 30 1761: Lord Bute came to Devonshire House. I related to him what had passed with the King and my difficulty, and that I had wished he might be one.[264] He smiled and shewed very plainly that he did not chuse or intend it. I then acquainted him that I had been with the Duke of Cumberland to inform him of the King's pleasure. He [Cumberland] said that he imagined the King and he did not understand the report of the lawyers in the same sense, for that it appeared

---

[261] The christening of the son of the 2nd Earl of Ashburnham.
[262] The 3rd Earl of Albemarle, an old military favourite of Cumberland.
[263] *escritoires.*
[264] Of the persons authorized to examine the late King's jewels.

to him that nothing in the boxes were his, that they belonged to His Majesty. Lord Bute was not in the least aware of the Duke's claim. I therefore said that I thought it was right to tell him for the information of the King, that the Duke imagined he [Cumberland] was entitled to all the jewels which the late King had purchased with his own money and that he had laid out when Prince of Wales: £10,000 or £20,000, which were the diamonds that were just come from Hanover.[265] I found this was very unexpected and he [Bute] was reserved upon the subject. He said he thought I should acquaint the King with it and that pendente lite[266] there was nothing for us to do. He combatted the Duke's opinion and thought he had nothing but was in the strong box.

I asked him [Bute] whether he had seen the Duke of Newcastle, who was very desirous to settle the list of the Parliament with him, and that as the time drew near it became very necessary. He seemed in no hurry to do it, said that he was sure his Grace would bring a list with people ready for every borough; that as the King and himself had both some friends to bring in, that the Duke of Newcastle would tell the people that he, Lord Bute, had turned them out and consequently throw the odium on him. [Bute] asked me if I knew whether Lord Hertford had asked the Duke of Newcastle to go Lord Lieutenant to Ireland;[267] [Bute] protested he [Hertford] had never said one word to him about it; he was sorry the Duke of Bedford would not go any more. I told him, he appeared to me to act wisely, for that country was come to such a pass that no man that was at ease or had any character to lose would care to go among them.

Jan 31 1761: Viry had been with Lord Bute the day before, who was shut up with George Greenville and Lord Temple, who *he said* came privately, for they had no coach or chairs waiting when they were gone. Lord Bute told him [Viry] that nothing had passed but common civility and good humour; that he [Viry] found Lord Bute very intent upon the Secretary of State, and did not care to talk with the Duke of Newcastle till that point was determined. He [Viry] confessed that he had been desired to say it was contrary to Lord Bute's inclination. He had thought so at first and that it was to comply with the King's inclinations. But that he saw plainly, he had it much at heart as looking on it as the means of making him sole minister,[268] and if that could be the case would insist upon more of his friends being brought into Parliament. He said he was desired to get me to acquaint the

---

[265] By a royal warrant, 31 Oct. 1760, T.S. 18/249, Part 1.

[266] Pending a suit.

[267] The 1st Earl of Hertford became Lord Lieutenant in 1765. On this occasion Halifax applied to Bute for the office and held it, 1761-3. Halifax to Bute, 2 and 26 Mar. 1761, Bute MSS. (Cardiff) Bundle 2, Nos. 112-13.

[268] The first admission by Viry to Devonshire of Bute's intention to oust Newcastle.

Duke of Bedford with what had passed and to see if I could persuade him to propose it to Mr. Pitt.

I could not help telling him that I was surprised to find they knew mankind and the carte de pays so little; that in confidence I would say to him that if it was opened there the transaction would be no longer a secret, and that his Grace [Bedford] would be the most improper man to break it to Mr. Pitt, as they were far from being well together.[269] Lord Bute had been extreamly civil to me and therefore I should be very ready to do him personally any service, and I saw the King so attached to him that for the sake of His Majesty and the peace of the country, I should do everything in my power to serve him that was practicable and for the real interest of both; that in public considerations I had never suffered private friendships or connections to stand in the way of the good of the whole, and therefore if ever his Lordship came to be in question, I should be very ready to give him any assistance in my power that was consistent with what should appear to me to be the true interest of the public. That when I had said this his Lordship might safely trust me; that as hitherto I was not to know Lord Bute wished to be Secretary of State, on the contrary that he rather disliked it, that it would appear odd for me to propose such a measure to the Duke of Bedford, who would naturally say: 'If you think it right, why don't you propose it yourself?'

If I was allowed to say that I had a hint given me, that such a thing would be agreeable to the King, it would make it a very different case; in short, I desired him [Viry] to talk it over again with Lord Bute and to find out more explicitly what he wished me to do. Viry said: 'Why, he thinks if he can be made Secretary of State at the instigation of you great people, and that though he really wishes it, yet that it should be pressed upon him, he shall be able to govern over everybody and that you must all support him, as he has taken the post at your request.'

Viry said he was sorry for him, that he had a good heart and was a man of honour, but that he wanted to govern and had not a head for it, and was afraid he would ruin himself. It was George Greenville that had put him upon being Secretary of State. Viry had spoken to Lord Bute upon the Duke's [Cumberland's] subject and told him that it was for the King's honour to act generously by the Duke, and that nothing would do him, Lord Bute, personally more service than the advising it. He answered whatever he might wish there was great difficulties in it, which Viry thought was the Princess.[270]

Feb 1 1761: [I] acquainted the King that the Duke imagined they did not put the same construction on the lawyers' report;[271] that H.R.H.

---

[269] Because of Pitt's refusal to support Bedford in Irish affairs.
[270] The Princess Dowager.
[271] See p. 73, n. 248.

did not apprehend that the jewels which were in the late King's boxes here belonged to him [the King] and that I thought it necessary to inform His Majesty, that the Duke understood that all the jewels which the late King bought while he was Prince of Wales and after he was King here, were given to him [Cumberland]. The King said that if they differed as to the lawyers' report, that they must explain more fully what they meant. I suggested that it would be proper to have the question stated in writing. The King was of that opinion, that as the Duke was most concerned, he ought to state what he expected, and ordered me to desire him to set the question down in writing. I told H.M. that if the Duke stated the question, he ought likewise to consider it, and that it should not be referred to the lawyers till the question was settled to their mutual satisfaction. The King approved and ordered me to wait on the Duke of Cumberland.

I acquainted H.R.H. with what had passed with the King. The Duke had no objection and said he would draw up his question, that he should desire might be laid before the lawyers. Accordingly he sent it to me the next morning.[272]

Feb 2 1771: His late Majesty is supposed to have left behind him, besides jewels which came to him from any of his lineal or colateral ancestors, and besides jewels belonging to the Crown of Great Britain, jewels bought by him when he was Prince of Wales and jewels bought since his accession to the Crown.

Question

What jewels belong to His Majesty and what to His Royal Highness the Duke of Cumberland, according to your report made to His Majesty? Jan 13 1761

I carried the above to the King which H.M. approved of. I told him that his Secretary of State[273] was the proper person to send it to the Attorny[274] and Sollicitor General.[275]

Feb 4 1761: Lord Bute came to the Duke of Newcastle, stayed upwards of three hours. [It] began very unpleasantly: the Duke said for an hour did not see his eyes; that if people were to be turned out of their seats in Parliament to make room for his [Bute's] friends the odium would be thrown upon him [Newcastle]. It ended at last in naming Mr. Britton,[276] Mr. Worsesley[277] and Lord Parker,[278] to be brought

[272] See also Memorandum on the question of the ownership of the jewels left by George II, Chatsworth MSS. 622.01.

[273] Holderness to the Attorney-General and the Solicitor-General, 3 Feb. 1761, T.S. 18. 249, part I. The matter was ultimately settled by George III buying out Cumberland's share.

[274] Charles Pratt, M.P.   [275] Charles Yorke, M.P.

[276] William Breton was not returned to Parliament.

[277] Thomas Worsley, a friend of Bute and the King.

[278] Viscount Parker, heir to the Earl of Macclesfield.

in, and Mr. Charles Townshend to be chosen for Harwich.[279] They then came to talk of changes: he [Bute] said there would be scarse any; the King indeed wished to have Mr. Legge turned out of the Treasury.[280] The Duke asked whether it might be accommodated with some other place, or himself put in to the patent of his wife's peerage.[281] He said the King would never confer any honour or grant the least favour to him. He did not say that if his Grace insisted he might not be able to keep him in his place, but he would not advise him to attempt it; that for his part he wished the King did not carry his resentment so far as it might look like personal pique of his for the ill usage he had received from Mr. Legge. Charles Townshend Secretary at War; his place[282] to be given to a popular man[283] that Lord Bute insisted should not be told to anybody at present.

Feb 6: Viry asked if I was satisfied with the conversation that Lord Bute had had with the Duke of Newcastle. I said: 'Yes'. He added things will not go well, till Lord Bute is made Secretary of State. I told him I had mentioned it to the Duke of Bedford in confidence: his Grace thought it very right, that appearing in the light of a Favourite would not be relished, a ministerial employment would disguise it. We were interrupted by the Duchess of Bedford coming in.

Feb 9: The Duke of Newcastle had a long and warm conversation with Pitt. The substance of it was that he [Pitt] would never have anything to do with Lord Bute as a minister and that he would not go on if he could have no access to the King but through Lord Bute.

Feb 12: Lord Bute told me that he had offered to Lord Temple to go Lord Lieutenant of Ireland with the strongest assurances of support both from himself and the King; that he had neither refused nor accepted. [I] advised him [Bute] to tell it the Duke of Newcastle.[284] He asked whether Lord Hardwicke would have gone if it had [been] proposed to him. [I] answered: 'Certainly not.'

Duke of Newcastle related to Lord Hardwicke and myself what Lord Bute had told him, with an addition that he [Bute] had said to Lord Temple that he wished to live in harmony and union with him and Mr. Pitt. He [Bute] knew the world said he only wanted to keep them till a peace was made and then to shake them off; that there was

[279] Townshend was at present member for Great Yarmouth.

[280] Legge, Chancellor of the Exchequer, had incurred the enmity of George III over the 1759 Hampshire election. That March Legge was dismissed without compensation, Bute explaining 'that it was the King's own disgust and dislike of the man; that it was not his Lord Bute's doing.' Add. MSS. 32919, f. 42.

[281] Legge's wife had been created Baroness Stawell on 21 May 1760.

[282] As Treasurer of the Chamber.

[283] Sir Francis Dashwood, 2nd Bart., M.P., a follower of Bute, who became Treasurer of the Chamber in March.

[284] Bute to Newcastle, 12 Feb. 1761, Add. MSS. 32918, ff. 465-66.

not the least foundation for it, that he meant a permanent system. His Grace [Newcastle] rather jealous that there might be too good an understanding between them [Bute and Pitt]. I assured him there was no danger of it and that I approved much what Lord Bute had done. Feb 13 1761: Lord Temple told me at Court of the offer that Lord Bute had made him, in the most flattering manner; that he wished to consult me upon it before he came to any determination; that it was a very honourable employment, at the same time it was attended with so many difficulties; that he was afraid to undertake it. I told him I was very glad it had been offered him in the handsome manner he mentioned; that certainly there was great difficulty attending it, and consequently if he succeeded the more honourable, and that I thought him the most proper person that could be sent; that I hoped this step of Lord Bute's was a preliminary towards a reconciliation between Mr. Pitt and Lord Bute. He said this had nothing to do with their misunderstandings; that there was not system nor [no] harmony among them.

I answered it was too true, and that some method ought to be found out to effect it; that I continued in the same opinion I had been in from the very beginning, that all business should be transacted between [the] Duke of Newcastle, Lord Bute and Mr. Pitt; that I had often thought business would perhaps go on better if Lord Bute was in a responsible office, yet it was a nice question and I was not clear whether it would do well or not. He [Temple] said nothing, wriggled about in his chair and plainly shewed his opinion against it. [Temple] said he never could be the minister, his birth was sufficient to prevent it, and being a Favourite rendered it more impracticable. [Temple] abused the Duke of Newcastle, how he could stay in when he saw the ground taken from under his feet every day, till he had none left to stand upon, and after having been the minister of the country, to continue when the whole power was taken from him.

I concluded with advice to agree, for considering how the King was made it would be impossible to tear Lord Bute from him; that the King thought he [Bute] had been of great service to him, called him his friend, that young men's sensations of honour were more delicate; that I was apprehensive of [if] any attack was made on Lord Bute, the King would run great lengths to support and the attempt might so sour the King's temper at the first out set of his reign, as might make both himself and his people unhappy; that therefore I was much for moderate measures, and by giving his Lordship a reasonable share of power prevent him from grasping at the whole; that the King was very young and nobody knew what might happen. He [Temple] declared his disapprobation of any such attempt; said that the Sesssion was in a manner over, but that next year we should see affairs would not go so smoothly.

Feb 19 1761: Lord Temple came to Viry to let him know the offer that had been made him; confessed that Lord Bute had made it in the handsomest manner, with the strongest expressions of regard from the King and himself towards him, said that it was an insidious offer done only because the country was in difficulties and they did not know who to send. If they had had a proper consideration for him, why did they not offer him First Lord of the Treasury or Secretary of State? He believed he should not have accepted either. But to make him that was Privy Seal, Knight of the Garter and so popular in this country such an offer, it was an affront. [Temple] abused the Duke of Newcastle that they [Pitt and the Grenville family] had the rope about his neck and had nothing to do but to pull it whenever they saw the proper time;* that they whipped him with one hand and caressed him with the other.* That there was nobody could support Lord Bute but Mr. Pitt and them; that the Duke of Cumberland would certainly prefer them to Lord Bute, for that they had never offended him but to please Leicester House, which he must know; that the Duke of Devonshire depended on H.R.H.; that he was indeed always for moderate measures and keeping things quiet, yet they should have him. In short [Temple] represented themselves as masters of the country. And that at a proper time they would shew it, though they might perhaps temporise for the present; that he nor any of his family had never asked a favour since the King came to the Crown. Viry instanced that they were all continued in great employments and what was done for George Greenville. He [Temple] said that was nothing.

Viry asked whether he should tell Lord Bute the conversation. I advised, by all means, that both the King and he might know the disposition of Lord Temple and that they might see how fortunate they had been in not throwing themselves into the hands of such a set of men. Viry said Lord Bute had wrote to the Duke of Newcastle to desire him to take Elliot (his particular friend) into the Treasury in the room of Oswald.[285] A Bitter Pill.[286]

Feb. 21: [I] asked Lord Temple if he had determined about Ireland. He said he was always of the opinion not to go; that he declined giving a positive answer in order to see whether he could reconcile to himself the undertaking; a plain intimation that it depended upon an explanation and agreement between Mr. Pitt and Lord Bute.

The Duke of Newcastle consented to Mr. Eliot's coming into the

[285] James Oswald, M.P., a Lord of the Treasury.
[286] Bute to Newcastle, 12 Feb. 1761, Add. MSS. 32918, ff. 465–6. To which Newcastle made a most compliant reply, Add. MSS. 36796, f. 75. His real sentiments appear in his letter to Hardwicke of 13 Feb. 1761, Add. MSS. 32918, ff. 500–1.

Treasury. He [Elliot] came to thank him; said that his inclination had been to have kept his old friends together but that Mr. Pitt had held such language in regard to Lord Bute, that he had given up the idea and should always think himself under obligations to his Grace.

Feb 22: Viry said that Mr. James Greenville had hinted to him their wish that he would endeavour to bring about a reconciliation between them [Pitt and the Grenvilles] and Lord Bute. He had declined it as being resolved to have nothing to do [with] them. I enquired what was the result of the long visit Lord Bute had made to Lord Temple. He [Viry] said *he did not know* but he believed it ended in nothing; dropped as if Lord Temple wanted to be a duke.

Lord Temple and Elliot had a long conference together at Court after the Drawing Room was over, in the Levee Room.[287]

Feb. 23: Lord Temple had desired to see Lord Bute. He [Bute] supposed it was to give his final answer about Ireland. I related what had passed between us on Friday on the subject and added it was plain he meant to go or not, as Mr. Pitt and he [Bute] could agree. He asked me what they would have. For his part he could not find out.

Feb. 25: Viry came to tell me at Lord Bute's desire that he had had a long conversation with Lord Temple, who professed to be much pleased with the honourable offer the King had made him, and Mr. Pitt had desired him to say the same from him, and to assure Lord Bute that they desired to live in friendship with him, and hope the former intimacy and cordiality would by degrees be renewed. But that Mr. Pitt would depend upon no person whatever, and would do his business directly with the King, and not through any other channel. Lord Bute replyed that was a thing of course to which nobody could have the least objection. Lord Temple assured him that they had made no connection or party with anybody. Lord Bute said: 'I have, I have endeavoured ever since the King came to the throne to make des *liasons* and friendships and have succeeded in it.'

Temple seemed surprised and disconcerted. Lord Bute told him that *the King wished much to make him [Bute] Secretary of State.* *(Viry was not to tell that to the Duke of Newcastle, only to say that the King wished to have him a minister).* The other [Temple] replied: 'If the King pleases there can be no objection.' Lord Bute desired Viry to tell me what had passed and to acquaint the Duke of Newcastle with it,[288] and to assure him that he would have no half confidence but that he

[287] An account of this meeting is given in Elliot to Bute, [22] Feb. 1761, Bute MSS. No. 73.

[288] Memorandum on Events (C.V.) 26 Feb. 1761, Add. MSS. 32919, ff. 285-9. It was during this meeting with Temple that, according to Viry, Bute said: 'I supposed, your Lordship does not mean to look up[on] me as a bare Groom of the Stole—the King will have it otherwise.' To which Lord Temple replied: 'Certainly, so, I look upon you as a Minister and desire to act with you as such.'

should be informed of all transactions relating to those gentlemen.
Viry said it was wished that I would propose to the King Lord Bute's
being Secretary of State, that I might depend on the King's secrecy.
I said that I was not, nor desired, ever to be in a situation to make or
unmake ministers, and that I thought the King's servants would have
reason to take it ill if I meddled in such concerns. And besides, if the
King was to keep the secret, I did not see what it was to do, for as
H.M. wished it, he had no occasion to be confirmed in it. If the King
asked my opinion, I should be very ready to give it him and such a
one as would be agreeable to Lord Bute. He then said would I speak
to Pitt? To that I had no objection, but as he was ill there was no
hurry. Duke of Newcastle told me that the King thought Lord Temple
was very cold and reserved when he came to thank him for the offer
of the Lieutenancy. [Temple] made professions of serving him in what
was for the good of the nation.

Feb 28 1761: Viry came to tell me that Lord Bute and the Duke of
Newcastle were not so well together; that Lord Bute had desired him
to acquaint his Grace that upon consideration the King did not
approve of making Oswald Lord Register;[289] that he had disputed the
point with him and at [   ].[290] But that if Lord Edgecumbe[291] dyed,
Lord North[292] might be Comptroller of the Household, which would
make room for Eliot at the Treasury. Viry disputed the point, said it
was unreasonable and declined going on the message. But when he
saw that he was determined to speak upon it himself, consented to go,
as he was afraid they [Bute and Newcastle] might quarrel. Accordingly he informed the Duke of Newcastle of it, who flew out extreamly
and said he would never come into [it], or in short was so warm that
he [Viry] would not take an answer but desired him [Newcastle] to
consider it and talk to Lord Hardwicke and the Duke of Devonshire
upon it.

I told him [Viry] that if he asked me, I must own to him that it was
a very unreasonable demand and that I did not think he [Newcastle]
could comply with it. I told Viry that Lord Bute should consider how
handsomely the Duke of Newcastle had behaved to his Lordship on
his proposition of Eliot, which he had readily come into at once and
of his own accord, without concert, being at Claremont[293] when he

---

[289] Newcastle had suggested making Oswald Lord Register of Scotland in compensation for his loss of a place at the board of Treasury. Memorandum, 27 Feb. 1761, Add.
MSS. 32919, ff. 314-17.

[290] Word crossed out and illegible in MS.

[291] 2nd Baron Edgecumbe, Comptroller of the Household. Dec. 1758 until his death
on 10 May 1761.

[292] Lord North, M.P., eldest son of the 1st Earl of Guilford and the future Prime
Minister, was then a Lord of the Treasury.

[293] Newcastle's seat in Surrey.

received the letter which he answered directly;[294] that it was directly cutting the ground from under his feet; that he had made him give up Mr. Legge and that if he was to disoblige Oswald and Lord North, he took from him his main support in the House of Commons, and would render him contemptable and be the ruin of him. However Viry desired I would talk to him [Newcastle] on the subject and also about his [Viry's] idea of the Secretary of State.

The Duke of Newcastle had sent to desire I would come to him before he went to Claremont. His Grace told me that he had had the day before three different conversations with Lord Bute, who related to him what had passed with Lord Temple, in which was nothing new and desired him to remember that he [Bute] had taken that step at his request and mine. The Duke of Newcastle told him that he was under great difficulties in his own family, and particularly on Mr. Roberts's account. That Lord Lincoln had been with him from Lady Catherine to tell him that if it was done, she nor none of her family should ever set their feet into his house; that he made the most contemptible figure that man could do; that when he had made the vacancy at Lord Bute's request by [providing] for Eliot, that he should not have weight sufficient to carry it for Roberts who had been disappointed before, but should have a man named to it without the least communication. And added that these difficulties made it very uneasy and almost impossible for him to go on.[295]

Lord Bute excused it, said it was the King's doing; that he was ready to come into any scheme to accommodate it; that there was the Master of the Household, would not that do as well? Duke of Newcastle said he thought it would be better to give it to somebody of more figure and it might be accommodated. They then talked upon the subject of Eliot. The Duke of Newcastle said that he was ready to do anything to please Lord Bute, but that he should appear ridiculous to have his Treasury composed of James Greenville and two Scotchmen,[296] that he would not be master of his own Board. Lord Bute said he did not see it; that the odium of two Scotchmen would lie at his [Bute's] door; that the King would not make Oswald Lord Register; that the pensioning Finlater[297] and removing Lord Morton[298] would

294 See p. 83.

295 Newcastle's sister-in-law Lady Catherine Pelham, widow of his brother Henry, espoused the claim of her late husband's secretary, John Roberts, to be chosen M.P. for Harwich. She involved her son-in-law the 9th Earl of Lincoln, Newcastle's nephew and heir, who had married his first cousin. The King had promised any vacancy to Charles Townshend but in 1761 both he and Roberts were returned.

296 At first Newcastle was ready to accommodate both Oswald and Elliot at the Treasury but Hardwicke warned him against having two Scots. Hardwicke to Newcastle, 14 Feb. 1761, Add. MSS. 32918, f. 513.

297 James Ogilvy, 6th Earl of Finlater (1714-70), Commissioner of Customs, 1754-61.

298 The 14th Earl of Morton, Lord Clerk Register of Scotland.

disgust the Scotch nobility. However he owned that his Grace had done everything he could expect in this affair, and that Eliot must wait, though he believed he would not stay in the Admiralty. I told the Duke of Newcastle that the thing must be done in some shape or other or discontent would arise.

Duke of Newcastle imagined that Duke of Argyle[299] had made the objection to Oswald, for at first the proposition was relished. Viry said Lord Bute was to see Oswald; hinted it was not impossible that Mr. Legge and he might in time be reconciled. The Duke of Newcastle had acquainted Mr. Legge with the King's resolution, that he should be dismissed from his employment, and that his Grace, Lord Hardwicke and I, had endeavoured to get him made a peer in lieu of it. He thanked his Grace, said he had expected it, was much obliged for his inter-position; that as to the peerage he would not take it; that he looked upon himself in a manner one already, which he owed to his Grace,[300] and that as to himself he did not think it worth paying the fees.

March 1 1761: [I] acquainted Viry that I had related to [the] Duke of Newcastle what had passed in regard to his idea of Secretary of State for Lord Bute; that the Duke of Newcastle was of the same mind with me; that he did not see how he could propose it to the King, but if H.M. mentioned it to him he should be for it.[301]

Viry saw Lord Bute and returned to inform me, that he took it very ill of the Duke of Newcastle. He admitted the King's having never talked to me on business was a reason why I could not so properly speak of it, but that his Grace was in possession of talking freely to the King on all subjects; that he had taken pains to make him well in the Closet, and in short, if this was not done things would never go well, and that the doing of it was to be the touchstone of their friendship.

I told Viry that Lord Bute appeared to be in the wrong; that as yet the Duke of Newcastle knew nothing of this transaction but as an idea of Viry's own, nay that it was supposed rather contrary to Lord Bute's in-clination. That therefore it could not be made a test of their friendship; on the contrary, Lord Bute would have reason to be offended with the Duke of Newcastle, if he was to propose any arrangement relative to him without previous communication; that if Lord Bute would signifye his wishes to the Duke of Newcastle it would be a different thing. That it was evident Lord Bute wanted to have the appearance, as if it was forced upon him, whereas the contrary appeared.

March 2: [I] acquainted the Duke of Newcastle at Court with what had passed with Viry, and that he must contrive by some method or other to mention the Secretary of State to the King, or we should be

[299] The 3rd Duke of Argyle, who managed Scotland for Newcastle.
[300] Legge was referring to his wife's peerage as Baroness Stawell.
[301] Newcastle Memorandum, 3 Mar. 1761, Add. MSS. 32919, f. 400.

in confusion. This passed in company with Lord Hardwicke. They both were averse to it and agreed it would be better to talk to Lord Bute and ask him whether it would be agreeable to him.

March 6 1761: Duke of Newcastle told the King[302] that he thought it his duty to lay some considerations before H.M. which he thought might be of service to him; that he had no view or prejudice to anyone. The King seemed impatient to hear what he had to say. He told the King that a new Parliament was to be chose, which he hoped would be a good one, but considering the difficult situation of affairs, the disappointments which some must have met with in the beginning of a new reign, the old party spirit which may from disappointments on either side revive again, the great increase of National Debt, the immense sum which must be raised if war continues, and ever the large sums which will be wanting if H.M. should be so happy as to bring about a peace this year, the difficulties of procuring a peace and the agreeing upon the terms of it, all these things considered it was very improbable that the present unanimity should subsist. That therefore a settled, firm, well-connected and well united administration was requisite for His Majesty's affairs, composed of people who by their station and the King's confidence were known to act agreeable to H.M.'s opinion; that when measures were agreed, they would be supported as known to be H.M.'s measures, otherways every man would vote as was most agreeable to the minister he liked best. The King approved of what was said.

The Duke of Newcastle added that he did not pretend to suggest or prescribe the particular manner of settling such an administration; that Mr. Pitt's ill health was such as rendered it impossible for him to do business with the King for weeks and months at times;[303] that his credit and influence were of great service to H.M. and therefore nothing ought to be done that should give him offence; that Lord Holdernesse carried on H.M.'s foreign correspondence but entered very little into home affairs or parliamentary business.

The King said: 'These are very material points, but what would you propose?'

The Duke answered: 'Nothing but my duty to your Majesty should have made me go so far, but Sir, you have a right to know all I think. If your Majesty approved of making Lord Bute Secretary of State, it might be of great service and by introducing him, you would have one in your confidence a man of ability, firmness and expedition. And this is the opinion of [the] Duke of Devonshire and Lord Hardwicke, with whom I act in the utmost confidence.'

[302] An account of what passed with the King this morning, 6 Mar. 1761, Add. MSS. 32919, ff. 481–7.

[303] Pitt was ill for eight weeks. Knyphausen to Frederick II, 23 Jan., 3, 20, 24 Feb., 13 Mar. 1761, D.Z.A., Rep. 96. 33. Vol. E, ff. 43, 56, 80–1, 84–5, 116–17.

The King thanked him, and said it was his own thought; that he had proposed it to Lord Bute the day the late King died, but he declined it as not chusing to throw himself into so much business and not knowing what the other ministers might think of it: 'I will try him again, though I have not mentioned it to him of some time; what you have said may have altered the case.'

Duke of Newcastle repeated that Mr. Pitt must be managed, in which the King acquiesced; proposed that [the] Duke of Devonshire should be sent to Mr. Pitt.

March 10 1761: Duke of Newcastle told Lord Bute it was necessary to consider how to carry into execution what had passed between the King and him.[304] Lord Bute said the King had constantly pressed him to come into the administration; that he had always refused and had at last obtained his promise not to press him any more; but upon what had passed with his Grace the King had pressed it so strongly that he could no longer refuse; that he saw the difficulties; however that did not discourage him. He flattered himself foreign powers would see what he did would be supported by the King. He was only apprehensive of Mr. Pitt's temper; that therefore he must know before he engaged, whether he might, in case they differed, depend upon the support of him and his friends. His Grace assured him he might. Lord Bute thanked him for what he had said of him to the King. Duke of Newcastle replied he had given his opinion very sincerely to the King, and that the Duke of Devonshire and Lord Hardwicke were of the same opinion.

Lord Bute said he would see Lord Temple on Thursday and acquaint him with it and let him know that the King intended to signify his intentions the next day to his ministers; that if Mr. Pitt was not well enough to come out, the King would send the Duke of Devonshire to him. He then desired to know, if Lord Temple asked him what he thought of it, what answer he should make to him.

The Duke of Newcastle desired he [Bute] would say that he submitted entirely to the King's pleasure and had himself no objection to it. He said he would endeavour to go on with good humour towards Mr. Pitt but hinted it was owing to the advice of his Grace and others. Duke of Newcastle shewed the necessity of Mr. Pitt's service. The other did not care to allow it, said his [Pitt's] popularity was sunk and was persuaded he never would go into opposition, but in all events would retire with some honourable provision. [Bute] said Mr. Pitt would never gain the King, and was convinced Mr. Pitt would acquiesce: 'What can he say? Will he say that I am an objectionable man? He won't.'

---

[304] Substance of what passed in my conversation with Lord Bute this day, 10 Mar. 1761, Add. MSS. 32920, ff. 64-70.

[Newcastle] mentioned Lord Holdernesse as Groom of the Stole. Lord Bute desired that his union with [the] Duke of Newcastle might be complete; that he would send his friends Sir Francis Dashwood and Mr. Dodington to him,[305] and hoped he would look upon them as his friends and support them in their boroughs. Lady Bute to be made a Baroness.[306] Duke of Newcastle convinced that Lord Bute means to act confidentially with him.

March 13 1761: Count Viry was with [the] Duke of Newcastle to tell him that Lord Bute is to be with Mr. Pitt at two.[307] That Mr. James Greenville accepts,[308] that there is only the affair of the Duke of Rutland remaining; that the King will have Lord Talbot have something, that *this is not Lord Bute's doing*. That the King will give Lord Talbot a great employment. That if the Duke of Rutland refuses, they will give another employment to Lord Talbot and make such reforms in the Steward's office as will not be agreeable.[309] This does not depend on Lord Bute.

That Lord Bute will leave Mr. Pitt master of foreign affairs, except where his Grace [Newcastle], the Duke of Devonshire and Lord Hardwicke shall think he goes too far. And in regard to peace he will act with them three. Groom of the Stole must not be left vacant. Duke of Leeds Chief Justice in Eyre, called to the Cabinet Council,[310] the office made equal to the Cofferer: additional £2,000 p.a.

Mr. James Greenville Cofferer.[311]

Lord Sandys[312] board of Trade with old salary £1500: no Cabinet Councillor.

March 15: Lord Bute called here: first thing he said was: 'It is a most amazing thing that these gentlemen are never to be satisfied. I hear Lord Temple talks discontentedly, and indeed Mr. James Greenville came to thank me that the King had thought of him for a post of such high rank as Cofferer, but that it had the appearance of making way for Mr. Elliot in the Treasury, was throwing him out

[305] Dashwood was to be returned by George Bubb Dodington for Weymouth and Melcombe Regis. Namier and Brooke, ii. 301.

[306] As Baroness Mountstuart of Wortley, see p. 56, n. 168.

[307] Bute had to inform Pitt of his appointment as Secretary of State, because Devonshire was ill.

[308] Cofferer of the Household.

[309] The King wanted the 3rd Duke of Rutland, Lord Steward, to succeed Bute as Groom of the Stole, so as to appoint the 2nd Baron (shortly 1st Earl) Talbot Lord Steward. But Rutland did not wish to be Groom of the Stole, a less dignified position. The way was found by making Rutland Master of the Horse in place of the 10th Earl of Huntingdon. Add. MSS. 32920, ff. 119, 158-9, 162-6. Also Bute to Devonshire, 14 Mar. 1761, Chatsworth MSS. 590/4.

[310] 4th Duke of Leeds, who became a Privy Councillor but was not of the Cabinet.

[311] Cofferer of the Household, the post vacated by Leeds.

[312] 1st Baron Sandys.

of business and that he did not mind a thousand pound a year more or less.'

Lord Bute said he could not help saying to him: 'Why, Jemmy, what is come to you, you used to mind £1000 p.a. There is no harm done, this great offer was made to shew regard to Mr. Pitt and your family. Nobody desires you to take it, the Duke of Newcastle had proposed another arrangement for Mr. Elliot.' Upon this reply, my Lord, he changed his note.

He [Bute] then spoke about the Duke of Rutland [and] was in great doubt what to do; that he could not bear the thoughts of hurting Lord Holdernesse, if he chose Groom of the Stole. Would the Duke of Rutland take a reversion of Warden of the Cinque Ports for life, on the death of the Duke of Dorset,[313] and a large pension in the interim? I told him the latter would not do: perhaps he might be prevailed upon to take the Cinque Ports at the Duke of Dorset's death. 'Why then,' said he, 'I must try to persuade Lord Talbot to wait for that event.'

He [Bute] talked a great deal about Pitt; that there were some things dropped by him [Pitt] at the latter end of the conversation that looked as if he really meant to go on: particularly he [Pitt] said: 'I have altered my mind about the East India expedition. It is known; and we are in danger of a war with Spain. We may want our great ships. I think it would be better to send only a sufficient force to take the neutral islands, for the French talk much of making peace on the terms of uti possidetis; now they are certainly at present in possession of them. 3000 men will effectually drive them out of them.'[314] Lord Bute said he was quite of his mind, but proposed that it should seem to go to the very last; that a Council should be called two days before they were to sail and stop it, which would keep the French in suspense.

He [Bute] said he would go and talk to Lord Holdernesse for he was resolved to satisfy him.

[Bute] returned [and] said Lord Holdernesse preferred Groom of the Stole to any post in H.M.'s service.[315] Therefore he would see Lord Talbot in the morning and send me word in what manner to talk to the Duke of Rutland.

March 16 1761: Viry came from Lord Bute, who could not prevail upon Lord Talbot to wait, and therefore desired I would persuade the

---

[313] The 1st Duke of Dorset, Lord Warden of the Cinque Ports, who had been born in 1688, lived until 1765.

[314] St. Lucia, Dominica, St. Vincent and Tobago, declared neutral under the Treaty of Aix-la-Chapelle, 1748. But the geographical position of Martinique had made easy a French colonisation. St. Lucia and Dominica were taken in 1761 and St. Vincent in 1762.

[315] Holderness to Bute, 14, 15 March 1761, Bute MSS. (Cardiff) Bundle 2, Nos. 56, 58.

Duke of Rutland to come into some exchange. He [Bute] was ready to agree to anything I should say was reasonable. I went to the Duke of Newcastle at Mr. Pelham's[316] lodgings, where I found the Duke of Rutland, who had heard that the King intended great reform in the Steward's office which he should not like, and therefore he would willingly change it for Master of the Horse, but did not care to take Groom of the Stole. I related this to Lord Bute in the King's antiroom. He said the King would not do it: 'You may imagine otherways, but there are some things I cannot do. If I could have got the Master of the Horse for any other person, I would have got it at first for Lord Gower.'

I advised him to try it. He came from the King, who agreed to it provided Lord Huntingdon consented; said the King would speak to me upon the subject, which he did. Lord Huntingdon came into it handsomely.[317]

April 9 1761: The Duke of Newcastle was with Mr. Pitt, who said that it was necessary that the King's servants should settle among themselves upon what terms they should make peace before a French minister should come over;[318] that he had formed his own opinion and come to a determined resolution that nothing should alter. That he would *make war*, to save or regain Hanover, *or rather continue*, but that he would never consent to give up the acquisitions that he thought necessary for this country to keep, for the sake of Hanover. He said his notion was to keep all North America and the Fishery on the Banks of Newfoundland.

The Duke of Newcastle told him that he was afraid the latter would be difficult to be got, as the French would with great difficulty be persuaded to give up so essential a point to their marine,[319] and that none of the powers of Europe would like that we should make a monopoly of the Bacaloo trade.[320] Besides that Spain claimed a right to fish there likewise,[321] which as we had refused to allow, would make them disposed to assist France rather than suffer us to get sole possession of a trade so necessary to them and other powers.

Mr. Pitt answered he was resolved, that he would immediately insist

[316] Thomas Pelham, second cousin to Newcastle.

[317] To vacate the Mastership of the Horse and become Groom of the Stole.

[318] Toward the end of Mar. Choiseul had forwarded to London proposals for a Congress to be held at Augsburg, to which Frederick of Prussia was agreeable, together with a separate negotiation between Britain and France over colonial issues. On Apr. 4 Britain and Prussia consented to the Congress and on Apr. 7 the Cabinet authorized Pitt to accept Choiseul's other proposal.

[319] For the importance of the Fisheries, see 'Questions and Answers Relative to the State of the French and British Fisheries at Newfoundland', Add. MSS. 35913, DLXV, ff. 75–92; P.R.O. 30/8/85, ff. 345–66.

[320] i.e. cod trade.

[321] See p. 59, n. 183.

on knowing the sense of the King's servants on this head, and if he was overruled he should desire to retire.

[Pitt] talked about naming plenipotentiary for the Congress: said he believed Lord Temple would not go; that he was the properest person, and would be a great loss to him, as he depended upon his judgement upon all occasions; that he knew his own character very well; that he was an odd mixture of a creature the most obstinate on one head and the most diffident on the other; that Lord Temple was a man of the greatest abilities and the most distinguishing head, that except one or two, he was fitter to determine a difficult cause in the Court of Chancery than anybody there, barring the knowledge of the terms and forms of law.

[Pitt] complained that the great change in government of making Lord Bute Secretary of State and the other arrangements had been settled without concert with him; that he would over look it and would go on with good humour, though if my Lord Bute had consulted him he should have advised him to have stayed where he was.* Mr. Pitt told Lord Bute upon the late King's death, that if he would take the Treasury he would assist and support him.*

April 18: The Duke of Newcastle's friend [Viry] had seen Mr. Pitt,[322] who laid the whole blame of Prince Ferdinand's miscarriage[323] upon the commissariat, the want of care, economy and attention in the Treasury, and plainly shewed an intention of attacking it. He also expressed great resentment against the Duke of Bedford and seemed determined to shew it. His friend [Viry] had given Lord Bute notice[324] of what passed, who he thinks made a right use of it.

April 20: Lord Bute wrote to the Duke of Newcastle[325] to acquaint him that the King returned to his former destination of the Scotch employments, but that if he could persuade Lord Moreton[326] to take a pension of £2000 p.a. to make room for his [Bute's] brother,[327] he should be much obliged to his Grace. The Duke of Newcastle pressed the necessity of keeping Lord Marchmont[328] in good humour as a very usefull man in the House of Lords. The other [Bute] replied there was no great occasion for that, as there were others that would support measures there, and instanced Lord Melcombe.[329] The Duke of Newcastle said that Mr. Pitt was very angry with him [Newcastle] on account of the assistance he had given his Lordship. The other [Bute]

---

[322] Memorandum (Secret), 18 Apr. 1761, Add. MSS. 32922, f. 32.
[323] Prince Ferdinand's spring campaign had initially miscarried.
[324] Viry to Bute, 17 Apr. 1761, Bute MSS. (Cardiff) 7/55.
[325] Bute to Newcastle, 7 Apr. 1761, Add. MSS. 32922, f. 24.
[326] The Earl of Morton.
[327] James Stuart-Mackenzie.
[328] 3rd Earl of Marchmont.
[329] The former George Bubb Dodington.

would not allow that to be the case but said, if Mr. Pitt talked of enquiry into the Treasury or commissariat, the enquiry would of course become general.[330] He urged the necessity of popular measures, that Pitt might not run away with the advantage of them, and said then the country gentlemen would not perhaps follow him.

The Duke of Newcastle was much out of humour with this conversation[331] and thought it a bad return to the proposition he had made of serving Mr. Mackensie. I observed to him that Lord Bute did intend to govern Scotland and would not let him interfere, and therefore would never make an arrangement where the two people promoted were to be his [Newcastle's] friends; that Mr. Mackensie['s] was recalled[332] in order to take the direction of Scotland.[333]* Lord Moreton refused a pension. Lord Bute said the King would take care of him and had ordered Mr. Pitt to write by the first post for him to come over.* April 22: Being desired to attend a meeting tomorrow to consider of a letter of Prince Ferdinand's[334] to regulate the plan of the next campagne, I told Mr. Pitt that I had desired to be excused from attending the meeting. In general [that] I had promised to be present when ever the grand point of peace was to come under consideration, thinking it necessary that all the King's servants should attend to take their share in it. He said this was a very material point and desired I would come; from thence we talked about the proposition from France.[335] I took the opportunity of telling him, that I thought it absolutely necessary that when a French minister came over,[336] that the King's servants should all appear of one mind, for nothing would so much retard the making or prejudice the peace itself as our enemie's perceiving that we were not agreed among ourselves. And as I had been informed since I came to town that there was danger of the King's servants differing in their opinions, I was desirous of letting him know mine beforehand. That I understood his plan was that we should settle among ourselves the terms on which we would advise the

[330] Newcastle, having put Bute in as Secretary of State, expected him to protect his department against Pitt's vindictiveness over the commissariat. 'My Lord Bute should be made sensible, that I have drawn all this upon myself, by the part I have acted with and towards him and consequently, that his honour and (I think) his interest are concerned to take a strong part in defence of the Treasury.' Newcastle to Devonshire, 19 Apr. 1761, Add. MSS. 32922, f. 66.

[331] Account of my conversation with my Lord Bute, 21 Apr. 1761, Add. MSS. 32922, ff. 108-10.

[332] From Turin, where he had been British envoy since 1758.

[333] In succession to the 3rd Duke of Argyll, maternal uncle to Bute and Stuart-Mackenzie, who had died 15 Apr. Bute to Stuart-Mackenzie, 21 Apr. 1761, Bute MSS. Bundle marked odd papers.

[334] Prince Ferdinand to Bute, 13 Apr. 1761, S.P. 87/40.

[335] See p. 73.

[336] Early in Apr., Britain and France had agreed to exchange special envoys.

King to make peace, and that the French minister should in the first conversation be told that on those terms we would make peace and on no other. He admitted that was his plan.

I told him I was sorry to differ with him, that such a resolution appeared to me premature and would rather tend to retard than accelerate the peace. That France had made us a proposition and therefore we ought to wait to see what she would say to our answer,[337] and what explanation she would put upon her own Paper, that we should then be able to form a judgement on what terms we might be able to have a peace, and that would be the time to consider whether they were such as we ought to accept or not.

Mr. Pitt was rather warm. He said he could not allow what I said; that either we were in a situation to receive the law or to give it; that he thought the latter was our case; that therefore it was our business to propose the terms and tell France on what conditions they were to have peace; that it was so at the Peace of Utrecht and it would be absurd to act otherways. I replyed I could not agree with him; that I hoped at least he would defer as long as he could bringing us to the point, as I should be very sorry to see a difference among us, and perhaps we might find all difficulties removed by the construction France should put on that Paper. He grew cool and seemed to acquiesce in the last proposition.

As Lord Bute would not allow to the Duke of Newcastle that Pitt had been of this opinion, I told him [Bute] what had passed.[338] He answered if that is the case, we shall all be obliged when the time comes to give our opinions and he [Pitt] will not find many with him. April 23 1761: We met at Council to consider a letter of Prince Ferdinand's demanding more assistance, proposing his plans of the campagne and desiring orders how to act. Mr. Pitt took notice of a paragraph in the close of it, in which he says that he was not satisfyed with the commissariat and that to them and the want of subsistance and waggons was in great measure owing the failure of his expedition to relieve Hesse.[339] He attacked the Duke of Newcastle most furiously, that the Treasury was answereable for their faults and that an enquiry ought and must be had upon them, and made a flaming speech against him.

The Duke of Newcastle replyed that he was desirous of an enquiry

---

[337] Pitt to Choiseul, 8 Apr. 1761, accepting the French offer to negotiate; printed in Thackeray, ii. 511–12.

[338] Account of my conversation with Lord Bute (copy), Newcastle to Devonshire, Add. MSS. 32922, ff. 108–10.

[339] By the spring of 1761 Prince Ferdinand had lost most of Hesse-Cassel to Broglie, for which he blamed Newcastle's mishandling of the commissariat. Prince Ferdinand to Holderness, 30 Mar. 1761, S.P. 87/40.

into it; that the Treasury had done everything in their [power] and did not doubt but their conduct would be approved. That they had already wrote over to have it enquired into and nothing on their parts had or should be wanting.[340] Pitt answered warmly. The Duke of Bedford replyed to him, abused the expedition into Hesse, and that Prince Ferdinand, as it had failed, wanted to lay the blame on the commissariat.

I proposed that this affair should be enquired into and that as Prince Ferdinand had found a fault, the Secretary of State should desire him to point it out that it might be rectified. Pitt objected, said it was offensive to Prince Ferdinand, that it was the business of the Treasury. He was at last overruled, Lord Chancellor,[341] Lord Hardwick and Lord Mansfield speaking strongly for it. Lord Bute mentioned the turning out the commissariat immediately. Duke of Bedford took it up very high, said it would be very unjust to punish unheard.* Lord Bute whispered me they were all put in by Prince Ferdinand.* And we concluded with referring that part of Prince Ferdinand's letter to the Treasury, and the Secretary of State writing to him to desire he would point out the grounds of his dissatisfaction with the commissariat.[342] Pitt much hurt, as it was plain he did not want to have the point cleared up but only that it might hang over the Treasury, in order if he was attacked to throw the blame on others. Lord Temple made a long speech entering into a state of the war from the beginning of their ministry: nothing to the present purpose, but prepared for some other occasion.

April 27 1761:[343] We met in Council on the Memoire from [the] Duc de Choiseul in answer to that sent from Mr. Pitt,[344] who took notice that it differed very essentially from the former one, and made the whole transaction more obscure and insidious. He read to us the answer he had prepared, in which he had inserted their own words in order to shew them how they had varied from their former proposition,[345] by now fixing down the Epoques to the times mentioned in their first Memoire,[346] in which they were stated as points to be treated

[340] Lords of the Treasury to Granby, 23 Apr. 1761 (copy), Add. MSS. 32922, ff. 145-8; Bute to Newcastle, 26 Apr. 1761, S.P. 44/139.

[341] 1st Baron Henley, Lord Chancellor 1761.

[342] Bute to Prince Ferdinand, 24 Apr. 1761, S.P. 87/40.

[343] As Newcastle and Hardwicke were both present, no correspondence between them was necessary. So far as the editors are aware, Devonshire's account stands alone.

[344] Choiseul to Pitt, 19 Apr. 1761 (*memoire* enclosed), S.P.F. 78/251.

[345] In his initial Memoire of 31 Mar. 1761, Choiseul had left the epochs open to future negotiation.

[346] Which followed the principle of *uti possidetis*, the dates being 1 May 1761 in Europe, 1 July 1761 in the West Indies and Africa, and 1 Sept. 1761 in India. Pitt would have preferred the epochs to have remained open, so as to leave room for further conquests. Thackeray, ii. 509.

of. Lord Hardwicke spoke for agreeing to their Epoques at once, the Duke of Newcastle the same.

Mr. Pitt answered them warmly and strong, said he would not come into it; that he thought this country in a situation to give peace to France, and if we were at first firm in our proceedings and did not yield to France, we should soon have a very good peace; that this would be a concession to them and would make them think that by chicane they might carry any points they had a mind to; that if he had the misfortune to differ from the majority of their Lordships, he had nothing to do but to acquaint H.M. with his opinion, and if greater people and of more weight than him were to overrule him he must beg leave to retire.

I told Lord Mansfield who sat by me that I thought a middle way might be found out, by adding some words to shew that we were ready to treat both on the Epoques and on the compensations etc. He said he thought so too. [I] proposed to him to mention it. [He] asked me if I would second him: 'Yes, if necessary.' Accordingly he threw it out and it was immediately approved of. I then proposed to Mr. Pitt that we might send over passports for Monsieur Bussy,[347] and acquaint them who was to be our minister, *Mr. Stanley,*[348] and that he should set out as soon as he received their passports. The Council were rising when I mentioned it to Mr. Pitt, who immediately approved of it. I said if he liked it, I wished he would mention it to the King. He answered: 'My Lord, if I had really the authority of a minister, or was accredited I would, but that is not my situation.' So then I proposed it: the Lords sat down and came into it.

May 11 1761:   Commissariat

It is said there never was such a scene of abuse, cheating, mismanagement etc. One says that in a few great articles he [Massone][349] could have said [saved] £500,000 and got an estate; that Colonel Pierson's[350] name is seldom seen in orders, Massone often, and he is understood to be the person to apply to on all occasions.

That the troops forage the country and give receipts without check or control for a great deal more than they have; that the contractors or commissaries buy these receipts at a great discount; that they charge the highest contract price. That the country is plundered and they hide, whereas if ready money was paid, the army would be better and cheaper supplied. That money is given to the foreigners who are

[347] François de Bussy, the proposed French envoy.
[348] Hans Stanley, M.P., was a great favourite with Pitt.
[349] General A. von Massow, assistant director of the Commissariat.
[350] Colonel Richard Pierson, Director-in-chief of the Commissariat.

deficient in numbers; the British Legion has been foraged complete the whole year, though very deficient.[351]

Hospitals ill taken care of.

May 13 1761:[352] Meeting on Mr. Stanley's Instructions:[353] Mr. Pitt began with desiring to know what instructions were to be given to Mr. Stanley. Lord President[354] of opinion that very little instruction was to be given him, for that the business must be done here with Bussy. Mr. Pitt then explained the points that he would have him instructed upon. First that he should declare to the Duc de Choiseul that the King's intention was that a separate peace with France should be concluded before and independent of the Congress. And that if France would not agree to that we could go no farther. The Duke of Newcastle objected, said that he feared insisting upon such a declaration from France would make them break off, for that she never would make such a declaration before she saw a probability of concluding; that in all the transactions with France, he had often seen them come into things, that if they had been at first proposed they would have refused.

Lord Bute thought Mr. Pitt was in the right, that we should declare our intention and the manner in which we understood this separate negotiation, but he was not for insisting upon the same declaration from France. I agreed with him. Mr. Pitt came into it. Lord Bute said that when France proposed a separate peace,[355] we could not agree to it as we had not the King of Prussia['s] consent,[356] but that was not the case now.[357] The next point was the uti possidetis. The Council were all of opinion that Mr. Stanley might say that the King consented to the proposal.[358] Mr. Pitt then wanted that we should give our opinions how we understood the uti possidetis, for he said he could not negotiate till he knew the intentions of the King. He said we must determine what we would do. If we confine the uti possidetis to conquests made on each Crown only, you then leave your allies to the Congress only for relief, and added for his part he had no objection. In the other way, you admit that the consideration of the losses of your allies shall be considered in the compensation offered by France. He added we might take either way. He would give no opinion but would

[351] Raised in 1760, consisting of five battalions. On 25 Mar. a whole battalion had been taken prisoner.

[352] Newcastle Memorandum, 13 May 1761, Add. MSS. 32923, ff. 49–50; Newcastle to Hardwicke, 13 May 1761, ibid., ff. 63–71.

[353] Stanley's Instructions of 18 May 1761 are printed in Thackeray, i. 506–9.

[354] Granville.

[355] In Jan. 1760, in reply to the earlier declaration of Britain and Prussia calling for a European Congress, see p. 34.

[356] Minute with the Prussian Ministers, 13 Mar. 1760; *Chatham*, ii. 29–30.

[357] Frederick had since consented to a separate negotiation between Britain and France, see p. 76, n. 258.

[358] To accept the principle of *uti possidetis*.

follow directions; that we must come to some determination or he should not know how to act, for that he could not transact with a French minister being ignorant of the intentions of his own Court.

Lord Bute said it was too soon for him to give an opinion on so nice a point and that we must first hear what Monsieur Bussy said. I was strong of that opinion. The Duke of Newcastle the same, and said that if we admitted to France that our allies were to be indemnifyed out of our conquests, they would make such demands as would moulder away all our conquests. Mr. Pitt was very angry at that expression, and desired the Lords would remember, that he should be for insisting on more advantageous terms than the Duke of Newcastle, who answered that might very probably happen.

Mr. Pitt and I had some altercation. I said that I was not prepared to give an opinion, nor could [not] be till I knew in what sense France meant their proposition. Pitt said he could not see that it made any alteration. All the Lords were against him except Lord Temple.[359]

July 11 1761: Lord Bute called upon me.[360] I told his Lordship that he had been very civil to me, and that therefore it was a return due to him, and likewise my duty to the King, to inform him of the situation that I apprehended our affairs were like to run into. The Duke of Bedford was much out of humour, and declared that he was come to a resolution not to come to Council any more, if they were to be overruled. [any more] That he [Bedford] saw no reason why we were all to give way to one man, [Pitt], and that he was rather displeased with his Lordship [Bute] for yielding so much to him.[361]

That the Duke of Newcastle was much hurt and much agitated;[362] that he saw his own situation so ticklish and so dangerous, that he did not know which way to turn himself. For that whether it was peace or war, his part was equally distressfull. For if the majority of the Council were with him for peace, and Mr. Pitt did not approve the terms, and he, Lord Bute, would not decide against Mr. Pitt, in that case he should be attacked the next Session, and what would become of him, with Mr. Pitt against him, and perhaps his Lordship and of course the King? He should undoubtedly be undone.

On the other hand, if he was overruled and warlike measures were to be pursued, the great burthen would fall upon him, as he was to raise the money.* It was the opinion of moneyed men in the City that

---

[359] Because of illness Devonshire could not attend the Councils of 20, May 16, 24 and 26 June. On 16 June the epochs relating to *uti possidetis* were decided, two months later than Choiseul had proposed.

[360] Devonshire to Newcastle, 12 July 1761, Add. MSS. 32925, ff. 28–9.

[361] Bedford to Newcastle, 2 July 1761, Add. MSS. 32924, f. 384. Newcastle to Devonshire, 28 June 1761, Chatsworth MSS. 182:77A.

[362] Newcastle to Devonshire, 4 July 1761, Add. MSS. 32924, f. 410.

few people would risk much in a new subscription credit, being hurt by the many bankruptcyes. Sir Joshua Vanneck[363] was of opinion that very little was to be expected from abroad, they having already laid out all their spare money.* That considering how much the stocks would fall and *other circumstances*, it would be impossible for him [Newcastle] to execute his office with credit to himself, and therefore it would be better for him to retire.

This being the situation of affairs, it would undoubtedly come to his Lordship [Bute] to decide what part he would take, and therefore it was necessary to prepare him for it. He [Bute] said he would go as far as any man in giving up his opinion for the sake of unanimity, and that if such terms were agreed upon as he could set his hand to, he should think himself bound in honour to support it, though he might have been of opinion that we might have got better terms. On the other hand, he confessed that, if the Duke of Newcastle was overruled and the war was to continue, *he should not be surprised to see him quit the Treasury*. (This was said in such a manner as made me think he was not very anxious whether he did or not.)

I observed to him that it would be very prejudicial to the King's affairs and unfortunate for his Lordship; that it was obvious to all the world the share he had [in] the King's favour, and likewise the influence; that for one I should have no objection to see him have that weight and share of power in this country that it entitled him to. But that if his Lordship made too much haste, he would defeat his own scheme; that the Duke of Newcastle and myself had both taken pains to bring our friends to be cordial to him, which must be a work of time, and ónly to be brought about by keeping well with the Duke of Newcastle. That by so doing he would have a good chance of succeeding him and keeping his friends, when his Grace should drop, which by the course of years must be soon. He asked me if I would have him prescribe any set of men and quarrel with all the Tories.

I said no, I was against any prescription whatever; that it was perfectly right to take in men of character and abilities from among them, but that if he attempted to take the whole party, he would by that means lose two thirds of the nation, and besides he might be assured that, if he and Mr. Pitt differed, that he would lose [a] great part of them. He said he had received a warm letter from the Duke of Bedford to the purport of what I had said to him; that he was determined to write him a very civil but strong answer.[364] He hoped when we came to talk over the terms of peace we should not much differ; that it was plain the Duc de Choiseul had by flattery got the

[363] A wealthy merchant banker in London.

[364] Bedford to Bute, 9 July 1761, Bute MSS. 478; Bute to Bedford, 12 July 1761; *Bedford*, iii. 22–5, 29–35.

length of Stanley's foot, and that he imposed upon him and his conduct full of chicanery. His opinion on the points in dispute as follows:

The Fishery, as by the Treaty of Utrecht; to give them some port for their Negro trade on their ceeding Senegar and Goree; Dunkirk as by the Treaty of Aix; to be firm on Nieuport and Ostend. [Bute] agreed that Mr. Pitt had done wrong in giving up the Treaty of Utrecht; blamed him for having set down specifick compensations, whereas we ought to have said, on such terms we will make peace and abide by them. He [Bute] said he would state all this to the Duke of Bedford and hoped they should not differ much.[365] I thought he seemed rather dry on the subject of the Duke of Newcastle.

Saw Viry, who said Lord Bute was too much guided by Dodington and Sir Francis Dashwood; confessed he did not behave well to Duke of Newcastle; said Elliot had dropped something, as if they could go on without him; desired me to talk to Lord Bute. I told him I had very freely and give[n] such advice as I thought best for him and most for the King's service.

July 14 1761: Lord Bute, before Mr. Pitt, said to the Duke of Newcastle, it was very extraordinary they heard nothing from France;[366] that Cressener's intelligence[367] said Prince Soubise[368] was ordered to detach troops from his army and named the regiments, in case we made any farther attempts on their coasts. Mr. Pitt complained that we lay inactive, while the French pushed on their conquests. Lord Bute said the Duke of Newcastle ought to prepare to raise the money for another year. The Duke replied that would be a very difficult matter. Pitt said he knew it was to be had. This is the Duke of Newcastle's account and looks something like concert [between Pitt and Bute].[369]

July 15 1761: (State of affairs) Duke of Newcastle, Lord Hardwick and Lord Bute were got together in the room where were all the foreign ministers and King's servants before the Levée. His Grace was giving

[365] In return for participation in the Newfoundland Fisheries on the Utrecht basis, France was to demolish the fortifications of Dunkirk in accordance with the Treaty of Aix-la-Chapelle. Britain could never have consented to the annexation of West Flanders, the price originally agreed by Austria for the French alliance.

[366] Choiseul was negotiating secretly with Charles III of Spain, with a view to an alliance, which culminated in the Second Family Compact, signed on 13 Aug. 1761. Also, he may have been waiting upon recent French successes in Germany. 'Intelligence' Versailles 16 July 1761, Add. MSS. 32925, ff. 91–3. But the British defeated the French at Wellinghausen on July 16.

[367] George Cressener, British Minister to Cologne, 1755–63. Intelligence from Cressener, 2 July 1761 (copy), Add. MSS. 32924, ff. 280–3; Cressener to Bute, 8 July 1761, S.P.F. 81/39.

[368] Charles de Rohan, Prince of Soubise.

[369] 'It is expected that Lord Bute and Mr. Pitt are agreed.' Newcastle to Hardwicke, 18 July 1761, Add. MSS. 32925, f. 156.

an account of a conversation he had had in the morning with Bussy, who complained that he was ill used, there having been a proposition sent to France without communicating it to him.[370] The Duke of Newcastle denied it, asked him the meaning, why we did not hear from them as they had promised. He confessed he could not tell the reason of it. The Duke told him that we should not sit still any longer and see France take all the Electorate, without availing ourselves in the part where we were strongest, and that these conquests in Germany[371] would not enable them to make a better [peace] than they could now; that we had both funds and money for carrying on the war another [year] and therefore if peace was not soon concluded another campaign would be inevitable. This led us into a conversation of the terms on which we might make peace.

Lord Bute stated: 'The Fishery with a place for them on the Banks of Newfoundland; Dunkirk as the Treaty of Aix; a port in lieu of Goree; Newport and Ostend not to remain in the hands of France after the general peace is concluded.' We all agreed to these terms.

Lord Bute said: 'Farther than this I will not go.' The Duke of Newcastle hesitated on that.

The other replied: 'I see your Grace will make peace on worse terms than I will.'

I then declared that I was for sending these terms to France and to acquaint them that we should not come into terms less advantageous than these, and that France should without loss of time send an answer. And that Mr. Stanley might hint that if he had not a favourable answer, he must expect to be recalled. At the same time I desired to have it understood, that I should remain at full liberty to give such answer as I should think proper to any proposition or reply that they should make.

July 16:[372] Met Duke of Newcastle and Mr. Pitt at Lady Yarmouth's. In conversation Pitt told him that he could raise the money better than any other man, but it could be done without him. He [Pitt] had when alone with her expressed great satisfaction with the King, that he had behaved extremely well with him, was firm, and would not make a bad peace. The King had that day refused to send 2000 men at Pitt's request from Belleisle to Martinico.

July 18 1761: Dined at Claremont: Duke of Newcastle much out of humour, shewed me a letter he had wrote to Lord Bute[373] recom-

[370] There is no evidence of this.

[371] The new French Commander, the Count of Broglie, had enjoyed some successes in Hesse.

[372] This paragraph relating to July 16 was entered by Devonshire before his account of July 15 and transposed by the editors.

[373] Newcastle to Bute, 17 July 1761, Add. MSS. 32925, f. 131.

mending the Bishop of Lincoln[374] for London, and likewise mentioning that he had received a few applications out of the country for places in the Queen's Household. He had received a very dry letter in answer;[375] that the Bishop of London had been so long declining, that he believed His Majesty had determined how to dispose of it,[376] unless his Grace's recommendation should make him change his mind; that the Queen's establishment was all full and when it came to be known, it would appear how little he had to do with it. [Newcastle] pressed me much to talk to Lord Bute, to tell him that it was impossible for him to continue in the King's service, treated in the manner he was by his Lordship, that there was no communication, that he could never see him, nor was consulted in any shape.

| July 24 1761:[377] | Mr. Stanley's letter[378] |
| 2 Sec. State | Duc de Choiseul understood facility [on the] Fishery not from Mr. Stanley.[379] P.[380] |

Lord President
Lord Hardwick
Duke of Bedford

Duke of Newcastle
Lord Halifax
Lord Anson
Lord Legonier
Lord Holdernesse

Duc de Choiseul had struck out of the Memorial the guarantee[381] of Spain, which Mr. Stanley had remonstrated against.

The Memorial not the Ultimatum of France

France desires peace, from necessity of her affairs malgré Spain and Austria. Canada,

---

[374] John Thomas, Bishop of Lincoln.

[375] The prospective Queen's Household. The King's marriage to Charlotte of Mecklenburg-Strelitz took place in September. Bute to Newcastle, 17 July 1761, Add. MSS. 32925, f. 133.

[376] Thomas Sherlock, Bishop of London, died that year after a long illness. Newcastle correctly suspected the King proposed to fill the vacancy without consulting him. Thomas Hayter, Bishop of Norwich, Preceptor to George III as Prince of Wales, was translated.

[377] Devonshire does not record himself as present and Newcastle sent him an account of the proceedings on 28 July 1761, Add. MSS. 32926, ff. 28–9.

[378] Stanley to Pitt, 14 July 1761, enclosing the French Memoire of 13 July S.P.F. 78/251. Two meetings were held to discuss the dispatch, the first on 21 July and the second as described here by Devonshire.

[379] In his letter of 14 July, Stanley denied having given Choiseul any hope of an eventual share in the Newfoundland Fisheries. Thackeray, ii. 543.

[380] Pitt.

[381] Choiseul, in the preliminary draft of his Memoire of 13 July, had made mention of Spanish grievances which he deleted when Stanley protested. Stanley to Pitt, 12 July 1761, S.P.F. 78/251.

Goree, Senegal.[382] She will acquiesce any unfortified port that her Fishery may not interfere with ours. Resign Nieuport and Ostend, cede advantages E. Indies, withdraw troops from Westphalia. Will not consent to the demolition of Dunkirk.[383]

Letter Cipher

8 July[384]
Duc de Choiseul: they had consented to engage with Spain on Prizes, Logwood, Fishery. Wished they could be settled with our peace.
Proposed I [Stanley] should talk with Grimaldi.[385]

Spain wants Minorca and has offered Puerto Rico in exchange.

12.[386]

Duc de Choiseul:
Alternatives in lieu of Cape Breton not in Paper but Bussi has instructions.[387]

Not necessary to restore Senegal and Goree, [if] it agrees in other things.
Owns he mistook about the King of Prussia's country, it being in the Empress.[388]

[382] Choiseul agreed to abandon Canada but expected the return of either Senegal or Goree.

[383] Dunkirk was not mentioned in the French *Memoire* of 13 July, though shortly before Choiseul had complained to Stanley: '... that the demolition of Dunkirk is a new condition which cannot be insisted upon according to the terms of uti possidetis already agreed on both sides: the Treaty of Utrecht having by your [Britain's] own avowal ceased at the war.' Stanley to Pitt, P.S. to 5 July 1761, S.P.F. 78/251.

[384] This entry is a précis of Stanley's dispatch, separate in cypher, of 12 July 1761, referring to a conversation between Stanley and Choiseul of 8 July.

[385] Marquis of Grimaldi, Spanish Ambassador in Paris, 1753–63.

[386] Stanley's dispatch of 12 July.

[387] Pitt with unanimous support in the Cabinet refused either Cape Breton or St. John. No territory sufficiently extensive to attract French colonisation could be allowed, no matter what the safeguards.

[388] In his dispatch of 17 June, Choiseul had agreed to evacuate all the French conquests in Germany, including the possessions of Prussia on the Rhine, Wesel, Gueldres and part of Cleves. Now, having drawn closer to Madrid, Choiseul repudiated his position on the ground that the areas involved had been administered in the name of the Empress, whose consent was necessary. Bussy to Pitt, 23 July 1761, P.R.O. 30/8/ 85, f. 199.

Memorial. Limits of Canada, Bussy has orders to settle them. If France is allowed a port for Fishery they will consent to an English Commissary.

1° The compensations determine Epochs Cede Canada with 4 conditions: allow their religion,[389]

2ᵈ the inhabitants may retire into French colonies and sell their effects and transport them.

3 Limits relative to Louisiana may be settled.

4° Drying Fishery on Banks of Newfoundland.

---

restore Minorca—

England restore Guadeloupe, Marie Galente.

5 Neutral island—2 Charaibbes remain as they are.[390]

England—Tobago, France—Santa Lucia.

6 East India Companies abstain from arms (?) a neutrality in time of war and not take part in the wars in the country.

7 American French colonies want Negros[391]— Evacuate Hesse, Hanover and the Electorate,[392] leaving the Meine open.

As King of France is engaged by treaty with the Empress, can't act to her prejudice, if peace is made can't allow that any troops of Prince Ferdinand's army should go to assistance of King of Prussia.

King of Prussia's country Lower Rhine were conquered in the Empress's name and therefore cannot be evacuated.

Prizes made before the declarations of war to be determined by the Courts of Law.

In equity to be restored.

Not to suffer the disputes between us and Spain to be talked on by France.[393]

[389] Permit the free exercise of the Roman Catholic religion.

[390] Caribbees. Dominica and St. Vincent.

[391] Hence Choiseul's demand for Senegal or Goree.

[392] Of Cologne, whose Elector was on the French side.

[393] Together with his Ultimatum of 13 July, Choiseul forwarded a separate Memorial detailing the Spanish grievances, which Pitt warmly rejected with unanimous Cabinet approval. Pitt to Bussy, 24 July 1761, S.P.F. 78/251.

Offensive proceeding.[394]

Dunkirk, Treaty of Aix.[395]

Fishery, to show facility, not to cede any island, or any territorial jurisdiction, no farther than as by the article of the Treaty of Utrecht.

Present

Lord President

Lord Privy Seal

Lord Chancellor[397]

Duke of Bedford

Duke of Newcastle

Lord Hardwicke

Lord Halifax

Lord Legonier

Lord Mansfield

2 Secretaries

Duke of Devonshire.

If England agrees to give no succour[399] they the same.

[Aug 13][396] what passed relative to Spain was out of sincere desire of peace: no offer of mediation. The King of France will always interfere as long as Spain approves.[398] He [Louis XV] will sacrifice his power, in consequence of supporting his allies: may not for ambitious views but will not suffer them[400] to be prejudiced. Duc de Choiseul offended at the imperious style.[401] Stanley assigned 3 causes:[402]* mixing Spain in the negotiation, retraction of Wesel, delay of answer, and* Duc de Choiseul* asked if it was impossible a rock to afford shelter for the barks of their fishery, that the total exclusion was what no minister could or durst come into.

Would consent to every limitation, an English commissary to reside there.

Reproach on France to let Prince Ferdi-

[394] Choiseul's championing the Spanish grievances.

[395] In his reply to the French proposals of 25 July, Pitt had informed Stanley that the demolition of the fortifications of Dunkirk in accordance with the Treaty of Aix, rather than the more stringent provisions of Utrecht, would be acceptable, rather than jeopardize the whole negotiation.

[396] A meeting summoned to discuss the French Ultimatum of 5 Aug. and Stanley's dispatch of 6 Aug. 1761, reproduced in Thackeray, ii. 577–8. The proceedings open with the reading of the dispatch.

[397] Sir Robert Henley, 1st Lord Henley, Lord Keeper June 1757 and Lord Chancellor since October 1760.

[398] In a letter presented by Bussy to Pitt on 5 Aug. Choiseul wrote: 'Sa Majesté Louis XV on à chargé de déclarer a V.E. que tant que l'Espagne l'approuvera, le Roi se mêlera des intérêts de cette Couronne, sans s'ârreter aux refus de la Puissance qui s'y opposerait.' S.P.F. 78/252.

[399] To their respective German allies.

[400] The interests of Spain.

[401] Of Pitt's letter of 25 July.

[402] Stanley to Pitt, 6 Aug. 1761: 'I then told him that the austerity of language which he called imperious and which I must call plain and ingenuous arose in my opinion from three causes, from the part he had taken contrary to my earnest and humble representations of intermixing the British disputes with Spain, from the delay of his last answer and from the appearances of retraction which his error about the return of Wesel carried with it.' P.R.O. S.P.F. 78/252.

nand's army loose against the Empress Queen.

Stanley never said anything on the Fishery.[403]

Minorca and Belleisle only a common topick and not meant to insist upon.[404]

[French] desire of peace universal: [they] think that England will grant it out of kindness.[405]

Don't wish it on *higher* terms for us.

An appeal to their nation against their government would have no weight.[406]

They are not reduced yet to receive the terms proposed.[407] King[408] for peace, chagrined at the turn the negotiation. Daupin and mistress[409] against peace; wishes well to Spain and Austria on religious views.

If the Articles relating to France were settled he [Choiseul] would not be difficult on other points.[410]

He does not mention engagements with Spain as obstacle to the peace.

France will never let their allies obstruct their peace if they see facility on their own favourite point.

[Stanley] asked him why he never mentioned Spain before: embarrassed.

The sole cause of the failure of this negotiation is the refusal of the entire Fishery.[411]

---

[403] According to Bussy, Stanley made vague promises, for which he had no authority, about the Fisheries. This, of course, Stanley denied.

[404] In his Memoire of 13 July Choiseul had offered to restore Minorca in exchange for Guadeloupe and Marie Galante and asked for the return of Belleisle without equivalent. Now he simply proposed that Britain and France retain their respective conquests.

[405] Here Devonshire comes very close to the actual wording of Stanley's dispatch. Stanley to Pitt, 6 Aug. 1761, Thackeray, ii. 577.

[406] A point made clear in Stanley's dispatch.

[407] Already in July Choiseul had warned Stanley 'that propositions had been opened to France in case she chose to continue the war.' The hint was 'they would have new allies,' indicating Spain. Stanley to Pitt, 5 July 1761, S.P.F. 78/251.

[408] Louis XV. [409] Dauphin and Mdme. de Pompadour.

[410] The Prussian territories and the Spanish grievances.

[411] Stanley to Pitt, 6 Aug.: 'I am fully and deeply convinced that the sole cause of the failure of this treaty is the determined resistance of the French as to the entire concession of the Fishery, although they have brought other matters already into the negotiation and will I doubt not ascribe the rupture to the more generous and popular motive of fidelity to their foreign alliances.' S.P.F. 78/252.

In this Council[412] Lord Hardwick began in taking notice that he thought the paper of points[413] did not quite agree with the sense of the last meeting.[414] Duke of Bedford likewise mentioned same and particularly in putting Minorca and Belleisle as compensations to each other. There was much warmth on this occasion on the part of Mr. Pitt. Lord Bute said that he understood we were all agreed on the point of the Fishery as stated in the Ultimatum,[415] and that we would not yield more.[416]

I said I never had understood it in that light; that I was for having an Ultimatum delivered to the French Minister; that he should be made to look upon it as such in order to bring the negotiation to a decision, but that I had expressly declared I would be at full liberty to consider their answer and not be tied up by the terms we had sent to France. I said that in former times, minutes used to be taken at all times to avoid mistakes, and that I hoped it would be done again in order to avoid such altercations for the future as had passed this day. Much heat passed. Mr. Pitt said that it was derogatory to a young King's honour to recede from what he had sent as his Ultimatum.

I expressed my surprise at that declaration, when he himself had made Dunkirk an absolute sine qua non never to be departed from in his paper of points, and in the letter to Mr. Stanley that accompanied it, he tells him to relax in that point.[417] The result was that he should write a letter[418] to Bussy in answer to one that he had received from him with the ultimatum from the Court of France,[419] to tell him that he was ready to talk with him on the subject matter of both Memorials.[420] This took its rise from Lord Granville having told us that Bussy had been with him and said that if Mr. Pitt would see him and talk over the Memorials they might still agree. Mr. Pitt was offended and added that what Bussy said to anybody but him must pass for nothing, and let the lord be ever so great he should lay no stress upon it.

[412] The same Council of 13 Aug. At this point, the reading of Stanley's dispatch of 6 Aug. concluded, the discussion opens.

[413] Pitt's dispatch of 25 July 1761 to Stanley containing the British reply or Ultimatum to Choiseul's *Memoire* of 13 July.

[414] Held on Friday, 24 July 1761. Hardwicke disliked Pitt's style, 'haughty and dictatorial', adding that if, after long deliberation, such 'liberties are taken the whole may as well be left to one man.' Hardwicke to Newcastle, 2 Aug. 1761, Add. MSS. 32926, f. 141.

[415] Wherein France was granted a share in the Newfoundland Fisheries provided the fortifications of Dunkirk were reduced.

[416] For Bute's essential compliance in Pitt's obdurate policy, see Bute to Pitt [24 July 1761], P.R.O. 30/8/24, f. 321; Newcastle to Hardwicke, 1 Aug. 1761, Add. MSS. 32936, ff. 125–6; Jenkinson to Grenville, 21, 25, 28 July 1761, *Grenville*, i. 376–80.

[417] See p. 106, n. 395.

[418] The letter Pitt drafted was discussed at the Council of 15 Aug., see p. 111.

[419] Bussy to Pitt, 5 Aug. 1761, S.P.F. 78/252.

[420] The English Memorial of 25 July and the French reply of 5 Aug.

Fishing Gulph St. Lawrence not of that consequence as we shall be in possession of the territory.

A small island where fortification no inconvenience: not C. [Cape] Breton.

----

to spend 20 or 30 millions for it.

----

to shew whether we were reasonable or not.

This country exhausted.[421]

Aug 14 1761: Lord Bute sent to desire to see me. When I came to him, he began with saying: 'Did you ever see such a day as yesterday? I find out that I am indeed a very young politician. If ever I thought any point had been finally settled it was that of the Fishery at our last meeting, but I was mistaken.' He then very calmly endeavoured to persuade me to be of the opinion not to make any further concessions on that head; that we ought after our successes to reap some advantage from the war; that we had given up *Sugar Islands*,* hinted out of complaisance to Mr. Beckford,* which brought a revenue of £4 or 500,000 to France, and had only a long barren tract of country[422] that did not produce £40,000 p.a.; that therefore if we had not the Fishery we really got nothing.[423]

I kept firm to my former opinion, that I had always kept myself at liberty to judge upon any proposition that should return from France; that it did not appear to me, that any facility had been shewn to her on the point of the Fishery; that Mr. Stanley repeated over and over again that France would never consent to give it up entirely;[424] that if we would relax something on that head, all other points might easily be adjusted, for which reason I was for going as far on that as I possibly could.

I was not for yielding Cape Breton or St. Jean whither, as they demanded permission for their subjects in Canada to retire with their effects, they might come and make a new settlement. I thought they

----

[421] The lengthy account of the discussion of Stanley's dispatch of 6 Aug. ends at this point.

[422] Canada.

[423] Bute suggests that Pitt had agreed to hand back Guadeloupe out of regard for Beckford and the West India interest. For the true situation see Namier, 273–82.

[424] In this connection, see Stanley to Pitt, 18 June, 1, 14, 30, July, 1 Aug. 1761, S.P.F. 78/251.

were too near our coasts. I was for giving them permission to fish in the Gulph of St. Lawrence (which could not be refused unless we called it a mare clausum), and let them have any small island, such as the Magdelaine or St. Pierre, under those sort of restrictions they themselves had proposed.[425] If the French were sincere they would take these terms as it comes nearly to their demands; that their fishing in the Gulph would not be of the same consequence as the coasts were in our possession; besides they might be obliged not to come within a certain distance of the shore.

When we had talked this over very seriously we entered on the subject of the administration. I told him that our situation at home appeared to me as serious as that abroad; that I feared we should break to pieces; that the Duke of Newcastle, though he had not absolutely said so, yet appeared to me to think seriously of retiring.[426] That he [Newcastle] saw warlike measures were to be pursued, which was contrary to his opinion; that the burthen of it must lie upon him in the Treasury, which would be accompanied with almost insurmountable difficulties, and add to this he despaired of living in friendship with you [Bute] and in your confidence. And therefore, however much he might wish to continue in employment, that he began to see the necessity of retiring.

Lord Bute replied very calmly that if his Grace would retire, he should be very sorry for it; that he saw his own situation would become much more difficult and dangerous, but the King was not to be left alone, and that he was determined to do everything in his power to serve him; that it would naturally oblige him to act more with Mr. Pitt, a man whom he never could nor would unite himself with; that he solemnly declared he wished to live well with [the] Duke of Newcastle. But that no one thing became vacant, but his Grace immediately put in for it,[427] and if it was not done immediately, a quarrell ensued and that he would not submit his Grace should have the entire disposal of everything.

I told him plainly that they appeared to me to be both in the wrong: the Duke of Newcastle was too eager in applying, and his Lordship was too cold in his manner of putting him off, which drew on altercation and occasioned ill humour. I had always wished an union between them as I thought it conducive to the King's ease and the welfare of the country. I hoped he would not take it ill if I told him

---

[425] Miquelon or St. Pierre: No fortifications and a resident English Commissary. Stanley to Pitt, 6 Aug. 1761, S.P.F. 78/252.

[426] Newcastle to Devonshire (most secret), 5 Aug. 1761, Add. MSS. 32926, ff. 187–93.

[427] Newcastle recommended John Douglas, Bishop of Salisbury, for the expected vacancy in the Primacy of York, only to be overruled again. Newcastle to Bute, 7 Aug. 1761, Add. MSS. 32926, f. 292; Newcastle to Devonshire, 12 Aug. 1761, ibid. ff. 382–3.

plainly that I thought it impossible for him to stand alone at present, and if he must have some support, I left it to him to judge which would be the least burthensome, the Duke of Newcastle or Mr. Pitt. And moreover it was my firm opinion that a ministry composed of his Lordship and Mr. Pitt would not go down in this country; that I had taken great pains to reconcile people to his Lordship, but that if such an union took place, I could not answer to persuade my nearest and best friends to support it. And therefore I could wish that he would consider well and manage the Duke of Newcastle, for that he could not do without him if the war continued.

He replied: 'My Lord, I wish to manage him both in time of war and peace.'

Friday Aug. 15 [14] 1761:[428] Objections to Mr. Pitt's letter by Lord Hardwick: the time of peace not yet come—disputes in America. An appeal to the public, which Court has most shewn an *eloignment* to peace, and that it had rather the appearance of a manifesto.[429] Lord President[430] said the same; called the letter a fine piece of oratory, a classical and elegant performance; that all his experience had taught him that in negotiation plain language and style did best and was of opinion it ought to be altered and made less offensive.

Mr. Pitt flew into a great passion; that he did not know what the Lord [President] meant in calling his letter a piece of oratory; that it was wrote in the plainest language;* it should not be *cobled* by any-one;* that he would not suffer an *iota* in it to be altered; that he would carry it to the King and tell him that this letter he was ready to set his hand to, but to no other, and that if H.M. did not approve of it, he must employ some other lord to frame another; that he would not bear the treatment he met with. He averred he had stuck literally to the sense of the Council on all occasions and he would not bear insinuations to the contrary; that he saw combinations of great Lords against him but for his part he would go his own way; that he was a British subject and he knew he stood upon British ground; that he had learnt his maxims and principles under the great Lord Cobham[431] and the disciples of the greatest lawyers, generals and patriots of King William's[432] days: named Lord Somers[433] and the Duke of Marlborough.[434]

The Duke of Bedford replied he did not know what made him so

---

[428] Devonshire's entry of 15 Aug. describes the Cabinet of the previous day, a continuation of the meeting of 13 Aug. which had ended in an instruction to Pitt to draft a reply to Stanley's dispatch of 6 Aug. containing the French Ultimatum of 5 Aug.

[429] Hardwicke criticised the letter as 'much too long and too irritating.' Hardwicke to Royston, 15 Aug. 1761, Yorke, iii. 320-1.

[430] Granville.   [431] 1st Viscount Cobham.

[432] William III.   [433] 1st Baron Somers, Lord Chancellor, 1697-1700.

[434] 1st Duke of Marlborough.

angry, but after what had fallen from him [Pitt] it was in vain for him [Bedford] to think of attending Council any more, and went away.

Lord Bute interrupted us by reading an intercepted letter which the King sent him from Choiseul to Havrincourt,[435] in which he says that England was so unreasonable that it was determined to carry on the war, but for certain reasons they should prolong the negotiation for a month or six weeks.[436] Probably that Spain might not be under the necessity of declaring herself till such time as her galleons might come home.

When most Lords had spoke, I said that I should take very little notice of the letter which was the subject of the meeting; that had I been [asked] to have given my opinion I should have been for making it less offensive, but that as Mr. Pitt had declared he would not suffer the least alteration, it was to no purpose to enter into it, and indeed the letter read by Lord Bute rendered it of less consequence. That I was still of opinion that we had not opened ourselves sufficiently on the point that France had most at heart, namely the Fishery; that it was very necessary we should clear up on what terms we would have made peace, to be able to justifye ourselves to the public whenever the negotiation was broke off. For I was convinced it would be the most unpopular act. That I had never been fond of attending meetings but what had passed these two last days[437] would make me much more averse to them. But that as long as I had the honour to come, I should always give my opinion like an honest man to the best of judgement, and what I thought most for the true interest of my King and country, and when I had done that I should rest contented and be very indifferent what anybody thought of it.

When other Lords had declared their opinions, I got up to go away. Mr. Pitt called me back [and] said as he must acquaint the King with the difference of opinions among [the] Lords, he should be glad to know mine, as he did not understand that I had given any. I said it was very true and desired he would acquaint H.M. that, as he, Mr. Pitt, had refused to make any alteration in his letter, it could not be said to come under our deliberation, and that therefore I could not give any opinion upon it. He then took notice that I had mentioned the word unpopular; that for his part he was not guided by it and that he did not call popularity what arose in the City from the cry of stockgobbers and those that were interested in subscriptions.

I replyed I was glad he had not intimated as if I had charged him

[435] Louis de Cardevac, Marquis of Havrincourt, French Ambassador to Sweden, 1749–62.

[436] Choiseul had written on 30 July 1761: 'Sa Majesté s'est determiné à continuer la guerre mais comme il est important de cacher encore un mois cette resolution à la cour de Londres nous entretriondrons encore quelques semaines la négotiation avant de la rompre.' Choiseul to Havrincourt (copy), Add. MSS. 32926, f. 67.

[437] The Council meetings of 13 and 14 Aug.

with it; that I mentioned it as a reason why we should be explicit on the terms on which we would make peace, as I was convinced the breaking off the peace would be very unpopular; that I did not take my notions from the cry of the City but from the universal voice of every part of England. I had gone through this year; that I did not charge him with being governed by popularity, and that I believed I was in no danger of being suspected of it.

Pro	Con
Lord Chancellor	Duke of Bedford
Lord Privy Seal	Lord President
2 Secretarys	Lord Hardwicke
Lord Halifax	Duke of Newcastle
Lord Legonier	Lord Mansfield

Duke of Devonshire, refused giving any opinion.

Aug 18 1761: Sent Lord Bute the Duke of Bedford's answer,[438] that he could not come to Council after what he had said without the King's express desire. Lord Bute appointed me to meet him at his office. He began with an account that after he was gone from Court the day before, (where we parted at three), he met a servant of Mr. Pitt's, who desired he would meet him at Court. They went to the King, where Mr. Pitt related the whole that had passed.

Bussy presented a Paper marking the bounds of Louisiana,[439] which took in the Ohio and [a] great part of what they used to call Canada, and that France would insist upon it. He said they had a right *immemorial* to fish in the Gulph of St. Lawrence. Mr. Pitt pressed him on that point saying that in rivers and gulphs the territories gave the right, therefore they could not have it previous to their conquests.

Bussy answered: 'Ma foy, Monsieur, je ne vois pas ce que ce mot ces à faire là.' [He] insisted upon the Fishery and an island with a territorial jurisdiction: if St. Jean or Cap Breton were refused, named Canso.[440]

Mr. Pitt having done, Lord Bute told the King before him that this was the most critical minute he had ever seen in this country; that the honour of his reign and the fate of his kingdom perhaps depended upon the determination of the Council. That therefore whatever his own opinion might be, when he saw so many Lords of great

[438] At a meeting with Devonshire on 16 Aug., the King had deplored the lack of harmony within the Cabinet, and suggested a further Council which Bedford might attend. As instructed, Devonshire gave a full account of this conversation to Bedford. *Bedford*, iii. 36–9. In his reply Bedford reaffirmed his desire to remain absent, unless personally summoned by the King. Bedford to Devonshire, 17 Aug. 1761, Chatsworth MSS. 286/8; Devonshire to Bute (enclosing a summary of Bedford's letter), 18 Aug. 1761, Bute MSS. 584.

[439] Entitled 'Sur les limites de Louisianne', 18 Aug. 1761 (copy), Add. MSS. 32927, f. 100.

[440] Cape Canso, by the strait of Canso, on the east coast of Nova Scotia.

consequence and character, of opinion to relax upon the point of the Fishery, as far as they thought consistent with the honour of the nation, he should as far as he could in conscience [and] for the sake of unanimity, give up his opinion; that he had done it on the point of the Newfoundland Fishery and that he should be inclined to do it in this instance. But then he should hope that [the] Lords would fix an ultimatum in their own minds how far they would go. Pitt looked angry at the first part but seemed to clear up at the last.

I told his Lordship, if he was of that opinion he would do right to advise the King to send for the Duke of Bedford. He wished me to write again and thought that would be sufficient. I assured him, not without the King's express direction. [It was] plain he did not choose to write. The King directed me to do it.[441] [He] desired me to relate this conversation to [the] Duke of Newcastle, Lord Hardwicke, etc. Aug 19 1761: (Council)[442] Read a letter from Lord Bristol.[443] Mr. Pitt gave an account of his conversation with Monsieur Bussy, who said, 'you must be content with cession of Canada.' Mr. Pitt replied yes, if the limits were settled and urged that there must be a neutral country and asked what he looked upon as Louisiana.

Bussy said: 'The cours du Ohio est à nous en remontant: between the right shore and Apalachians Mountains neuter—que des les bords du lac toute est Louisianne.'

Mr. Pitt desired then to know his sentiments as to [the] Fishery. We understood that France wished to have it on the foot of the Treaty [of] Utrecht, which Mr. Stanley was authorised to negotiate on condition that Treaty was preserved to us in Dunkirk.

'You say a right immemorial pour pêcher: on what principle?' [Bussy] gave up the expression.

Mr. Pitt allowed in open seas right to all nations: in gulphs and lakes the territories give it.

He [Bussy] insisted on a right.

'What do you mean by abri?'

'We demand Cap Breton or St. Jean.'

'What do you mean or any other port?'

'I don't know of any other island: we mean a territorial possession, perhaps Canso.'

---

[441] Devonshire to Bedford, 18 Aug. 1761: 'I have had much discourse with Lord Bute and we shall not differ tomorrow, for whatever may have been his former opinion, you will find he will give it up and be with me.' Bedford MSS. XLIV. 8, f. 136. Bedford replied consenting to attend. Bedford to Devonshire, 18 Aug. 1761, Chatsworth MSS. 286.9.

[442] Newcastle's notes on this meeting: 'An account of what passed yesterday at Council' 20 Aug. 1761, Add. MSS. 32927, ff. 131–2.

[443] Probably Bristol to Pitt, 27 July 1761 (rec. August 18), reporting his talks with Wall on Italian affairs and on the logwood question, S.P.F. 94/163.

Neutral islands.[444]
Senegal and Goree.[445]
Allies:
Bussy as firm upon the succour as upon the resitution.[446]
Prizes.[447]
Ostend and Nieuport: France did not mean to keep it.[448]
Cessation of arms.
When he [Bussy] gave his Paper.
Mr. Pitt asked him if these were the ancient or new limits of Louis-ianne.
Bussy: not the old ones for they were much larger.[449]

Whatever concessions we make to go for nothing if the negotiations breaks off.

Where are the intermediate nations?

Why, they must be somewhere about the Apalachian Mountains.[450]

To reject their boundaries of Louisiana.[451]

Does France think she now offers what she did in her original proposition?[452]

To give them as the Duc de Choiseul[453] desired a Rock: if sincere there it is for him, if he does not accept it, plain he meant more.

Yes, and gives up much for conciliation.

Canada contains:
Lakes Huron, Michigan and Superior marked by Monsieur Vaudreuil[454] on a map and given to General Amherest[455] as the Government he surrendered.[456]

[444] To be equally divided, the apportionment fixed by treaty.
[445] Both demanded by Pitt.
[446] Choiseul refused to evacuate Prussian territory on the Rhine and insisted that France and Britain withhold support from their German allies once a treaty was signed.
[447] Captures made by Britain before war was declared.
[448] On the last day of 1758 France and Austria had signed a revised treaty of alliance, by which Louis XV renounced his interest in West Flanders.
[449] Once the French had lost Canada, they adopted a very extended theory concerning Louisiana, which brought the retort: 'all which is not Canada cannot be Louisiana.'
[450] The territories of the Indian nations between the Mississippi and the Thirteen Colonies.
[451] As fixed by Choiseul in Bussy's Paper, Louisiana comprised most of the Indian lands, the Ohio valley and even Lakes Michigan and Superior.
[452] Of 17 June 1761. [453] A base for French fishermen.
[454] Marquis of Vaudreuil, last Governor of New France.
[455] Sir Jeffrey Amherst, Commander-in-Chief of the British army in North America.
[456] By the Capitulation of 8 Sept. 1760. Here the line drawn by de Vaudreuil followed the Ohio and Wabash rivers, from the confluence of the Ohio and the Mississippi to the source of the Wabash, thence continuing along the height of land to Lac Rouge at the headwaters of the Mississippi.

An island under
certain restrictions.

No fortification.

Confirmed by Monsieur Mirepoix's[457] Memorial signed by him.

Not to suffer any
other nation to dry
fish on it.

Ohio part of France we have looked on the river as belonging to Canada and necessary for communication with Louisiana.

Worse terms the
longer the war is
continued.

Lord Hardwick:

Cap Breton, or St.
Jean, too near.[458]

The question not giving up an original right. It is whether you give better or worse terms.

You get a country and leave them part of the Fishery.

Mr. Pitt proposed to order Stanley in case the French persisted in these boundaries of Louisiana to break off the negotiation. Duke of Newcastle objected to that. Duke of Devonshire seconded him. They were of opinion that the whole concessions on both sides should be stated, for France would never recede from one point till she saw what she would get upon another. The latter declared for more facility in the Fishery giving them an abri, and the island of St. Peters[459] or any other of that sort. Lord Chancellor and Lord Halifax[460] came into it. Mr. Pitt said he disapproved but would for the sake of unanimity come into it.

Aug 21 1761: Lord Huntingdon, Groom of the Stole, came to Lord Ashburnham who was in waiting and told him that he would put on the King's shirt. His Lordship replied, to be sure if he pleased, but then he must take the whole waiting. The other said: 'No, I will only put on the shirt.'

Lord Ashburnham said: 'I give you notice, if you do it, I shall quit the room, that the King may not be left without somebody to attend him.'

Lord Huntingdon put on the shirt: the other retired. The Levée over, Lord Ashburnham desired an audience [and] told the King he hoped H.M. did not think he meant any disrespect to him. The King very civilly said no, that he had told Lord Huntingdon he should not decide for him unless he could shew a precedent.

Aug 24: Lord Huntingdon told Lord Rockingham[461] who was then

[457] Duke of Mirepoix, French Ambassador in London, 1752–5.

[458] 'Whatever concessions ... too near' a lengthy marginal note by Devonshire.

[459] St. Pierre.

[460] 2nd Earl of Halifax, President of the Board of Trade.

[461] 2nd Marquis of Rockingham, a Lord of the Bedchamber since 1751, who became Prime Minister, July 1765–July 1766, and February–June 1782.

come into waiting, that he had received direction from the King not to put on the shirt, except he took the whole waiting, and that he would always give notice in writing the day before, but he would inform his Lordship that it was his intention to take it upon all great occasions. Lord Rockingham told him that it was new, and he would talk to the rest of the Lords of the Bedchamber on this declaration. Many of the Lords were much dissatisfied, thought it lowering their employments, and that they could not stay.

Lord Bute told me he had heard from the King, that they [Lords of the Bedchamber] had had a meeting and had signed a paper, which would give great offence to the King if it was presented. (He said the Duke of York had given the King the information.) He believed he would turn them all out. Duke of Newcastle and I both spoke to Lord Rockingham, to desire him to be quiet and not speak to the King that day, but to no purpose. Lord Bute went to him and desired the same; that it would be time enough to remonstrate when the thing happened. Lord Rockingham said that was sufficient for him but it might fall upon other Lords. Lord Bute answered he was persuaded not. So the affair seemed to be at an end.

At night[462] I received a letter from Lord Bute[463] that the King was very angry, would insist upon the rights of the Groom of the Stole, and turn out all the Lords that did not comply. I returned the answer on the other side.[464] [I] met Lord Bute at Court, who said the King had a Paper which he intended to give me to communicate to the Lords of the Bedchamber. His Lordship was wrong, I argued, that the late King had piqued himself on raising the Bedchamber by getting men of the first rank and fortun[ate] to take it, and that if it was lowered, they certainly would not remain in; that it was a very cheap way of keeping them steady to support government. He [Bute] said Lord Huntingdon would give them no trouble, and I might assure them so.

I replied: 'If the King gives me authority to say so.'

He said: 'That he will not do.'

[Devonshire answered]: 'Then I shall certainly not commit myself.'

I went to H.M. who gave me the Paper,[465] talked very reasonable, said it was all owing to Lord Huntingdon's manner but that he was now very humble, and would give no more trouble. I told the King there would be no difficulty in his waiting now, to shew his right; that if he took a week's waiting sometimes, nobody would say anything: but that if he took a day's waiting from any Lord, it would raise the

---

[462] Of 26 August, from the date of Bute's letter.

[463] Bute to Devonshire, 26 August 1761, Chatsworth MSS. 530/11.

[464] Devonshire to Bute, 27 Aug. 1761, ibid. 260/339.

[465] Paper from the King to be shown by Devonshire to the Lords of the Bedchamber, 27 Aug. 1761, Chatsworth MSS. 622.3.

flame again. I added that Lord Rockingham wished he would take tomorrow, that it might fall in his week.

The King was pleased with that and said he would order it just as I thought best. I shewed the Paper to the Lords: they acquiesced. Lord Huntingdon sent to Lord Rockingham that he would wait the next day if convenient. The other answers he had no objection.

I asked Lady Augusta[466] how the King came to be so warm, when yesterday he seemed quite easy about it. She said he was quite so till Lord Bute came and talked it up; that he was not of a temper to be moved till the other made him so; that Lord Bute had been very warm upon the subject the night before. [This] did not correspond with the concern mentioned in his letter to me.

Aug 28: I acquainted the King that I had shewn the Paper to all the Lords I could meet; that they desired their humble duty and to assure H.M. they had never disputed the right, only the exertion of it, and were very thankfull for the latter part of the Paper, which gave them reason to hope it would not be improperly exerted.

I talked much to Lord Bute of the consequence of disobliging so many of the first people. He said if it had come to the point, very few would have quitted. I told him he was mistaken, for if five or six of the most considerable Lords had thrown up, which I knew they would, the rest would have been ashamed to have stayed, and when it was known that they had quitted because the office was made beneath them, that he would get nobody to take it that was worth having. I then advised him to be cautious in his expressions; that if I had shewn his letter, it would have enraged them all; that such Lords would not bear to be told the King *would force them to submit*; that I was as much for keeping up the King's dignity as he could be, but that it might be done without using such strong terms. He agreed and excused his letter, as it was only privately conveying the King's intentions to me. Dispute between Groom of the Stole and Lords Bedchambers from Aug 21 to Aug 27 1761.[467]

Sept 10 1761: Mr. Stanley had said in his letters of the 1st[468] that the disposition of the French Court was such as he thought would justify his not taking leave, though they did not agree to every Article.

By the letters received from him this day[469] he seems to be frightened, and desires fresh instructions and that he was to have his final answer in a day or two. After the Drawing Room was over I was going away, but Lord Bute who was talking with Mr. Pitt, called to me to desire I would stay. When their conversation was ended, he said

[466] Princess Augusta, eldest sister to George III.
[467] Endorsement by Devonshire.
[468] Stanley to Pitt, 1 Sept. 1761 (secret), S.P.F. 78/252.
[469] Stanley to Pitt, 4, 6, 8 Sept. 1761 (received 11 September), ibid.; Newcastle to Bedford, 13 Sept. 1761, *Bedford*, iii. 43-6.

that Mr. Pitt seemed determined to retire. He [Pitt] was very calm and in great good humour, said that he saw so many Lords great in themselves and in their influence in the House of Commons, differing so much in opinion from him, and inclined to make more concessions for the sake of peace than he could come into; that it was impossible for him to remain; that for the sake of unanimity he had gone as far as his conscience and even his *sleep* would permit him, and therefore as he could not execute any orders for making further concessions, he must throw himself on the King's generosity for the care of himself and his family: *protested he meant to give no trouble*.

He [Pitt] threw out the danger he, Lord Bute, would be in as a Secretary of State. His Lordship was alarmed at what he had said, desired I would acquaint the Duke of Newcastle, that he should think seriously whether it would not be better to let Mr. Stanley come away. For if the peace could not be made, his stay would do no good and only drive Mr. Pitt out, who had taken his part ever since the news of the junction of the Austrians with the Russians,[470] and seeing that his hero the King of Prussia would be crushed, he wanted to draw himself out of the scrape and leave the burthen upon them. That he [Bute] did not see and wanted to know who the Duke of Newcastle would put in his place. And therefore, if the answer was not satisfactory, he wished Stanley might be recalled, and he thought his coming away would not retard the peace long, from the inability that all sides were in to carry on the war. I communicated what passed to the Duke of Newcastle. He was very averse to Stanley's coming away, treated what Mr. Pitt said as a menace and that he had frightened Lord Bute and made him change his opinion. The King had told the Duke of Newcastle that Pitt proposed to him the recalling Mr. Stanley, but he had been against it, which he took to be the cause of Mr. Pitt's desiring to retire. Lord Hardwicke was for Mr. Stanley's being recalled if France did not accept our terms, especially as far as related to our national disputes, and thought it would shew such a want of firmness in us as would make them more obstinate. I was of his opinion.

Sept 11 1761: Mr. Pitt said the same to [the] Duke of Newcastle and me that he had said to Lord Bute the day before; abused the Duke of Bedford, that he had held such a language of peace at Council and to foreign ministers as prejudiced our cause; that by the relaxations we had given into we had made it impracticable either to make peace or continue the war. That he desired to retire, would give no opposition, not to appear in the House of Commons the next Session unless he was calumniated.

Sept 16 1761: The King enquired how the meeting[471] had gone off.

---

[470] In Silesia at the beginning of Sept.; Mitchell to Bute, 1 Sept. 1761, S.P.F. 90/78.
[471] The Cabinet meeting of 15 Sept., see p. 120.

Lord Bute had given him a fair relation. [The King was] pleased with the Duke of Newcastle et cetera, laughed at Lord Temple's shewing his readiness for the Treasury.[472] [The King] told me that Prince Ferdinand had wrote two letters to Mr. Pitt,[473] containing a plan for carrying on the war the next year, depending on him for recruiting the army and recommending Sloper[474] for preferment; that he had wanted to take his pleasure upon them, but he had refused to enter into the consideration. Lord Bute very angry that Prince Ferdinand [that he] did not apply to him in whose department[475] he was. Mr. Pitt asked him what should be done in consequence of them. The other replied he had not time to think of them, and told the King, he would overlook it for the sake of his service but *Manet alta mente repostum*. Duke of Newcastle told the King *il faut fermer les yeux Sire* oui *mais seulement fermer*. Pitt and Lord Temple very bad at Court.

A Courier from Choiseul to the French army taken, his letters to Broglio blaming him much;[476] tells him that he had covered himself with infamy at the same time that he has covered Prince Ferdinand with glory. That with a superior army he has suffered himself to be beat and disobeyed orders; that therefore he desires he will remain the rest of the campaign upon the defensive. He tells his brother,[477] he has wrote so strong a letter to Broglio, that he must look upon him no longer as a friend; that it is in vain to think of undertaking another campaign.[478]

A letter from the Dutchess of Duras[479] to her husband, says peace is over through the insolence of the English, who not only have insulted their nation but treated impertinently their King during the negotiation; that they do not know what to do for they have neither money nor ships and shortly they shall have no men; that our insolence will be as great if not greater another year and they shall not be in a better condition to resist us.

Present:
Lord Chancellor
Lord President

Sept 15 1761:[480] Lord Bristol to Wall acquainting him that England had returned the Paper which France had delivered

---

[472] Temple had hinted to Bute and others his readiness to become First Lord of the Treasury should Newcastle retire.

[473] Prince Ferdinand to Pitt, 5 and 7 Sept. 1761, P.R.O. 30/8/90, Part 2.

[474] Captain William Charles Sloper, A.D.C. to Prince Ferdinand.

[475] The Northern Department, of which Bute was Secretary of State.

[476] Choiseul to Broglie, 27 Aug. 1761 (intercepted), Add. MSS. 32928, f. 117.

[477] The Count of Stainville, subsequently Duke of Praslin, French Foreign Minister after Oct. 1761. He and Choiseul were not brothers but cousins.

[478] Choiseul to Stainville, 27 Aug. 1761 (intercepted), enclosed in Yorke to Bute, 13 Sept. 1761, S.P.F. 84/493 and Add. MSS. 32928, f. 119.

[479] The wife of the Duke of Duras, former French Ambassador to Spain.

[480] Newcastle Memorandum, 15 Sept. 1761, Add. MSS. 32928, ff. 185-8.

Duke of Devonshire
Duke of Newcastle
Lord Holdernesse
Lord Halifax
Lord Bute
Lord Hardwicke
Lord Temple P.S.[482]
Lord Anson
Lord Legonier
Mr. Pitt
Lord Mansfield

relative to our dispute with Spain.[481] That we were ready to treat amicably with them but would not suffer France to interfere; that with regard to Spain's claim of the Fishery we would never admit it.

Mr. Wall: Catholic King does not deny the step of the mediation of France, did not mean offence.[483]

---

3 Art. of Greivances.
Claims of ships taken.[484]
Fishery—a negative.
Evacuation of Musquito shore not before logwood promised.[485]
The whole dispatch in a very extraordinary style.

Bussy Memoire[486]
delivered this day
                    Art 1[488]

Renews declaration that nothing it contains should be valid if no peace.[487]
Had said would cede all Canada: renews the same offer.
The line shewn by Mr. Stanley is in the most enlarged sense, agrees to it.[489]
A year for emigration[490] too short.
England talks of dependancies, should explain what it means.[491]

---

[481] Bristol to Pitt, 31 Aug. 1761, S.P.F. 94/164, Part I.

[482] Privy Seal.

[483] Wall to Bristol, 28 Aug. 1761, enclosed in n. 481.

[484] Spain had been unable to obtain redress in the Courts for the depredations against her merchant marine by British privateers.

[485] See p. 59.

[486] 'Memoire de la France sur la reponse de l'Angleterre remise au Duc de Choiseul le 1er Septembre par M. de Stanley,' dated Sept. 9 and submitted by Bussy 15 Sept.; printed in Thackeray, ii. 619-23.

[487] In the preamble Choiseul insisted that in the event of no treaty the entire negotiation would be without prejudice to either party.

[488] The reference is to Article I of Pitt's Ultimatum of Sept. 1.

[489] The boundary between Canada and Louisiana drawn by de Vaudreuil and submitted by Pitt in his Ultimatum of 1 Sept. See also p. 115.

[490] Britain had agreed a period of one year during which French settlers could leave Canada with their possessions and migrate elsewhere under the French crown.

[491] By the word dependencies Pitt meant that Canada must comprise the relevant coast-line and all islands in the vicinity of the St. Lawrence and Newfoundland, especially Cape Breton and St. John.

Art 2	Limits of Louisiana in the English Memoire 2 paragraphs neither clear nor just.
Bussy told Mr. Pitt that he understood they meant in great part their own original proposed line.	Propose Indian nations between Lakes and Missispisi within the drawn line shall be neuter under protection of France. The other side of the line under English protection.
	Traders on each side forbid to go beyond respective lines. The Indians may trade on each side.
Art 3	Cede Senegall on condition of having Animaboo and D'Akea.[492]
Art 4	Contains many objects; joins Fishery with demolition of Dunkirk,[493] which they won't allow.
except preserving Port *Marchand*.[494]	Propose agreeable to the letter of Mr. Stanley.
Mr. Pitt asked [Bussy] whether his Court would take the Article of the Treaty of Aix. He said he did not think it.	As to the Fishery: Treaty Utrecht confirmed Fishery in Gulph acknowledged. They agree unless in case of accident they will neither fish or dry their nets. But they must have liberty to fish in every part of the Gulph.
	St. Pierre, the smallness of it and its neighbourhood to Placentia render it inadequate as it may occasion dispute. Renews demand [for] Canso, if not, asks Miguelon, *two leagues*;[495] only 50 guards to support police.
	Won't fish on other parts of Newfoundland, provided they may fish on island of St. Pierre.[496]
Art 5	Neutral islands, agreeable to Mr. Stanley.[497]

[492] Anamabu and Dakar.

[493] A share in the Newfoundland Fishery on condition that the fortifications of Dunkirk were demolished in accordance with the provisions of the Treaty of Aix-la-Chapelle. See p. 106.

[494] Choiseul proposed to retain the harbour which, he claimed, was too small to receive men of war.

[495] The length of Miquelon.

[496] Under the Treaty of Paris of 1763, St. Pierre and Miquelon were ceded to France as *abris*.

[497] France accepted the division of the Neutral Islands, provided St. Lucia and one other were hers.

Art 6   Agree.[498]

7   Agree.[499]

8[500]   On this refers to the 7th of his ultimatum,[501] not in his power to evacuate what belongs to the Empress.[502]

9   Ask explanation as not clear: supposes what is not known to both Courts.[503]

France does not think that England can prevent her allies to join the King of Prussia. France can not make sacrifices of its own country and not keep its engagements with its allies,[504] 10. Art. proposed with their consent.

---

10   France thinks their demands as to Pures [Prizes] just and adheres.[505]

11   Preliminaries signed: King[506] will sign a declaration not to keep Ostend and Newport.

12   Agreed.[507]

13   Should be settled at the time of the peace.[508]

14   No difficulty.[509]

Mr. Pitt:

Relaxations fatal.

Ultimatum sent, Lords departed from it.

Stanley letters King[510] cause of peace, our stiffness advantage to her allies.

Spoilt future negotiations. France will think Lords will do in 1762 as 1761.

He no weight; hopes the King will be supported, hinted Lords discourse out of doors.

---

[498] Article VI offered France the return of Belleisle together with Guadeloupe and Marie-Galante.

[499] Article VII affirmed that Minorca be restored to Britain.

[500] That France evacuate Prussian territories along the Rhine.

[501] The French Ultimatum of 5 Aug. See Thackeray, ii. 566-9.

[502] See p. 104, n. 388.

[503] The treaty obligations of Britain and France to their respective allies.

[504] Devonshire's *précis* from the French *Memoire*: 'Le Roi détermine, pour le bien de la paix, à faire les sacrifices les plus considérables, est en même temps irrévocablement résolu de ne rien accorder, dans le futur Traité de paix, qui soit contraire aux stipulations auxquelles il s'est engagé avec ses Alliés.' S.P.F. 78/252.

[505] Return of compensation for French ships taken before the declaration of war.

[506] Louis XV.

[507] Hostilities to cease on the ratification of the peace preliminaries.

[508] The future of the French East India Company.

[509] Over the release of prisoners of war.   [510] Louis XV.

Duke of Newcastle:

Reason why France has not made peace: Treaty signed 15 days ago.[511]

Of opinion if those concessions had been sooner made it would have [been] better. France has rose in her demands from encouragement from Spain.

I will do my best, not answer for raising the money.

Impossible to have a loan for more than 12 millions.

Moneyed people against the recall of Mr. Stanley.

———————

Lord Granville:
Desired to know the state of our force within call.
Lord Anson:
Cruiser and convoys 5 of Line

Downs—	1	Frigates 58
off to Havre	2	
Com. Keppell[512]—	28	
in port and under sailing orders— >	20	
	56	
two cast—	2	
	54	
under Admiral Saunders[513]	11—	12—
East Indies——	14	
Jamaica—	6	
Leewards—	8	
North America—	6	
Plantations—	2	
Foreign Convoys & Cruiser	4	
	105[514]	

Lord Hardwicke:
To narrow the war, the German expence.
Sorry what has passed formerly has been mentioned:
cannot be of opinion that the concessions are the cause of the retractions in the French Memorial.

---

[511] Devonshire suggests that Pitt's obduracy over the Fisheries led to the Second Family Compact between France and Spain, signed on 15 Aug. 1761.

[512] Commodore Augustus Keppel.

[513] Sir Charles Saunders, Commander-in-Chief the Mediterranean.

[514] These totals do not correspond with the figures.

The union with Spain the cause.
Lord Temple:
14 millions may be procured easily.
The advantages that have arisen to this country have arisen from the totality of the war.

Agreed to recall Mr. Stanley.

Mr. Pitt:
Warm, did not know whether it was better to recall Mr. Stanley or not: that if Lords hereafter intended to come into worse terms for this country, it might be better to submit now; that he desired to know on what conditions they would make peace hereafter: one made on our last proposal not to be justified. Seemed to want a pretext to retire.
Duke of Devonshire:
Said he differed strongly with him; that the relaxations were not the cause the peace was not made; wished unanimity and therefore would not enter on the subject at a time when the assistance of everybody would scarce be sufficient to extricate this country out of perhaps the most desperate state it ever was in; would not bind himself as to any terms on which peace was to be made hereafter. When that time came, should compare the conditions proposed with the situation of the country and the means of carrying on the war.
Mr. Pitt endeavoured to explain himself off and said he had declared his opinion and resolution and that was sufficient for him.
Sept 16 1761: A[   ]⁵¹⁵ told me Bute had been to them⁵¹⁶ by seven the two mornings after the wedding, to know their thoughts of the Queen.⁵¹⁷ [The King] under great anxiety, would give them no intelligence. The next day locked their door: not to be disturbed. Lord Bute very uneasy at the King and Queen going alone to Richmond and his not being of the party, the King having in a manner forbad him, saying the night before: 'I shall see you [on] my return to town.'
A[   ] desired to sound the King, who asked the reason why he came not to go.
[Ashburnham?] answered: '*His business would not let him.*' The King does not care to let anyone see the Queen. The King did not like the Duke of York should come into the Queen's state apartments before the Drawing Room.

---

515 Probably Ashburnham.
516 The Lords of the Bedchamber.
517 Charlotte of Mecklenburg-Strelitz, whom the King had married on 6 Sept.

Sept 18 1761:[518] Spanish Memorial:[519] Will never give up the right each court has of interfering in their respective disputes.

Union intimacy and near relation with F[rench] King.

They are acquainted with the steps taken by France to effectuate a peace.

The dear price and the sacrifices she has made would have miscarryed in them if a rupture with Spain.

France thought it a fair step in regard to England to acquaint her of it.[520]

6 years ago Spanish governors ordered to check the encroachments of the English.

England desired those orders might not be carried into execution[521] ever since we have sollicited redress in vain.

If England had endeavoured independantly to settle their peace with Spain, their union with France would have been no obstacle.

Notification:[522]

King of Spain in ascending the throne expresses his desire of living in friendship, congratulates on the conquest Quebec, but cannot help looking with a watchfull eye on the conquests that affect the equilibre of that country.

Reply:[523]

Desirous of cultivating harmony and shewing France to have been the aggressor.

Spain demand Fishery and said they had acquainted France with their demand.[524] Answered we are concerned and surprised at such a communication,[525] and that at no time we could allow that right.

---

[518] Hardwicke's Minute, 18 Sept. 1761, Yorke, iii. 275–6. Newcastle's Memorandum, 18 Sept. 1761, Add. MSS. 32928, ff. 227–32. Hardwicke makes clear that he was present, although his wife was mortally ill and died the day following. Devonshire was probably not present, which may account for his not writing his account until after his entries for 25 Sept. This has been transposed by the editors for the sake of chronological order.

[519] Wall's Declaration of Aug. 28, see p. 121.

[520] The alliance between both branches of the House of Bourbon, which Versailles could not afford to abandon.

[521] In accordance with the request of the British Minister, Sir Benjamin Keene, the orders for the destruction of illegal logwood settlements, issued in 1754 by Ensenada were suspended pending further enquiry. Keene to Sir Thomas Robinson, 17 June, 31 July 1754; Wall to Keene, 15 Sept. 1754, S.P.F. 94/147.

[522] See p. 25, n. 11.

[523] Draft of an answer to d'Abreu, 13 Dec. 1759, S.P.F. 94/160.

[524] Fuentes to Pitt, 9 Sept. 1760, ibid. 94/162.

[525] Pitt to Bristol, 26 Sept. 1760, ibid.

Intelligence:[526]	Fuentes exhorting his Court to take part in the war that this was the time.
	Mention a Convention signed in August likewise that the connection was made before the first Memorial from France was presented.
Mr. Pitt:	Consideration what steps should be taken in regard to Spain, a dangerous and arduous situation.
	The safest method is to take that course which is least liable to objection though attended with danger, manfully and systematically.
Lord Mansfield:	Any intelligence that leads to prove Spain having taken any engagements with France for coming into the war?
Mr. Pitt:	None but the strongest union expressed and Mr. Stanley's letter[527] mentioning their undertaking the defence of Martinico.
	The fear is for their fleet; 12 men of war are sent out to convoy them.
	France cannot finish their affairs without our points are settled....
Mr. Pitt:	No doubt with me that Spain is France [more] than that the Isle of France is, a union in the House of Bourbon; loss of time loss of opportunity. Whatever is dangerous will be more so 6 months hence; no safety but acting with vigour. Procrastination will increase the danger.

	The[528] fact is proved, the treatment we have had shews what we are to expect. The question is that France and Spain are joined: what is to be done? I wish to hear the opinions of Lords before I form my own.
Lord Granville:	I would avoid extremes, weigh our own strength; consider we have great effects in Spain and what the consequence would be

[526] The intercepted letters between Fuentes and Grimaldi, printed in *Chatham*, ii, 93–7, 139–44.

[527] Stanley to Pitt, 19 Aug. 1761, S.P.F. 78/252.

[528] Pitt continues, or resumes after a short break.

in a hasty step.[529] I am at a loss how to steer between the two extremes for want of materials.

Could we give them an immediate great blow, it might be worth while, but where are we we should fail?

Lord Hardwicke: The question no less one whether we should enter into a war with Spain joined to our other enemies, a strict union as one united House of Bourbon, and to consider the navy of Spain as the remaining navy of France and whether we ought not to try to destroy it. I am not for proceeding with too great delay, nor with too much precipitancy. Union not a sufficient cause of war.

Does there appear any engagement that Spain must enter into the war? Mr. Stanley hints it,[530] I don't know on what authority. Passages in intercepted letters not sufficient to ground war upon.

Sir G. Byng[531] ordered: Consideration in entering into a war with Spain very different from any other power; many houses of English; care always taken to apprise them to withdraw their effects. Treaties of commerce with Spain most advantageous, you suspend them all the moment you break.

The advantages from the trade of Spain of such consequence that it should lose and not be able to regain. I doubt whether the im-

[529] The treaty with Spain negotiated by Pelham in 1751 reaffirmed most-favoured-nation treatment for British exports, which had originated with the Anglo-Spanish Treaty of 1667. War with Spain could not be undertaken without severe detriment to British mercantile interests.

[530] Stanley to Pitt (private), 2, 6 Sept. 1761, includes the following sentence: 'I have recently seen an article drawn up between France and Spain in which the former engages to support the interests of the latter equally with her own in the negotiations of the peace with England; it was entitled article 10. I am as yet a stranger to the other nine but shall endeavour to get them.' S.P.F. 78/252. Stanley was relying on espionage.

[531] The editors can find no Sir G. Byng in 1761. This could be a reference to Sir George Byng, later 1st Viscount Torrington, who in 1718 was ordered by the 1st Earl Stanhope, then Secretary of State, and Pitt's uncle by marriage, to undertake a pre-emptive strike against Spain reminiscent of the action Pitt was proposing in September 1761. On 11 Aug. 1718 Byng destroyed the Spanish fleet off Cape Passaro and thus wrecked the ambition of Philip V of Spain to upset the Italian provisions of the Treaty of Utrecht. Possibly Pitt interrupted Hardwicke's discourse and 'ordered' is used in the sense of 'cited'.

portant conquest of Canada would repair that loss.

I wish some method of treaty might be thought of not to give up his [King of Spain's] dignity: the greatest princes have shut their eyes when necessary for their interest.

Spain made some sort of excuse that if they had thought it would give offence they would not have done it.[532]

They likewise mentioned that the King will give his word that till the cutting logwood is adjusted they will give us leave to take it.[533] Our trade with Russia remains in that state.[534] At the time we demolish settlement we can't justifye, Spain should give a Letter or some order that we should have the log-wood.[535]

6 ships ready to receive orders.

3 ready beginning of October.

4 October.

4 not manned.

4 just arrived from Com. Douglas[537]

What is your strength?[536]

What is the way to make the danger less?

What effects it may have on your trade do not operate on this occasion.

No power so vulnerable to our fleets as Spain.

[532] Wall in a note to Bristol on 28 Aug. 1761 had suggested that the injection of Spanish grievances into the negotiations between Britain and France would not have been attempted had his government realised the offence. Bristol to Pitt, 31 Aug. 1761, S.P.F. 94/164, Part I.

[533] Wall in his conference with Bristol on Aug. 28 had undertaken on behalf of Charles III that British logwood cutters could operate freely until an agreement was reached.

[534] Britain was not at war with Russia, although the Empress Elizabeth was at war with her ally Frederick of Prussia. The Baltic trade was a deterrent to an extension of war, and Spain might provide a parallel.

[535] Here Hardwicke's discourse ended and he left early because of his wife's illness. Hardwicke to Newcastle, 20 Sept. 1761, Add. MSS. 32928, ff. 259–62.

[536] A question presumably addressed by Pitt to Anson.

[537] Sir James Douglas, Commander the Leeward Islands station.

Mr. Pitt: I am still of opinion that an immediate action gives us the best chance to extricate ourselves.

Number of Men[538] 83,300— Acquiesced in their partiality till such time as we had broke the force of France, wishing then that Spain would give us an opportunity to punish them.

15,490—Complement of ships at home Best chance to order Lord Bristol away and your fleets to take every Spanish flag. If the means to do this are doubtful will it not be more so next spring. I am for it *now*.

11,590 bore
9,269 Mustered
2,321 —difference
3,900 difficiency
4640

Lord Temple:

The immediate Declaration: doubt whether we have sufficient grounds: no overt act. Do your Lordships flatter yourselves it is in your power to accommodate the affairs with Spain?

Spain has threatened during the course of the war this not a time to put them in practice. Logwood is but a pretext.
Stanley says the [   ][539] will undertake the defence of Martinico.[540]
Mr. Pitt proposed the immediate recall of Lord Bristol.
All Lords against it. He then read a Paper[541] which contained his reasons which he said he would give the King, signed by himself: Lord Temple desired to join in it.
No other Lord with him.
Agreed to increase the squadron at Martinico to 15 of the line and to send 3000 men more from Belleisle there.[542]

Present Sep. 18—
Lord Chancellor
Lord President
The Papers being laid before the Lords by H.M.'s commands and they being asked what might be advisable to be done, there-

---

[538] The estimated strength of the Spanish military establishment.

[539] Blank in MS. but the reference must be to Spain.

[540] Pitt was planning to send Commodore George Rodney to take Martinique.

[541] A brief memorandum dated Sept. 18 and entitled 'Advice in Writing'. This contained Pitt's arguments in favour of immediate war with Spain. *Grenville*, i. 386–7.

[542] Which had surrendered on 7 July 1761.

Duke of Newcastle
Lord Holderness
Lord Halifax
Lord Hardwicke
Lord Temple
Lord Anson
Lord Mansfield
Lord Legonier
Mr. Pitt
Duke of Devonshire.

upon were unanimously of opinion that before any hostilities should be committed a notification should be given to the Court of Spain tantamount to a declaration of war, and Lord Bristol recalled. They were also unanimously of opinion that reinforcements should be sent to the West Indies and Mediterranean, as if a war with Spain was certain, and proposed [that a] number of ships [seven] of the line and [3000][543] land forces should be immediately sent to Guadeloupe. Mr. Secretary Pitt proposed (here insert his Paper) in which Lord Temple concurred, the rest of the Lords present doubting of the propriety of such a measure, and having deliberated thereupon till late at night, desired to consider farther thereon till Monday.

Sept 19 1761: Settled at Devonshire House: present Duke of Newcastle, Lord Bute and Lord Mansfield, not carried into execution.[544]
Wall approbation.[545]
3 points:
If Catholic King wars, King of France engaged to assist.[546]
Step taken, Spain amity.
Union counsels and interests with House of Bourbon, causes to take accessory meaning.
Three order[s] sent to Earl of Bristol to be recalled.[547]

Sept 20: The King spoke to the Queen to kneel at Chapel: she did not.

[543] Blank in MS.; see however the figures given in Add. MSS. 35710, f. 304.

[544] At the informal meeting of Sept. 19, Bute suggested that all opposed to Pitt's policy of war with Spain set down their objections in writing. After some discussion this plan was abandoned, it being decided that each minister give his reasons to the King verbally, which took place at a special audience of 26 September. W. Hunt, 'Pitt's retirement from office, 5th Oct 1761', *E.H.R.*, xxi (1906), 124–5.

[545] Wall's approval of Choiseul's Memorial of 15 July endorsing the Spanish grievances.

[546] Refers to the statement in the French Memoire of 15 July: '. . . il [King of France] ne peut pas dissimuler à l'Angleterre le danger qu'il envisage et qu'il sera forcé de partager si ces objets qui paroissent affectir sensiblement S.M. Catholique déterminent la guerre.'

[547] No orders were sent to Bristol at this time. He was ordered on 2 Nov. 1761 to ask for his passports in a despatch from Pitt's successor the 2nd Earl of Egremont.

I

In one of the letters [Bristol] said Spain would let us cut logwood till the manner of furnishing us with it was settled.

Mr. Pitt:[548] No treating under force of the declaration therefore no middle point. Nothing less consistent with the King's dignity.

Have we a fleet ready to act offensively immediately?

———————

2

You don't leave them to opt. We are not in a state to precipitate this nation in another war. Ought not to make a war unavoidable. Preparations to reinforce Admiral Saunders.

Lord Temple: Middle term the worst of all, consider the price you give. The loss of the campaign a loss not to be retrieved.

———————

3

Lord Bute: What Spain means to do consequence of her declaration?

4

[Pitt]: Experiment to be made no time lost.[549]

5

Every step taken as if a war was determined.

Lord Mansfield: Manly spirited resolution and as history shews productive of great events.

[548] The notes jotted down by Devonshire on the Cabinet meeting of 21 Sept. Why these do not follow immediately on his account of the meeting is unclear.

[549] Newcastle to Hardwicke of 21 Sept. 1761 also makes clear that Pitt spoke later, stressing the need for immediate action and that no time was to be lost. Hunt, *E.H.R.*, xxi, 124–5.

| | Doubt of the justice of declaring war. |
| Whatever scheme | Whether they really mean it. |

Whatever scheme might be undertaken: the Admiral[550] dispatch a vessell to receive orders and might act directly.

Doubt of the justice of declaring war.
Whether they really mean it.
Wall, though he avows the measure done with their consent, yet he endeavours to fight it off.
That the King of Spain would not have done it if he thought it would have offended the King of England.[551] Ought not to take the first step to make the war unavoidable.
To give all necessary reinforcements as if the war was certain.
To give Spain an election and to bring them to a categorical [answer].
Spain revenue 50 million.

Lord Temple replyed in a very inflamatory declaration, as if he was in the House of Commons. While he was speaking, Mr. Pitt took out his Paper (which he had shewn to the King not signed) and set his hand to it, and when Lord Temple had sat down gave it him who also signed it. They then delivered it to Lord Bute. The Duke of Newcastle answered Lord Temple very properly. They both got up and went away.

Mr. Pitt the former day[552] had said he could execute orders, though he would not be a party to them. This day he refused doing it; said the other Secretary might do it; instanced his having signed Papers in Lord Holdernesse's department when his Lordship was at Bath.[553] They both got up and went away, seemingly in very ill humour.

Lord Bute said to me: 'If we persist they will resign.'

I replied [that] I could not help it; that for one I had given my opinion as I thought best and Mr. Pitt should not make me change it; that if we were to yield to him, he would threaten us every day to quit, in order to carry his wild ideas into execution. [I] beged his Lordship to be stout and not shew any fear of them, which would be the only means to bring them to reason.

Monday/Present:[554] The same Lords[555] are of opinion not to advise H.M. to begin immediately a war with Spain as thinking such a measure not sufficiently founded either in justice or prudence, but that a farther tryal ought to be made, and therefore humbly submit it to H.M. that a Memorial should be sent to Lord Bristol to be delivered

---

[550] Saunders.

[551] See p. 129, n. 532.

[552] 18 Sept.

[553] At the turn of 1758-9. Pitt to Keith, 2 Jan. 1759, S.P.F. 91/67.

[554] 21 Sept. For Newcastle's notes on this meeting, see his letter to Hardwicke written later that day, printed in Hunt, *E.H.R.* xxi, 124-5.

[555] Hardwicke and Granville were not present.

to Monsieur Wall, stating the desire that His Majesty has shewn to cultivate the friendship of Spain, and to act with the greatest openness and sincerity upon all occasions. And as a proof of it His Majesty declares that with regard to the three points that are set up as matters of complaint: in regard to the two first[556] H.M. can give no other answer than what has already been given, but as to the third he has always been ready to adjust in such manner as might be agreeable to both parties. And is satisfied that the settlements on the coasts of the Bay of Honduras et cetera should be evacuated, His Catholic Majesty stipulating that the British subjects should cut logwood till such time as the method in which we are hereafter to be furnished with it shall be settled between the two Crowns.

His Majesty having thought it agreeable to candour and good faith to explain his sentiments clearly and categorically upon these points, [he] expects the same from the candour and good faith of His Catholic Majesty: that he will explain himself as to some parts of the extraordinary Paper delivered by Mr. Wall[557] and the proceedings therein avowed, which cannot but have given H.M. great doubts of the intentions of His Catholic Majesty, and therefore desires to know whether His Catholic Majesty is under any engagement to take part with France in the present war against England, or whether His Catholic Majesty intends to live in friendship with the King of Great Britain.

That Lord Bristol should be instructed to intimate to Monsieur Wall, that in case he does not receive a satisfactory answer on these points, the harmony between the two Courts so much to be desired cannot subsist any longer, and that such a refusal will be considered as a declaration of war.

Lord Bristol to be likewise instructed, that in case the Court of Spain avows their intention to make war, or avoids and refuses to give an explicit answer, his Lordship is immediately to come away giving notice to the merchants of the rupture and acquainting Admiral Saunders of it.[558]

Provisional orders to be sent to Admiral Saunders, to be by him forwarded to America, and information given to Governor of Gibraltar.[559]

---

[556] The capture of Spanish prizes, the Newfoundland Fishery and logwood in Honduras. Britain never accepted that Spain had the slightest claim to participate in the Fisheries, a point on which Pitt had the unanimous support of the Cabinet. The British attitude over prizes was generally unsympathetic. Answer to the Spanish Memorial, presented to Fuentes on 1 Sept. 1760, Thackeray, ii. Appendix, 486–95.

[557] See p. 136.

[558] That afternoon of 21 Sept. Pitt drafted his orders to Rodney for the Martinique expedition.

[559] 8th Earl of Home, Governor of Gibraltar, 1757–61.

Draft of a Paper, and consideration on Mr. Pitt's protest in Council: Sept 18 1761.

Sept 21: The Council met on the subject of the Promemoria of Wall to Lord Bristol. Mr. Pitt proposed the recall of Lord Bristol again and to follow it with an immediate declaration of war. Those that had opposed it the 18th continued of the same mind. In that meeting, he [Pitt] said, that though he should enter his protest, yet he would execute any resolution we should come to: now he said he would not do it, that the other Secretary[560] or other Lords used to the business might.

no reason   Pitt instanced when Lord Holdernesse was at Bath, he had done the *business of his department.* They[561] signed their paper and withdrew.[562]

The next day being the day of the Coronation,[563] the King was at the House of Lords soon after eight. He expressed great surprise at the proceedings of Mr. Pitt and Lord Temple, asked me whether they would go out. I told him I did not see how they could stay if Mr. Pitt would not do the business of his department. The King seemed to express his wish of getting rid of them.[564] I represented how much it was to be wished, if the war continued, that Mr. Pitt should continue in employment. At the same time, if they quitted upon this point,[565] I thought the ground was not tenable and hoped they would not have much following; that I was strong against yielding to them and thought they were more likely to stay if they saw we were not afraid of them. The King was of the same opinion and much displeased with them. Lord Temple talked with great seeming friendship to Lord Bute and wanted to cajole him; The other told him he saw plainly they were to contend with each other in that House.[566] Lord Temple replied he meant nothing less.

Sept. 23: Came a letter the day before from Mr. Stanley[567] with an account of a long conversation with [the] Duc de Choiseul. He says that if he [Choiseul] will give him in writing what he has said to him [Stanley] by word of mouth, he shall think it his duty to stay, though he should receive the orders he expects to return home. For he [Choiseul] told him that the island of Miguelon should not be an obstacle;

---

[560] Bute.   [561] Pitt and Temple.

[562] Newcastle to Hardwicke, 21 Sept. 1761, makes clear that Bute expected Pitt's resignation at this point; Yorke, iii. 325-6.

[563] 22 Sept. 1761.

[564] George III to Bute, 19 Sept. 1761, Sedgwick, 63.

[565] Pitt's demand for a declaration of war against Spain.

[566] The House of Lords. Following Pitt's resignation on 5 Oct. Temple attacked Bute bitterly 'in that House' on 14 Nov. 1761.

[567] Stanley to Pitt, 15 Sept. 1761, S.P.F. 78/252.

Spain should be dropped and some expedient found out to set Prince Ferdinand's army at liberty to go to the assistance of the King of Prussia.[568] There was likewise a private letter[569] which Stanley desired might only be shewed to the King, who made Mr. Pitt leave it with him that the Duke of Newcastle and I might see it. It gave an account of a conversation with [the] Duchess of Grammont,[570] containing the strongest assurance of her brother's desire of peace and how necessary it was for him; said that Fuentes had done much mischief but that Spain should not be in the way, and tending to remove the most material difficulties. After Court, the Chancellor, Duke of Newcastle, Lord Bute, Lord Anson and Lord Mansfield met at my house to consider what was to be done to justify our dissent from Mr. Pitt.[571] It was at first proposed to draw up a minute agreeable to a former paper settled here,[572] but after consideration it was determined to have no minute taken, but that every Lord of the Council should acquaint the King with his opinion; that [to] draw up papers against one another would be introducing a very bad custom and that might be productive of much inconvenience.

Sept 24: All the Lords of the Council waited on the King and gave him their reasons why they were of a different opinion from Mr. Pitt and Lord Temple. The King was much satisfied with them, pressed much to know whether I thought Lord Temple et cetera would go out. I told him they were much out of humour but it was impossible to say what they would do; that they had meant to force us into the measure but as we had continued firm they must either yield or retire. Lord Temple had said to somebody that Mr. Pitt could not stay but that was no reason for him as he did not hold the pen.

Mr. Pitt pressed much for an embargo on Ireland,[573] blamed the Duke of Bedford strongly to the King.[574]

Sept 25: A letter from Stanley[575] in which he said he had received his orders,[576] had got his passport and was coming away. The King observed that he [Stanley] said he had sent a copy of his letter to the

[568] In view of the Family Compact, this was chicanery.

[569] Stanley to Pitt, 15 Sept. 1761 (private), S.P.F. 78/252.

[570] Choiseul's sister.

[571] Newcastle to Hardwicke, 23 Sept. 1761, Add. MSS. 32928, ff. 325-6. Hardwicke was absent because of the recent death of his wife.

[572] On 19 Sept, see p. 131, n. 544.

[573] Because of the continued defiance of the Irish Parliament over money bills. Halifax to Pitt, 11 Oct. 1761, S.P. 63/416.

[574] Pitt had clashed with Bedford, Lord Lieutenant of Ireland June 1757-Mar. 1761, over policy in Feb. 1758 and Dec. 1760.

[575] Stanley to Pitt, 19 Sept. 1761, S.P.F. 78/252.

[576] Pitt to Stanley, 15 Sept. 1761, Stanley MSS. 10.M55/127, No. 44.

Duc de Choiseul[577] and flattered himself that it was done to give the Duke [of Choiseul] an opportunity of stopping him.

Lord Bute said if Mr. Pitt went out we ought to think of making a strong and solid administration; that I had heard him propose Mr. Fox; that upon talking with people he found it would not do to give him the place of minister in the House of Commons;[578] that he would be for gratifying him in order to have his assistance. That the only way he saw was what the Duke of Newcastle would not come into, to make George Greenville Chancellor of the Exchequer. I mentioned it to [the] Duke of Newcastle, who said it was impossible, hurt to refuse Lord Bute anything. I told him that I had asked his Lordship [Bute] whether he should like to have the Duke of Bedford Secretary of State. [Bute] replied, surely he would not take it; if he would, whatever difficulties or danger of disagreement there might be, he would wave them in such a crisis as this; that no personal consideration should weigh in the scale of the public.[579] I told him that the Duke of Newcastle was very averse to George Greenville. He said he expected it and that he would not propose it to him.

I saw the King before the Council. [Oct. 2]. He told me he had had Stanley with him above an hour, but could make nothing of him. He [Stanley] owned that he was convinced the Duc de Choiseul always meant peace and had acted *de bonne foi*; that if our last terms had been offered sooner, they might perhaps have done; of opinion Spain would declare war. The King asked him from what intelligence he formed that opinion. [Stanley] refused to answer. In short the King convinced that Mr. Pitt had secured Mr. Stanley.[580]

The same confirmed by the Duke of Newcastle and Lord Bute.[581]

[577] Stanley to Choiseul, 20 Sept. 1761, printed in *Mémoire Historique sur la negotiation de la France et de l'Angleterre* (Mouton, reprint 1966), 184-5.

[578] Bute ought to have realized that Fox, by his panic resignation of 15 Oct. 1756, had forfeited all claim to popular esteem. Newcastle would never have endorsed his return or have accepted Grenville at the Exchequer. As he explained to Hardwicke in his letter of 26 Sept.: 'The moment Mr. Grenville is Chancellor of the Exchequer, it is to him only, to whom the King and his minister will apply; and it is he, who will have singly the King's confidence ... I should not pass one easy moment in the Treasury after that was done.' Newcastle to Hardwicke, 26 Sept. 1761, Add. MSS. 32928, ff. 362-3.

[579] It would seem that Devonshire was alone in suggesting Bedford as Pitt's successor. By his opposition to Pitt, Bedford had put spine into Bute and he was without doubt one of the 'great lords' to whom Pitt disparagingly referred at the Council of 2 Oct., the last he attended as Secretary of State.

[580] George III to Bute, Sept. 1761, Sedgwick, 65.

[581] Newcastle and Hardwicke saw Stanley after his interview with the King. Hardwicke to Newcastle, 30 Sept. 1761, Add. MSS. 32928, f. 440. Hardwicke, Memorandum, Add. MSS. 35421, f. 102. 'I saw the King .... Duke of Newcastle and Lord Bute' entered by Devonshire after his account of the Council and transposed by the editors for the sake of chronology.

Grimaldi to Fuentes. Oct 2 1761:[582] Present:[583]	France should not make peace without our [Spanish] disputes are accommodated.
Lord President	Not appear as a sine qua non.
Lord Privy Seal	
Duke of Devonshire	Fears the English will agree to their [the
Duke of Newcastle	French] Memorial and then the negotia-
Earl of Hardwicke	tion will break off on our account.
Earl of Bute	
Lord Anson	
Lord Legonier	
Mr. Pitt	
Lord President:	What are we met for? Not of opinion that Spain means to go to war, and therefore ought not to force them into it by any act of violence. Mr. Stanley told me that Spain would go into the war. Don't see anything to authorise such a step.
Duke of Newcastle:	Of the same opinion.
Lord Hardwicke:	The same.
Duke of Devonshire:	The same. The Paper delivered by G[eneral] Wall not a Memorial.
Lord Mansfield:	The same.
Lord Bute:	The same.
Lord Anson:	The same.
Lord Legonier:	Spain has near 60,000 foot and 15,000 horse. Whether it is advisable to throw this force into the scale of France? Queen Ann's war begun in conjunction with Austria et cetera.
Mr. Pitt:	Fortnight elapsed and no advice formed to give the King, contrary to the dignity of the King.
essential interest	contrary to the *honour of the* nation. Matter in this bag such as if a proper answer not immediately given, criminal to Secretary of State, left to sleep.[584]

[582] Grimaldi to Fuentes, 13 Sept. 1761 (intercepted and a translation read), *Chatham*, ii. 141. Grimaldi did not wish the failure of the negotiation with France to be attributed solely to the Spanish grievances.

[583] Mansfield also present.

[584] Devonshire's version of Pitt's speech corresponded closely to Newcastle's account, printed in Hunt, *E.H.R.*, xxi, 132.

Indignity clear, ruinous in point of safety. I will not be responsible for measures I do not *direct*.

Saw a union among so many great lords, that it was no longer fit for him to remain, that he had supported the war, and the nation for four years on his shoulders called to it by the voice of the late King and without arrogance might say by the voice of the people.

[Pitt] had retrieved the affairs of this country:

every scheme he had proposed come into, but [   ][585] thrown out, and if any one had failed [he would have been] liable to have been impeached.

Lord Temple:

Such a different way of thinking in the Council from him that he could no longer be of it.

Got up and went away.

Lord President:

Told Mr. Pitt that he [Pitt] could not justifye withdrawing himself from the service of his country at this crisis, declaring he was to have the direction of the whole. [Pitt] was taking more upon himself than any man had a right to, approaching to infalibility.

Mr. Pitt answered him with good humour, acknowledged the obligations he had to

——certainly meant at Lord Bute.

his Lordship and indeed to every one of the *Old Ministry*.

Oct 4 1761: The King asked me if I did not think Lord Talbot looked very much down at Chapell. That is said he on account of his friend, meaning Temple.[586] The King seemed much pleased that Mr. Pitt was going out.

Saw Charles Townshend,[587] much out of humour with Duke of Newcastle and Lord Bute; the former no one could trust, the latter had shewn him no communication for three months, till he saw danger of a rupture with Mr. Pitt and then [Bute] shewed him the two Spanish Papers.[588] Clear of the opinion of the Council that they did

[585] Word illegible.   [586] The circumstances of their friendship were personal.
[587] Secretary-at-War since Mar. 1761.
[588] Probably Wall's Declaration of 28 Aug., see p. 126, and Bristol's letter of 31 Aug., see p. 121, n. 481.

not warrant the commencement of hostilities: said he would support government.

Mr. Pitt had gained Stanley by immense flattery, that his letters[589] were fulsome to the last degree especially since he was about coming away.

Oct 5: Mr. Pitt resigned the Seals to the King, made great professions, that he should retire to Hayes[590] and remain a private man the rest of his days; that so far from opposing, he should be ready to support government but never meant to set his foot in the House of Commons the next Session, unless he was attacked. The King was civil to him and expressed a readiness to serve him or his family. He said he could take nothing at present. He desired that any mark of favour he might have hereafter might be as a reward for future services, not for past.[591]

Lord Temple gone to Stowe.[592]

Oct 6 1761: Met the Duke of Newcastle and Lord Bute at St. James's. His Lordship told us that George Greenville would not take the Seals: he had a delicacy in taking his brother-in-law's place.[593] [Bute] threw out difficulties and the ill humour of the City with a gloomy face.[594] After some time he brightened up and said, he had prevailed on Mr. Greenville to give up all thoughts of being Speaker; that being consulted in affairs, he might take the lead in the House of Commons continuing Treasurer of the Navy. Duke of Newcastle approved and much pleased as the idea of making him Chancellor of the Exchequer was dropped.[595]

His Grace acquainted us that he had seen the Governor of the Bank[596] who said Mr. Pitt going out would have no bad consequences with the better sort of people: he did not know what it might do with the mob. That the Bank would lend the same they did last year viz: £2,000,000 on malt and £750,000 on land; that stocks rose as they imagined in the City that there would be more probability of peace. Mr. Walpole[597] had confirmed the same thing and said Mr. Pitt being out might have an effect on a Lord Mayor's shew but nothing else.

---

[589] Pitt to Stanley, 11, 15 Sept. 1761; Stanley MSS. 10.M55/127. MS. Nos. 41, 44.

[590] Pitt's home in Kent.

[591] Pitt's observation must be linked with the request he shortly made for a peerage for his wife Lady Hester, which would enable him to remain in the House of Commons.

[592] Temple's seat near Buckingham.

[593] *Grenville*, i. 410–14.

[594] Earlier that day Bute had written anxiously to Newcastle: '.... that the storm runs high in the City and I hear some of them Pitt's supporters are rash enough to say they will have their minister again. This may subside, but a weak administration .... will not tend to silence it.' Add. MSS. 32929, f. 75.

[595] On the rearrangements see K. Schweizer, 'John Stuart 3rd Earl of Bute and George Grenville, October 1761', *Historical Journal*, xvii. 2 (1974), 435–42.

[596] Bartholemew Burton, M.P., was Governor, 1760–2.

[597] Thomas Walpole, M.P., a prominent banker.

He [Newcastle] then said Monsieur Fuentes had been with him [and] made the strongest professions of the disposition of the Catholic King to live in friendship with us; that it had been industriously given out in France that they meant to declare war and join with France against us; that nothing was farther from their thoughts, they would not act *si sottement*. On the contrary he had orders to treat; that the point of the Fishery would not be insisted on, or we should not break upon it; and that we should be furnished with logwood. Lord Bute shewed a letter from Lord Bristol[598] received this morning, agreeing to what Monsieur Fuentes had said.

The Duke of Newcastle being gone in to the King, Lord Bute said that he saw his [Bute's] situation very dangerous; that though Mr. Pitt spoke fair yet the opposition and the attack would all be upon him; that he was sensible his situation in this country either as to property, friends or weight was not equal to it, and though he had the favour of the King, yet that was not sufficient. He hoped and depended on my friendship and assistance. I told him he would certainly have it and the assistance of everybody and that the unjustifiable manner in which Mr. Pitt had acted would unite all the most considerable people to support government. He then mentioned the making Lord Egremont Secretary of State. I answered, a very good and proper man,[599] but what would become of the Duke of Bedford if it was not offered to him? He said he did not see why he should take it ill, expressed suspicion of a league offensive and defensive between him and the Duke of Newcastle and *that there was a run in the City against the Duke of Bedford. And he was afraid if a man who was thought ready to make any peace was to have Mr. Pitt's place, it would be very unpopular; said *Lord Mansfield had suggested it to him*.[600]*

I endeavoured to persuade him [Bute] there was no such thing, [as an alliance between Bedford and Newcastle], that they were very well together from having agreed in sentiments about the peace. It was plain he was not satisfied with the Duke of Bedford but when I urged his consequence, he said he wished the Duke of Rutland could be gratified in some other shape, and the Duke of Bedford might be Master of the Horse.[601] *The truth: Lord Bute at the beginning of this reign had made great court to [the] Duke of Bedford and imagined he had got him to himself; finding it not so was a little piqued at him.*

[598] Bristol to Pitt, 14 Sept. 1761, S.P.F. 94/164, Part I.

[599] The 2nd Earl of Egremont had no political experience except as Lord Lieutenant of Cumberland since 1750.

[600] Bedford had incurred hostility because of his part in forcing Pitt's resignation. Bute suggests that Egremont as Pitt's successor was Mansfield's suggestion, which has not previously been known. Egremont was appointed Secretary of State for the South on 8 Oct.

[601] Bedford had never shown a desire for household office.

He [Bute] then complained about the unreasonableness of my Lord Hardwicke and his family; that if the Attorney[602] went out, Mr. Yorke[603] would be Attorney and from his abilities the Seals[604] open to him,[605] and yet they were not satisfied: it was really too much.[606] I urged Lord Hardwicke's consequence and his great knowledge in business, which was such that you could not do without him, independant of his long connection with the Duke of Newcastle, and added that if they [Newcastle and Hardwicke] came into his scheme of transacting the business between the two Secretaryes [Bute and Egremont], the Duke of Newcastle and Mr. Greenville, that they [the King and Bute] ought to add his Lordship [Hardwicke] to them: he made no objection to it.

When the Duke of Newcastle returned, Lord Bute told us that he was the day before half an hour with Mr. Pitt, found him very gloomy and low. When he took his leave of him, Lord Bute said to him that they had long lived as friends and hoped they should continue to do so. Mr. Pitt assented to it civilly *but exclusive of politicks*. Lord Bute said that the people in the City began to get about Mr. Pitt, and that Wood[607] said he grew more gloomy and out of humour every minute; that therefore it was necessary to lose no time in endeavouring to find out what would gratify him; that he could not get him to name anything.[608] He thought the King was disposed to act generously. Lord Holdernesse had £4000 p.a.;[609] this should at least be £5000.[610] What did we think of making him [Pitt] Governor of Canada? It would be shewing that we meant to keep possession of it at a peace and would be flattering him as it was his own conquest. The only difficulty was whether it being a new created place it would render him incapable of setting in Parliament. I approved of the thought and

[602] Charles Pratt, M.P.

[603] Charles Yorke, M.P., Hardwicke's second son.

[604] The office of Lord Chancellor.

[605] Pratt was Pitt's protegé and on the formation of the Pitt and Newcastle ministry in July 1757 had been appointed Attorney-General over the head of Yorke, who had to be content with becoming Solicitor-General. With Pitt out of the way Hardwicke hoped to get Pratt removed and see his son Attorney-General, in which event the office of Lord Chancellor might be his. Lord Chancellor Henley could have been given a sinecure.

[606] Bute was annoyed because Newcastle and Devonshire were pressing him to appoint Hardwicke Lord Privy Seal in succession to Temple. Hardwicke was no longer interested and liked a frequent retirement to Wimpole, his seat near Cambridge. Newcastle to Devonshire, 9 Oct. 1761, Add. MSS. 32929, ff. 139–42.

[607] Robert Wood, M.P., who had in 1757 abandoned a distinguished career as Homeric scholar to serve as Pitt's under-secretary. He remained in office until 1763.

[608] Bute to Pitt, 6 Oct. 1761; *Chatham*, ii. 146–8.

[609] The pension granted Holdernesse in return for his enforced resignation in Mar. 1761 to make way for Bute.

[610] That Pitt must receive an emolument of at least £5000 p.a.

suggested that there might be a clause in any Act of Parliament to take off that incapacity,[611] which would still be more flattering to Mr. Pitt. He then named Lord Kinnoul's place[612] as the greatest employment next to a Cabinet Counsellor, that his Lordship might have the value of it for life.[613]

Lord Bute thought Lord Temple would quit. I told him if Mr. Pitt took anything he certainly would not. He replied: 'It is impossible: would that noble Lord, after he has told you he would not come among you to Council any more, keep a Cabinet Counsellor's place? Why, it would be taking a pension.[614] Oct 7 [6][615] 1761: Lord Bute wrote to Mr. Pitt offering him the Governor of Canada or the Chancellor of the [Duchy of Lancaster] with £5000 salary. [Pitt] said he could take no office, hinted at something for himself and [his] children.

Lord Bute told Viry that he looked upon Mr. Pitt as his enemy for the time to come, and it was the same thing to him whether he met him on foot in the streets or riding in a coach and six. Oct 8 [9][616] 1761: Lord Bute called on Lord Hardwicke, told him the great things that had been done for Mr. Pitt and his family,[617] shewed him his answer of last night: very stiff and laboured and affectation of great submission and flattery to the King, so as to disclaim all obligation to any other person.[618] Lord Hardwicke submitted to his Lordship whether it might not be proper to send further instructions to Lord Bristol, to express the King's satisfaction at their [the Spanish] declaration, and to attempt to make them explain the tendency of their new treaty with France, and his Lordship to negotiate here with douceur

---

[611] A suggestion Bute acted on when he wrote to Pitt that day.

[612] Kinnoul was Chancellor of the Duchy of Lancaster, 1758-62.

[613] A pension equivalent to the salary.

[614] Devonshire was wrong and Bute was right. Pitt's request for an endowed peerage for his wife Lady Hester was granted but Temple resigned.

[615] 7 Oct. in MS. but Bute wrote on 6 Oct. Bute to Pitt, 6 Oct. 1761; Pitt to Bute, 6 Oct. 1761; *Chatham*, ii. 146-50. On the evening of 6 Oct. Elliot called upon Pitt. To him Pitt expressed his desire for an endowed peerage for his wife.

[616] 8 Oct. in MS. Hardwicke to Charles Yorke, 10 Oct. 1761, refers to Bute's visit taking place 'yesterday noon'. Yorke, iii. 330. Hardwicke to Newcastle, 9 Oct. 1761, Add. MSS. 32929, ff. 144-5.

[617] A peerage for Lady Hester Pitt as Baroness Chatham together with a pension of £300 p.a. upon the lives of Pitt himself, his wife and their eldest son.

[618] Pitt to Bute, 8 Oct. 1761, Bute MSS. (Cardiff) Bundle 5, No. 53. The *Gazette* of 10 Oct. announced the resignation of Pitt and Temple, together with the endowed peerage for Lady Hester. It was long suggested that by publishing these honours and the resignations in the same number, Bute sought to undermine Pitt's reputation for disinterestedness. But as Pitt had requested the peerage and the pension, the announcements came quite naturally. The *Gazette* did include an intelligence report from Madrid stressing the peaceful intentions of Spain, which there is reason to believe Pitt resented. K. Schweizer, 'Lord Bute and William Pitt's Resignation in 1761', *Canadian Journal of History*, viii. 2 (1973), 111-25.

with Fuentes. He seemed to taste it. Lord Bute observed upon Pitt's behaviour with some asperity and upon his claim of *direction*.

Oct 12 [13][619]: Lord Hardwicke saw Mr. Pitt very civil and in good humour.

He [Pitt] did not know how much he should attend Parliament: supported supplies publicly and privately, men, ships and money: no disturbance to administration. If his resignation should be misrepresented, [he] would justifye it. [He] did not assert so strongly the resolution of Spain to declare war, but put it on their secret union with France.

Justified Lord Temple's resignation.

Oct 20 1761: Duke of Newcastle informed Lord Hardwicke[620] that he had acquainted Lord Bute that all was fire and flame in the City; that Mr. Pitt's letter[621] had brought back all his old friends and that there was to be a meeting this day of the Common Council to instruct their members in the most violent manner to support war and warlike measures with some compliment to Mr. Pitt.[622] Lord Bute unconcerned: said he did not trouble himself about it, or enquire what Mr. Pitt did.

Duke of Newcastle told him [Bute] that an agent of Mr. Pitt's said there was no union at Court. Lord Bute made no reply. He [Newcastle] then told him [Bute] the Spanish Ambassador's disposition to accommodate everything, and that we might see all he [Fuentes] had said on the subject was in Mr. Wall's Paper given to Lord Bristol.[623] [Newcastle] asked him [Fuentes] whether they intended to break with us or not. He did not directly answer the question but talked as if that could not be their intention, as their conduct had shewed notwithstanding their Family Treaty of 1743.[624] which he told his Grace the last time he saw him, contained all the stipulations in the Treaty with regard to their reciprocal engagements.[625] Fuentes complained that no answer had been given to Wall's Paper[626] and would conclude that some orders had been sent to Lord Bristol.[627]

---

[619] 12 Oct. in MS. but see Hardwicke to Newcastle, 13 Oct. 1761, Add. MSS. 32929, f. 227.

[620] Newcastle to Hardwicke, 20 Oct. 1761, bm Add. MSS. 32929, ff. 406–7.

[621] To rebut popular criticism, Pitt had on 15 Oct. addressed an open letter to Alderman Beckford, his chief City supporter, explaining his resignation and justifying his acceptance of a pension. The letter was published in the major newspapers and swiftly restored his popularity.

[622] Bedford to Newcastle, 19 Oct. 1761, *Bedford*, iii. 53.   [623] See p. 126.

[624] Treaty of Fontainebleau, the first Family Compact, 25 Oct. 1743.

[625] Fuentes was disingenuously arguing that the provisions of the second Family Compact of 15 August were covered by the Treaty of 1743, which was untrue. The new Treaty required that Spain enter the war on the side of France by 2 May 1762.

[626] See p. 126.   [627] To ask for his passports.

Upon this Lord Bute said the King had ordered Lord Egremont to prepare a Letter[628] expressing H.M.'s desire to correspond with their assurances, to treat, and settle all the depending disputes amicably with each other, *provided if or when they had made it appear to the King that there was nothing offensive contained in their last Treaty with France.* Lord Bute said this had been agreed at St. James's. Notwithstanding the Cabinet Council of us four, I [Newcastle] knew nothing of it.[629] I [Newcastle] begged the communication might not be too strongly insisted upon, that doing the thing was our point; that the moment our disputes were amicably settled, there was an end of the effect of their Treaty, viz. their junction with France. This did not convince.[630]

The Duke of Newcastle found by Mr. Mackensie[631] that strong measures and strong declarations were to do everything to prevent the junction of Spain and France, and bring about a peace in six weeks. They are not aware of the danger of the present situation; said vigorous measures would have a great effect and in a short time we should see *carpet ground.*

Nov 1 1761: When I came to town, found the Duke of Newcastle and Lord Bute very much out of humour with each other, always bickering that one was minister, and the other was minister. It appeared plainly to me that it was owing to Lord Bute's jealousy of [the] Duke of Newcastle, who [Bute] from the moment Mr. Pitt resigned grew alarmed at his Grace's weight in the Parliament and the nation.

[I] talked on the subject both with Lord Egremont and Mr. Greenville. They agreed on the necessity of the union and confidence among the King's servants. The latter said, they had got into a sort of Picqueering the one saying you are minister for you have got the both Houses of Parliament, the other you have the King; that this sort of language could do no good and was productive of much harm. That for his [Greenville's] part, he had come into the situation he was in not by choice, ambition of power, or interest, but at the request of the King and Lord Bute, that could he see any other *Succedaneum,* he should not be sorry to retire, but was this ministry to break he could not see any scheme that would do. What would immediately occur to

---

[628] The draft of a despatch sent eight days later. Egremont to Bristol, 28 Oct. 1761, pro S.P.F. 94/164; (copy) Chatsworth MSS. 260/353.

[629] Devonshire is paraphrasing Newcastle to Hardwicke, 20 Oct. 1761, Add. MSS. 32929, ff. 406-7. On the following day, Newcastle complained further to Hardwicke that Bute, together with Egremont and Grenville, were taking the decisions. Newcastle to Hardwicke, 21 Oct. 1761, ibid., f. 421. Newcastle to Devonshire, 12 Oct. 1761, Chatsworth MSS. 182/205. Two days later Newcastle was again grumbling over Grenville's amendments to Hardwicke's draft of the King's Speech. Newcastle to Hardwicke, 23 Oct. 1761, Add. MSS. 32929, f. 472.

[630] Newcastle and Devonshire do not appear to have grasped that the Spanish grievances were a deliberate and insincere pretext.

[631] James Stuart-Mackenzie, M.P., brother to Bute.

everybody would be Mr. Pitt coming in sole minister, but after what had passed in Council, he did imagine there was 8 or 10 of the first persons in this kingdom that would not think it consistent with their honour to set in Council with him. In that case he should think he could not be mad enough to undertake the administration, or if he did that he could carry it on.

I replied that what he had said shewed the necessity of keeping united the present ministry; that if one had the Parliament, the other the King, they ought by a thorough confidence and union to unite their mutual powers in jointly carrying on the administration. I was free to own that though the Duke of Newcastle and I had at times differed, yet my family before me, and I myself through life, had acted upon the same principles with him, and that my friendship for him was sincere and great. At the same time I had strictly examined myself, and did not think that I suffered my regard for him to influence my opinion, and without partiality I could not help saying, that I thought Lord Bute was in the wrong. What could his Lordship desire more, than that a man who had been for many years in a manner sole minister of this country, and should declare to him,

'My Lord, I know you have the King, I won't attempt to disturb you in the full possession of it, I desire to act with you and under you, to ask nothing but through you, only let me have that weight and credit that will maintain me with honour in the post I am in.'

That it was certainly a fortunate circumstance for his Lordship to have such a man to stand as a screen between him and the people, that they [Pitt and Temple] had made a great run at the Duke of Newcastle in the City, with a view to be sure to intimidate him and induce him to retire, flattering themselves that if they could carry the point they should easily get the better of Lord Bute, and therefore it was very ill-judged in his Lordship at a time that he ought to be encouraging his Grace, to act such a part, as would rather tend to make the Duke of Newcastle think seriously of the threats against him.

Viry told me that Lord Bute's jealousy grew to an extream height, that he was persuaded he was a man of honour and would do right. But that his conduct towards the Duke of Newcastle was very wrong, and would hurt himself.

Nov 2: I was told that Lord Bute sent Martin[632] to the Attorney General[633] to assure him that he had the greatest regard for him, to hang out the Seals[634] or anything he could wish, that his friendship to

[632] Samuel Martin, M.P., Secretary to the Treasury since 1758.

[633] Pratt.

[634] The office of Lord Chancellor. A knighthood was conferred upon Pratt on 22 Nov. Hardwicke got his way in consequence of the death on 15 Dec. of Sir John Willes, Lord

Mr. Pitt ought to be no obstacle, for he himself had the greatest regard for him and loved him. This had no effect upon Mr. Pratt. Soon after Lord Bute took him aside at Court and repeated the same, with adding that he saw no reason why Mr. Pitt and he might not be friends; that there was a particularity in Mr. Pitt's temper that made it difficult to act with him sometimes, but nevertheless he should be very ready to act with him.

This was confirmed by one that the Attorney told he was concerned in a treaty between Mr. Pitt and Lord Bute.

Very Doubtfull.[635]

The King asked me what I now thought of Mr. Pitt. I owned to him I had been mistaken, that I did not think Mr. Pitt would have accepted favours from the Crown and act immediately offensively.[636] The King replied, nothing so bad they will not do.

Nov 2: Lord Shelburne asked Lord Temple's leave to wait on him in a morning in a Frock.[637]

D.C.[638] Lord Temple told Lord Shelburne that he applauded him for his friendship to Mr. Fox, for he was a most amiable and worthy man and that he thought him very ill used.[639]

The first time the King and Queen went to Leicester House of an evening, Lord Bute came in. The King asked him if he had any business with him. He said there were letters of consequence that he did not chuse to send without shewing them to His Majesty. The King took him into another room and when he had read the letters wished him good night.

King would not let Lord Bute stay, as he did not chuse he should sit down before the Queen.

King never goes to Leicester House without the Queen.

Chief Justice of the Common Pleas. Pratt was forced to succeed him, which necessitated his departure from the House of Commons. Yorke became Attorney-General in Jan. 1762.

[635] A treaty between Pitt and Bute was very unlikely.

[636] An allusion to Pitt's letter to Beckford, see p. 144, n. 621.

[637] A frock denoted 'an upper garment worn chiefly by men; a long coat, tunic or mantle.' Hence frock-coat or frock-uniform, being undress uniform. Shelburne was a Colonel in the Buckinghamshire militia, which Temple as Lord Lieutenant commanded.

[638] Duke of Cumberland, to whom Devonshire presumably owed the information in this paragraph.

[639] Fox had recently tried unsuccessfully to obtain a peerage for his wife Lady Caroline.

Nov 7 1761: Lord Bute mentioned to me that Sir George Saville had refused the Comptroller's staff rather in an unhandsome manner, hinting the times were unsettled.[640] The Duke of Newcastle had told him I wished an employment for one of my brothers, and if I chose it was at my service.[641] He then mentioned the Privy Seal, said the reason why he had put it in commission was the apprehension of giving it the Duke of Bedford immediately, as it would have looked too pacifick. But after they had abused his Grace at [the] Lord Mayor's show,[642] he thought it necessary for the King's honour to shew him his countenance and favour. I mentioned Lord Hardwicke. He [Bute] said he heard he would not take it. I told him I had reason to think so and therefore I wished him to make the offer, and I thought he might do it safely. He said he would.

Nov 10 1761: Mr. Greenville insisted that Mr. Fox should take no part in the debates of the House of Commons.[643] Lord Bute under difficulties how to tell him [Fox], sent Lord Shelburne to open it to him, who made such a piece of work of it, that Fox could not make out what he meant.[644] He [Fox] said for his part, he did not intend to be always answering Mr. Pitt, that he should be glad to sit still. At the same time, if ever the Crown was attacked and administration wanted his assistance, he should be ready to give it.[645]

Present the	A meeting at Lord Bute's office.[646] Mr.
Duke of Newcastle	Greenville very desirous that the Spanish
Lord Egremont	papers.[647] should be laid before the House
Lord Bute	of Commons, if called for. Lord Hardwicke
Lord Hardwicke	spoke against it, urged the impropriety

[640] Sir George Savile, M.P., connected with Rockingham and Newcastle. Newcastle to Rockingham, 3 Nov. 1761: 'It is certainly a very honourable offer to him and comes in an honourable manner. I conclude they wish to get some of our considerable friends over to them.' Add. MSS. 32930, ff. 299–300.

[641] It seems that Devonshire did not recognize Bute as a danger to Newcastle.

[642] On 9 Nov.

[643] Grenville feared Fox, lamenting to Newcastle: 'What a figure shall I make. Mr. Fox has superior parliamentary talents to me; Mr. Fox has a great number of friends in the House of Commons, attached strongly to him. Mr. Fox has *great connexions*, I have none ...' Newcastle to Devonshire, 31 Oct. 1761, Add. MSS. 32930, ff. 225–6.

[644] An early instance of Shelburne's maladroitness, which led to a breach with Fox and was responsible for that general distrust which hindered him through life.

[645] Assured by Bute that his wife would receive the coveted peerage 'before the end of the next session,' Fox agreed to attend the House of Commons, give Grenville every support and 'enter no sort of engagement with anyone else whatever.' Shelburne to Bute, 31 Oct. 1761, Bute MSS. (Cardiff) Bundle 5, No. 57.

[646] Held on 10 Nov. Newcastle to Hardwicke, 9 Nov. 1761, Add. MSS. 32930, f. 374.

[647] Copies of the correspondence relating to the disputes between Britain and Spain, most of which was printed by the government in one volume entitled *Papers Relative to the Rupture with Spain* (1762).

Lord Mansfield

Mr. George Grenville

Duke of Devonshire

pending the negotiation, and the offence it might give to Spain and the bad precedent.

Lord Egremont doubtfull; all the rest against.

He [Grenville] then proposed giving extracts. The Duke of Newcastle opposed it. He was told that Mr. Pitt would say they were unfair extracts, and would take upon himself to prove it; that he would then be forced to give them all in his justification. It ended in their being to be refused.

Nov 11 1761: Mr Greenville expressed great uneasiness at being overruled about the Spanish Papers; said that there was not a single man of business among the Commons that thought they had any ground to stand upon in refusing them. Lord Mansfield proposed to him and Lord Bute to have a meeting for the House of Commons at Mr. Greenville's house to consider whether they ought to give them or not. He [Grenville] insisted that Mr. Fox should not be at it.

Nov 12: Met Lord Mansfield at Newcastle House early in the morning. His Grace [Newcastle] told us Lord Hardwicke was excessively angry and said he would attend Council no more, if when the King's servants had settled a measure, the gentlemen of the House of Commons were [to] determine the rectitude of it. Lord Mansfield condemned the meeting and said what he had proposed was that some of the Commons should meet the Lords to hear their reasons. When I told this to Lord Bute he said it was no such thing. However George Greenville refused having the meeting himself.

Nov 16 1761: I was with Lord Bute to tell him that my brother would accept H.M.'s most gracious offer with the greatest pleasure.[648] He told me that there was a most extraordinary dispatch from Lord Bristol, who had desired Mr. Wall to tell him whether there was anything offensive against England in the treaty they had made with France; that he had flown out into a most violent passion and talked a language that denounced war against us.[649] Lord Bute was very desirous that we should instantly return a strong and spirited answer, or else Mr. Pitt would justly charge us with giving up the honour of the nation, and that I should spirit up the Duke of Newcastle. [I] went to his Grace who agreed in opinion with Lord Bute.

Lord Hardwicke sent him [Newcastle] word that Lord Temple had been with him the night before for above an hour in good humour, and throwing out as if Mr. Pitt and he should be very glad to join with his Lordship and [the] Duke of Newcastle. At Court Lord Coventry[650]

---

[648] Lord George Augustus Cavendish was appointed Comptroller of the Household.

[649] Bristol to Egremont, 2 Nov. (received 14 Nov.), S.P.F. 94/164, Part 1. Egremont to Newcastle, 14 Nov. 1761, Add. MSS. 32931, f. 41.

[650] 6th Earl of Coventry, a Lord of the Bedchamber.

came to the Duke of Newcastle with a proposition from Lord Temple and Mr. Pitt that they were ready to join his Grace. He [Newcastle] said he had given a refusal but that Lord Coventry was to come to him the next morning. I begged him not to listen to it and likewise to inform Lord Bute of it; that he would not act an honourable part if he did not. Viry said that Lord Bute saw the necessity of keeping well with the Duke of Newcastle and would do everything that was right. Lord Temple sent Duke of Newcastle word that Lord Bute meant to get rid of him apeace, as he had done of them.

Nov 18 1761: [I] waited on the King to thank him for his goodness to my brother. He was very gracious and civil, asked me what I had heard of Mr. Pitt's speech the first day of the Session.[651] I told him that, by the best information I could get, it was a very able and artfull performance and, under the specious appearance of good humour and acquiescence, laid the foundation of general opposition, and full of inflammatory matter that might be taken up whenever it suited his purpose. He then asked me if I thought Mr. Pitt could give much disturbance.

I replied that it would not depend on Mr. Pitt but on H.M.'s ministers; that if they would agree, that is to say, the Duke of Newcastle and Lord Bute, he would be of no consequence, but if they differed, he would get the better of them and take possession of H.M., as he [Pitt] had done of his [the King's] grandfather, which I should be very sorry to see.[652] That the Duke of Newcastle was very well disposed; that it was certain he had jealousies but Lord Bute might very easily manage him by a little attention and confidence and early communication of what he was doing, and a smile from H.M. would do more than all. It was certain he had been so long a minister that he would not know what to do with himself out of employment, and therefore would be very glad to remain, and only desired that he might have the appearance of that degree of credit that would enable him to stay with honour to himself.

The King seemed convinced of the necessity of their union and hoped they would agree.

Lord Bute made the offer of Privy Seal to Lord Hardwicke who declined it. The King afterwards repeated it with many gracious expressions. His Lordship seemed pleased with the offer, and owned to me that he should have thought he had reason to take it ill, if nothing had been said to him.[653]

Lord Bute then offered it to [the] Duke of Bedford who said he was

[651] In the debate on the Address of 13 Nov. Barrington to Newcastle, 13 Nov. 1761, Add. MSS. 32931, ff. 19–20.

[652] A further reference to the events of 1746 and 1756. See also pp. 8, 66.

[653] Bute and the King offer the Privy Seal to Hardwicke after Devonshire's assurance of 7 Nov. that a refusal was certain.

indifferent whether he had any employment or not, but that he would leave himself to H.M.'s pleasure, but must first speak to [the] Duke of Newcastle and Duke of Devonshire. We both advised him to take it.[654]

I persuaded [the] Duke of Newcastle to let me tell Lord Bute of what had passed about Lord Temple, desiring secrecy and not to mention it as a direct offer.

Viry said George Greenville would have managements for his family, intimating as not desperate in his expectations from Lord Temple.[655]

	The House of Commons: Dec 11 1761.[656]
	Motion for Spanish Papers by Mr. Cook[657] seconded by Mr. Beckford.
	Mr. Grenville against and Mr. Robinson very well.
Lord Strange:	intended to have been again, but as moved for it: Parliament the constitutional advisers of the Crown, a right to them because not private intelligence; has confidence in the King not in ministers, whoever they are, are split and distracted.
Mr. Wilkes:	for the motion, not to gratify idle curiosity, but to satisfy the alarms of the people: a panegyric on Mr. Pitt.
Sir Francis Dashwood:	differs with Lord Strange. Parliament has the right to demand Papers but must judge whether proper: does not see the use.
	Does not know of faction in the ministry, hopes there is none anywhere else. Why not confide in the ministry? Ill consequence of seeing Papers: they may be what the City of London should not know.
Lord Frederick Campbell:	sees no faction in government. If there is the King will put an end to it, but if so, is that a reason for seeing these Papers? Because they are distracted, shall we be so too?

[654] Bedford became Lord Privy Seal on 25 Nov. 1761.

[655] Grenville's adherence to Bute when Pitt resigned caused a breach with his brother Temple.

[656] Devonshire's account of the debate in the House of Commons of 11 Dec. 1761 on the motion put forward by Pitt's adherent's George Cook and William Beckford that the Papers relating to the negotiations with Spain be put before the House. George Grenville and Thomas Robinson led for administration.

[657] George Cook.

Lord Middleton:[658]	against
Mr. Nugent:	hopes Lord Strange mistaken about factions. If they [there] are, hopes they will cease. A war with Spain felt here as much as at Madrid.
Mr. Dempster:	motion foolish or factious, the former if only to reconcile contradictory news-papers, the latter if to make a Prime Minister.
Mr. Gascoigne:	for the motion; confirms faction being in the ministry. Though Whig and Tory destroyed, worse because personal parties substituted in their stead.
Sir John Glynne:	against: no good effect from shewing Papers.
Mr. Rigby:	more sorry if this motion should be complied with than surprised at its being made; trusts to this administration acting with spirit; has heard an Alderman stand up and, (among other monstrous things), adopt a first minister. Why, if instructed, not his brethren do so too? Full as capable. Who are the Administration? Officers of State, late resignation a proof of union, which he hopes will last because two against twelve, among all the different language alike to the King. But what our loyalty, if we impose a first minister, what the loyalty of the great City of London who are famous for adoring the King?
Mr. Pitt:	when Parliament loses its temper, loses its dignity and becomes barbarous and violent, will do all he can to sooth it. Surprised at Mr. Rigby's speech. Fears his partial friend, (Beckford), thinks more of him than he does himself. Defends his expression for a Prime Minister. If the tendency of these Papers was to make one, he would dissent but does not think it much to be feared when he looks round the House. Agrees with Mr. Rigby about administration being in Great Officers. Thinks Lord Egremont would not continue if denied the guidance. He [Pitt] was to be responsible against his own conscience: this he insisted on having. Did he,

[658] 3rd Viscount Midleton.

during his being not minister but drudge, ask, or propose anything but through proper departments? Will Duke of Newcastle deny it? Will Lord Anson, who he complimented? Devoted to the King under great difficulties; great opinion of it; but thinks some experience must be wanting. The Bottom of the Bottom of this affair should not be divulged; when did twelve men think alike? Queen Elizabeth encouraged divisions in her Councils, a right in it. When he and Lord Temple left the Council, never was more unanimity.

Encomiums on Lord Bristol, able and punctual. Any minister that treats in part about the Fishery will be impeached. Calls the Gazette[659] abusive. Puts the issue on two points, either rupture or accommodation. If rupture, we have lost opportunity never to be recovered: if an accommodation, can there be union between us? No! (she [Spain] will impute it to France appearing in her favour and not to our regard to her).

Colonel Barry:[660] has listened an hour to Mr. Pitt for instruction and amusement: disappointed in both. He [Barré] cannot rouse, animate or divert, has no arts to deceive with; as a friend to his country, shall vote against it. This motion the consequence of [Pitt's] resignation: observes the little confidence had in the King by Mr. Pitt. Called to order by Mr. Pitt, who only affirmed duty to the King. (Several persons spoke to order on the propriety of naming the King. The Solicitor-General[661] said it might not be used to influence, but might with respect and duty. Pitt agrees with him). Colonel Barry said opposition right in general, but when coming without principle and in a flat [contradiction] to his whole former life. By popularity [Pitt] raises himself and then turns no friend to his country, though he may strike his breast, lift his eyes to heaven, and strike

[659] The *Gazette* of 10 Oct. 1761, see p. 143.
[660] Colonel Isaac Barré.
[661] Charles Yorke.

the table with ever so much energy. (Called
to order by Beckford, who is answered by
Rigby and Barry goes on).

Has often heard Beckford deviate from the
question, but has not his excuse as he can't
allow himself quite distracted. If he sees a
sacrilegious hand tearing out the bowells of
his country, he cannot sit content; his intentions pure as Mr. Pitt's; his [Barré's] front
not broad enough to have contradiction
wrote upon it.

If ever called to support the King will not
desert when most wanted.

Passed in the negative: no division.

Jan 6 1762:[662] I came to town on New Year's Day: everything seemed
very quiet and well at Court. Lord Bute desired the Duke of Newcastle
and I to come to his office this morning. Lord Hardwick was out of
town: there was besides Lord Egremont, Mr. George Greenville, and
Lord Anson and Lord Legonier. After some conversation about taking
the most effectual methods of distressing and attacking the Spaniards,[663] which ended in the resolution of attacking Havana, Lord
Bute threw out the recalling the British troops [from Germany]. The
Duke of Newcastle opposed it with great force and warmth.[664] Lord
Bute answered him.

I spoke my opinion strongly against the measure; that it was making
the King act a most dishonourable part in abandoning his allies and
leaving them to the mercy of their enemies, when they had suffered so
much on our accounts in a cause entirely foreign to them; that no
power would ever again trust this country; that for the sake of bringing
home 20,000 men, we should dissolve an army that had obliged France
to employ in Germany a force that she called 150,000 men, and that
in my opinion the consequence would be that France, absolute masters
of the Continent, would dictate to the Dutch and every other power
in the same manner as she and Spain are treating Portugal. *France
and Spain threaten Portugal to seize their country unless they will
take part with them in the war against England.* That they would
force even Holland to assist them to invade this country, which they
might threaten from Denmark quite to Cadiz, and that the moment
the troops returned, this country would be in a state of hot water,
always in apprehensions of being invaded.

[662] Egremont Memorandum, 6 Jan. 1762, P.R.O. 30/47/21.
[663] War had been officially declared on Jan. 4.
[664] Newcastle to Hardwicke, 10 Jan. 1762. Add. MSS. 32933, ff. 179–82.

Lord Bute said he did not mean to come to any resolution at present, he only wanted to know our opinions on so important a point, asked me if I knew what the Duke of Cumberland thought. I replied I had had some casual conversation with him on the subject but had no authority to say what his opinion was, but I believed he thought pretty much in the way of those who were for the old system.

Jan 7 1762: Acquainted H.R.H. with Lord Bute's question. He said I was very cautious but I might have boldly answered for him, and desired me to acquaint Lord Bute that it would always be [a] matter of great concern to him to differ in opinion with H.M.'s ministers or his measures, but that upon this point he thought his honour so much engaged to his old friends abroad, and the point so detrimental to the true interest and honour of this country, that if he was the only man, he would divide the House [of Lords] upon that question. I promised him he should not be single. He said he was much dissatisfy'd with Mr. Fox, that he was entirely gone over to Lord Bute, and he thought acting a very weak part; that he had wished to keep him to the Duke of Newcastle and us.

Jan 8: Told Lord Bute the Duke's answer. He then talked of Viry's negotiation through the Sardinian minister at Paris, Monsieur Soldano,[665] who had intimated to the Duc de Choiseul that we were disposed to make peace, and that as there was no great seeming difference between us when the negotiation broke off, it might be easily accommodated if France was really disposed to peace. The Duc seemed to listen to it and gave encouragement. He said Viry was to write again by George Pitt,[666] who was to go by Paris in his way to Turin; that he was to say that we should be ready to treat on the same terms; that no ministry, now Mr. Pitt was out, could make a much worse peace than he had proposed, and that as to Spain our differences were so trivial they might easily be adjusted.[667] We only asked to cut logwood till such time as Spain would settle how they would give it to us.

Feb 1 1762: Being confined with a severe illness, saw nobody. During that time, the question about recalling the troops was much agitated. The Duke of Bedford gave notice to the ministers that he would

---

[665] The Bailli de Solar, whom Devonshire here termed M. Soldano, Sardinian Minister in Paris. On 17 Nov. Bute had re-opened the negotiation with France through the channel of Viry writing to Solar. This was known only to George III. The Cabinet remained in ignorance until now, when Devonshire was apparently one of the first to be let into the secret. A complete transcript of the correspondence between Viry and Solar is in four volumes (9-12) of the Shelburne papers in the Clements Library, Ann Arbor, Michigan.

[666] George Pitt, M.P., recently appointed British envoy at Turin, 1761-8.

[667] Viry to Solar, 13 Dec. 1761, 5 and 12 Jan. 1762, Shelburne MSS. Vol. 9, ff. 13-16, 36-7, 39-41.

certainly move for it in the House of Lords.[668] Mr. Rigby called for the Hessian master roll in the House of Commons, as preparatory to the same step there. Lord Bute called upon me, was much against the Duke of Bedford's motions, and seemed a good deal come off from the idea of recalling the troops.[669] He talked of Rigby and of a party forming.

I told his Lordship it was in his power to stop it, for it had taken its rise from him, for his conversation made everybody think that in taking that side of the question they were doing what was agreeable to him. He answered they would find it otherways. He then complained of the Duke of Newcastle's intention of entering into the merits of the question; that it would lay him under great difficulties, for he should likewise be obliged to declare his, and that it would have a very bad appearance for the world to see the differences of opinion in the King's ministers. Whereas, if the Duke of Newcastle would be quiet, he would answer the Duke of Bedford and propose the previous question. I told him his Grace was full of complaints; that he had been a minister of 40 years and served two Kings, but never had had such language held to him; that he had imagined his Lordship meant to turn him [out]. Lord Bute smiled and said it never entered into his thoughts; that all he had meant to convey to his Grace was that if he took that part in debate he must likewise consider what part he must take.

Lord Bute said some of the warm militia people were for compulsive clauses against those counties that have not raised the militia, that he had been strongly against them.

The Duke of Newcastle was easily persuaded to let Lord Bute have the management of the debate.[670]

Feb 5 1762: The Duke of Bedford made his motion,[671] answered by Lord Bute, who proposed the previous question very theatrically, talked much of himself and the King. Lord Temple took him to order for it, and spoke very artfully and well. *Lord Wycombe*[672] made a bad speech, said in King William's time this nation was influenced by Dutch measures, and in the late reign by German ones. The Duke of Newcastle answered him well on that subject and justified the late reign. The previous question was carried 105 to 16.[673]

Earl of Shelburne

[668] Bedford, dissatisfied with Bute's failure to overrule Newcastle and Devonshire and to end at once the war in Germany, proposed bringing matters to a head by moving in the House of Lords for the immediate withdrawal of British troops. Newcastle to Hardwicke, 16 Jan. 1762, Add. MSS. 32933, f. 320.

[669] Bute to Bedford, 30 Jan. 1762, *Bedford*, iii. 72–3.

[670] Newcastle to Devonshire, 4 Feb. 1762, Chatsworth MSS. 182/220.

[671] See Sir James Caldwell to Lord Newton, 20 Feb. 1762, P.R.O. 30/8/70/5, ff. 26–49; *Parliamentary History*, xv. 1218–20.

[672] Shelburne, who sat by right of his G.B. peerage.

[673] Devonshire lists Bedford, Lord Privy Seal, together with the fifteen peers who followed him in voting against administration, noting particularly those with employments.

Duke of Bedford, Privy Seal.
Duke of Richmond, Regiment.[674]
Duke of Bridgewater.
Earl Talbot, Lord Steward.
Earl of Essex.
Earl of Dunmore.
Earl Waldegrave, Lord Warden of the Stannaries.[675]
Earl of Orford, Lord of the Bedchamber.[676]
Earl Gower, Great Master of the Wardrobe.[677]
Earl Pomfret, pension £1200 p.a.
Lord Weymouth, Lord of the Bedchamber.[678]
Lord Ducie.
Earl of Warwick.
Lord Vere.
Lord Fortescue.
Lord Wycombe, Aid du Camp.[679]

Lord Bute much hurt at the division. The King took no notice of Lord Weymouth nor Lord Shelburne. Lord Bute told the Duke of Newcastle that the Duke of Bedford sheltered them or else the King would make some example; that he was most angry with Lord Waldegrave and Lord Weymouth. The King said to me that Lord Shelburne's manner of speaking of the late King and King William was very indecent.

The Duke of Bedford very angry with Lord Bute, told Duke of Newcastle that his Lordship had deceived him, having informed him that he had given orders for the transports to be ready to bring the troops home;[680] that he had wrote to Mr. Yorke to know what the Dutch would do,[681] well knowing they would do nothing, with a view to get the better of the opinions and silence the Dukes of Newcastle and Devonshire.

Feb 5 1762: The Dutch ministers have today spoke a more becoming language to Monsieur D'Affry.[682] He [d'Affry] had orders to acquaint them that his master was informed England had pressed them for succours; that there was a strong rumour that the States intended an

---

[674] Col. the 72nd Regt. of Foot since 9 May 1758.
[675] Lord Warden of the Stannaries since 1751.
[676] Lord of the Bedchamber since 1755.
[677] Great Master of the Wardrobe since 1760.
[678] Lord of the Bedchamber since 1760.
[679] A.D.C. to the King.
[680] The editors know of no documentary evidence of such orders.
[681] On 12 Jan. Bute had instructed Sir Joseph Yorke, British Minister at the Hague, to ascertain from Prince Louis of Brunswick, guardian to William V, Prince of Orange, who was a minor, whether the Dutch were prepared to enter the war on the British side.
[682] The French representative at the Hague.

augmentation[683] which His Most Christian Majesty could not but look upon with a jealous eye, as tending to depart from their neutrality. The Pensionary[684] and Greffier[685] both expressed their surprise at these notions: said the Republick was a free state and independent, and not obliged to consult any power upon their interior conduct, or the measures they should think prudent to take for their own safety.[686] The East India [negotiation] will end in the way the King wished.[687] They will desire the King that the English Company should not assist the Nabob of Bengal[688] during the negotiation. All armament for India is dropped.

Accounts from Vienna represent that Court as much embarrassed,[689] which makes us hope for an explicit answer to Prince Louis's[690] insinuations.

We don't understand the sudden silence on the attack of Portugal: some suspect the Empress-Queen has interfered.[691]

Feb 22 1762: Duke of Newcastle to Lord Hardwicke:[692] Lord Bute very angry with the Prussian ministers and extremely displeased with the King of Prussia himself for his letter to the King, in which he was to lay his whole thoughts and plan before the King. Instead of that, it is a very short one, breathing war more than ever; that the present disposition of Russia was the most favourable for the King and himself;[693] that by pushing on the war, the King would decide his command over the seas, and the King and His Prussian Majesty would defeat the greatest combination of powers against them that ever was known. The war with Spain was a lucky incident: no hint at peace, only some general declaration about it. War was the question.[694] In a

---

[683] Of their naval and military forces.

[684] Peter Steyn.

[685] Henrik Fagel.

[686] Yorke to Bute, 5 Feb. 1762, S.P.F. 84/495.

[687] The negotiation initiated by the Dutch East India Company following their defeat by the British in Bengal in 1759. Yorke's dispatches to Bute, S.P.F. 84/493 and 495.

[688] Mir Jaffir Ali Khan.

[689] See intelligence in Yorke to Newcastle, 2 Feb. 1762, Add. MSS. 32934, ff. 145-7.

[690] Prince Louis of Brunswick.

[691] The proposed Spanish invasion of Portugal never got under way. Britain sent a contingent to Lisbon as by treaty bound. Maria Theresa disliked the Family Compact between France and Spain with the implied diversion of French resources towards the invasion of Portugal. Also, she was negotiating a marriage between the Archduke Leopold, the future Emperor Leopold II, and a daughter of Charles III.

[692] Newcastle to Hardwicke, 22 Feb. 1762, Add. MSS. 32935, ff. 9-13.

[693] Elizabeth, Czarina of Russia, had died on 5 Jan. 1762. Her successor Peter III, an ardent admirer of Frederick of Prussia, at once withdrew from the war.

[694] The Treaty of Westminster guaranteeing a subsidy to Prussia of £670,000 p.a. had just expired. Bute, supported by the entire Cabinet, was considering not the renewal of the treaty but the continuation of the subsidy by parliamentary grant.

decyphered letter of the King of Prussia to Kniphausen,[695] speaking of
the proposals or ideas of the present ministers, he says they ought to
be sent *a la Petite Maison*[696] (Bedlam). The Prussian ministers acquainted Lord Bute that as there master was willing to take the
subsidy of £670,000 in the way it had been offered, they insisted to
know whether they were to have it or not, and that it might be voted
immediately. Lord Bute took it up high, complained that the King of
Prussia had given no answer to the questions put to him to know his
plan;[697] that the great event in Russia required much consideration;
that we must know what turn that would take, and made the measure
of the subsidy doubtfull.

*Kniphausen told Lord Bute that he had talked with Mr. Pitt and
the heads of all the factions in this country and they were all for his
master. Lord Bute replied he would do better to talk to the King's
ministers and not cabal with factions: they quite quarrelled.*

Duke of Newcastle told the Prussian ministers that the event in
Russia was happy or otherways, as it might tend to promote peace;
that if it was to encourage us to continue the war it was making a
wrong use of it; that the subsidy did not press and must be delayed till
we had answers from Mr. Keith[698] and Mr. Mitchell, with an account
what use the King of Prussia meant to make of this event in Russia
towards bringing about a peace. Lord Bute proposed writing to the
Prussian ministers, that not having received the lights we expected
from their master, and not knowing his sentiments, how the present
event in Russia might be applied to negotiating and promoting peace,
we must wait for answers to these questions before we could do
anything as to the subsidy.[699]

Lord Bute said General Yorke had been pressing for an authority to
assure the Republic that H.M. would support them if they were
threatened or attacked by France.[700] Duke of Newcastle said he was
strong for such an assurance, and in that case Prince Ferdinand's
army ought to come down to the frontiers of Holland. Lord Bute asked
him if he thought he could pay and support an army of 70,000 men.
He replied, if the expence of Portugal does not go beyond what appears
at present, and there are no other new expences, I am of opinion I can
support them for this present year, but could he another year, he could
not tell, he could only answer for this year.

[695] Frederick II to Knyphausen, 29 Jan. 1762 (intercepted), Add. MSS. 32934, ff.
62–3.

[696] The wrath of Frederick arose from the British demand that he make peace when
his fortunes had been transformed by the accession of Czar Peter III.

[697] Bute to Mitchell, 8 Jan. 1762, S.P.F. 90/79.

[698] Robert Keith, British Minister at St. Petersburg, 1757–62.

[699] A letter to this effect was sent four days later. Bute to Knyphausen and Mitchell,
26 Feb. 1762, D.Z.A., Rep. 96. 33. F, ff. 69–71.

[700] Yorke to Bute, 19 Jan. 1762, S.P.F. 84/495.

Lord Bute was well pleased and seemed to give in to the measure to order General Yorke to give assurances of support to the Republick in case they resist the menaces of France, and to keep our army under Prince Ferdinand for this campaign to act according to events on the side of Hesse [and] Hanover or on the lower Rhine.

Lord Egremont is to write to Lord Halifax to know whether these Irish Roman Catholicks will enter into the King of Portugal's service.[701] We shall have 2000 German deserters and they say the 5000 Swiss sent 1000 per month to any port we shall name. Duke of Newcastle for Williamstadt in Holland and send 2000 by sea to Embden[702] to recruit our army.

Feb 23 1762: Viry said that Lord Bute coold about the peace; that George Greenville had been with him, talked that our situation was altered and by being firm we might get a better peace. Lord Egremont likewise held a different language. Viry was desired to send the proposals[703] as soon as they came to Lord Egremont, and to take no notice of them to the Duke of Newcastle or anybody, till such time as Lord Bute should direct him. But he said he would take a copy of them and send it me directly. I advised him [Viry] not to seem too warm for the peace, which might make Lord Bute think him prejudiced in favour of his negotiation and consequently lessen his weight with him. I told him if the terms were reasonable we would force them to be accepted, but I suspected Lord Bute would rather be adverse, that in case the peace should be unpopular the odium might be thrown upon us, and if it proved otherways he would then assume the merit of it. Viry said he was afraid that would be his scheme.

March 3 1762: Lord Bute talked to me on the subject of the Duc de Choiseul's letter to Solar[704] and the answer to Viry.[705] He said they were insolent to the last degree, that there ought nor could be any answer sent to them. Lord Egremont in the same style. I said when I had considered the Papers I would give my opinion. The Duke of Newcastle strong for not putting an end to the negotiation.[706]

Lord Bute before he went from Court said he thought Lord Egremont should write an answer to Viry, saying that if France continued

---

[701] Halifax, Lord Lieutenant of Ireland, had informed Egremont that the Irish Catholics, anxious to prove their loyalty, were prepared to serve on the Continent. Halifax to Egremont, 6 Feb. 1762; Egremont to Halifax, 23 Feb. 1762, *Calendar of Home Office Papers*, 154–5, 159. George III to Bute (early February), 1762, Bute MSS. (Cardiff) 8/398.

[702] Emden in East Friesland.

[703] Choiseul's reply to Viry's letter of 12 Jan., see p 155.

[704] Choiseul to Solar, 23 Jan. 1762, Shelburne MSS. 9, ff. 46–9.

[705] Solar to Viry, 1 Feb. 1762, P.R.O. 30/47/1; copy in Add. MSS. 32924, ff. 121–4.

[706] Devonshire found the French papers 'not at all satisfactory' and Choiseul's note 'mere verbiage . . . . full of impertinence.' But he thought the negotiation should continue. Devonshire to Bute, 4 Mar. 1762, Bute MSS. (Cardiff) Bundle 1, No. 206.

in such a disposition there was no talking to them.[707] And he said that he would write another letter to Viry that the time for peace, he saw with concern, was not come, expressing strongly our desire for it, but at the same time that we were not in a condition to be obliged to sue for it. And therefore while France held such haughty language, it was in vain to think of treating with them. He hoped a letter to this effect might renew the negotiation if France meant to treat.

March 19 1762: Duke of Cumberland told me they concluded at Leicester House I should die, and Lord Bute had determined to take my place. One present said to him: 'How can you do it? You cannot attend as you ought, you know the Duke of Devonshire does not much love attendance, and yet thinks it necessary to be always there when in town.'[708]

He replied: 'Very true.' but the King's particular goodness to him [Bute] would make the attendance easy, or excuse it.

March 19: Monsieur Fagel has received an answer from Madrid to his letter.[709]

March 26 1762: Duke of Newcastle, Lord Hardwicke, Mr. George Greenville and myself met at Lord Bute's office. His Lordship said he had desired us to come to consider what was to be done in regard to our situation with France, threw out that we might send a proposition to renew the negotiation publickly,[710] but for that purpose there must be a general meeting of those persons that used to attend. That he was very glad that Lord Egremont's letter had not been sent,[711] for what would people say if we had made such offers after the success of Martinico, and therefore he imagined the negotiation of Count Viry should be dropped and no answer sent. For that it would be very bad to have two negotiations going on at the same time.

I asked him if I did not misunderstand him in his intention of giving no answer to the Court of France, that though perhaps it might not be so proper now to be offering concessions on our part, yet that I was strong for having some answer made to Count Solar, shewing our desire for peace on reasonable terms. Duke of Newcastle strong of the

[707] Newcastle to Hardwicke, 3 Mar. 1762. Preliminary drafts of the letter Bute suggested were discussed at Cabinet meetings of 9 and 18 Mar. But following news of the capture of Martinique, which arrived in London on 21 Mar., no letter was sent.

[708] This is the merest gossip. Bute, far from desiring Devonshire's place as Lord Chamberlain, was deep in an intrigue to oust Newcastle, whom he proposed succeeding at the Treasury. Newcastle had just learned that Samuel Martin, Secretary to the Treasury, was supplying Bute with figures and information intended to force his resignation.

[709] Fagel, after consulting Yorke, had written early in February to Wassenaer, asking him to make informal enquiries as to the disposition of Spain towards peace. Yorke to Bute, 16 Feb. 1762, S.P.F. 84/495.

[710] So far the negotiations were known only to the King and Cabinet.

[711] Egremont's preliminary draft of 21 Mar. 1762, Add. MSS. 32936, ff. 1–8 (copy).

same opinion and Lord Hardwick, George Greenville for making no answer, and debated it with us three. *George Greenville owned his scheme of dropping the German war and then this country would be able to continue the war[712] for some years.

Duke of Newcastle replied he should have nothing to do with such a plan but whoever was in his place would find themselves mistaken if they entertained such notions.* Lord Bute said very little and soon gave in to a proposition to take out the sketch of the terms of peace in Lord Egremont's letter, and letting the rest of it go as a note to Count Viry to form his dispatch, but which he might send to Mr. Solar.[713] He [Bute] was pleased with turning the letter into a Memorial as he avoided by that means the signing it. Lord Bute seemed in my opinion to be with, as in his own mind, but made the proposition to please Mr. Greenville, knowing we should overrule it.

March 27: My old friend [Viry] told me that he knew for certain that Lord Bute's scheme was to make the Duke of Newcastle declare the impossibility of carrying on the war, and then he would make peace, and if it was blamed excuse himself by saying the Duke of Newcastle had declared it was impossible to continue the war. He was much out of humour with him, said he saw great duplicity in him.

The King a few days ago gave the Duke of Newcastle a Paper of queries relative to some private duties that belong to the Crown, wrote in his own hand, and said he had done it from his grandfather's accounts and some papers he had in his own hands.[714] It was manifestly drawn by a man of business and the Duke of Newcastle knew that Martin,[715] one of his secretaries, had been the week before a great while with Lord Bute. His Lordship acted a very unfriendly part to the Duke of Newcastle and it was abominable in him to make the King chicane, to say no worse of it.

Lord Chancellor[716]	Declaration of the Czar to his allies: the
Duke of Newcastle	Czar looks upon it as his duty to take
Lord Hardwicke	care of the safety of his subjects; desirous
Lord Legonier	to stop the effusion of blood, and there-
Duke of Devonshire	fore wishes to make peace, and to contri-
Duke of Bedford	bute towards so salutary an end for his

[712] The maritime and colonial conflict only.

[713] Viry to Solar, 27 Mar. 1762, Shelburne MSS. 9, ff. 88–96.

[714] The original paper, in George III's hand together with the replies. Add. MSS. 33040, ff. 309–11.

[715] Martin to Bute, 18 Mar. 1762: 'Mr. Samuel Martin to the Earl of Bute. The Duke of Newcastle suspects that he has given his Lordship some hints about the King's extra revenues in the Exchequer: which he will not disown.' Bute MSS. (Cardiff) Bundle 4, No. 66 (copy); Register of Bute's Correspondence, Add. MSS. 36796.

[716] Council, 29 Mar. Newcastle's Minute, 29 Mar. 1762, Add. MSS. 32999, ff. 454–5.

Lord Bute   own people and for all Europe, is willing to
Lord Mansfield   give up his conquests.[717]
Mr. George Greenville A hint to the House of Austria not to push
                       for farther conquests probably of Silesia.[718]
Lord Bute: what the Council ought to advise the King upon this
transaction.[719]
Mentioned that though this nation had met with great success yet he
wished that it might be thought adviseable to take some step towards
making peace with France.

Court of Vienna:
charged the Emperor [Czar Peter III] with having taken a [un] pas
précipité in granting a Cessation to his hereditary enemy, offered Czar
money to carry on a war against Denmark.[720] [Peter III] very angry
at these two points, said he had money of his own but if he wanted any
that Court [Vienna] should be the last he would apply to.[721]

Lord Bute: repeated his desire of peace, asked the advice of the
Lords who were all more conversant in business than them [him],
whether we might not proceed on the uti possidetis, the two ultimatums each Court stating the terms they would propose. Mentioned the
same message to be sent to Spain.

The King has seen the copy of the Dutch Minister at Madrid
signifying the pacifick temper of Spain.[722] You may answer that the
King is disposed to the same purpose and will listen with pleasure to
any proposals of that sort.[723]

If England makes war a contre coeur, she must propose a general
peace. If England would accept the terms she might have had in
August, and offer reasonable propositions to Spain, a general peace
might be brought about.[724]

---

[717] Declaration issued to the assembled Foreign Ministers in St. Petersburg on 23 Feb.
1762, Add. MSS. 32935, ff. 467–8 (copy).
[718] The withdrawal of the Czar from the war must prevent Maria Theresa recovering
Silesia.
[719] It was unanimously decided that Keith express the 'highest satisfaction' with the
Czar's Declaration. Bute to Keith, 9 Apr. 1762, S.P.F. 91/69.
[720] Over the Schleswig-Holstein dispute in which the Czar as Duke of Holstein-
Gottorp had a personal interest.
[721] Keith to Bute, 12/23 Feb. 1762, S.P.F. 91/69.
[722] Jan Lodewijk Wassenaer, Dutch Ambassador to Spain, 1747–62, to the Greffier
Fagel, 1 Mar. 1762 (copy) enclosed in Yorke to Bute, 19 Mar. 1762 (secret), S.P.F. 84/
495.
[723] Bute to Yorke, 9 Apr. 1762, S.P.F. 84/496.
[724] 'Extrait du Madrid', 1 Mar. 1762, in Yorke to Bute, 19 Mar. 1762, S.P.F. 84/495.
Minute, 29 Mar. 1762, Stowe MSS. S.T. 103, ff. 12–14.

The Lords were of opinion that the King should compliment the Czar on the generosity of his proceeding and express his desire of contributing towards a general peace on reasonable and equitable terms.

The Council were of opinion as the Court of France offered negotiation last year which was unsuccessful His Majesty, *thinking the present moment the most proper to shew his moderation and desire to put an end to the calamities of war, *in a manner suitable to his dignity,* offers His Christian Majesty to renew negotiation and to send respective Ministers, the two last ultimatums the basis. Each Court may propose the alterations they think necessary from the different changes that may have happened in their respective situations.

March 29: Lord Hardwicke whispered [to] Lord Bute and [the] Duke of Newcastle while at Council, that he thought the transaction with Viry should be communicated to all the Lords. Duke of Newcastle against it, the other no objection. I proposed deferring it till the next meeting, when the declaration to be sent to France should be laid before as agreed to, but Lord Bute said he would communicate the substance of it to the Duke of Bedford as soon as the Council rose.[725]

Lord Bute said that a resolution had been taken to blow up Belleisle[726] but stopped; desired to know the opinion of the Lords whether in the present moment is should be done. The Lords of opinion, not.

To make the same offer to Spain and to take up the negotiation where it broke off.

March 31: Duke of Newcastle said the Duke of Cumberland had owned to him that he had talked to the Duchess of Bedford at the opera about the Council. She said the Duke of Bedford had not told her one word.[727] However the next day a broker bought a considerable quantity of stock for Mr. Fox and Mr. Calcroft.[728] Munichausen informed him [Newcastle] that Lord Bute opened his dispatches.[729] The pretence was to see Kniphausen's letters,[730] but it certainly was with a view to look into General Yorke's correspondence with the Duke of Newcastle. *Kniphausen's letters were looked into before.*[731]

---

[725] It was agreed that Egremont, ignoring the negotiation through Viry and Solar, write to Choiseul, offering to treat on the basis of the ultimatums of 1 and 9 Sept. 1761, 'subject to such variations as may naturally arise from the alterations of circumstances on either side.' Cabinet Minute, St. James, 29 Mar. 1762, P.R.O. 30/47/21; Add. MSS. 32999, ff. 454-5; Egremont to Choiseul, 7 Apr. 1762, Add. MSS. 38198, ff. 115-19.

[726] The proposal was to withdraw the garrison and demilitarize. Troops were needed for service in Portugal.

[727] Gertrude, Duchess of Bedford, had a reputation for telling the duke what to do.

[728] John Calcraft, M.P.

[729] See 'Memorandum relating to the Prussian Letters, 31 Mar. 1762', Add. MSS. 32936, f. 229.

[730] To gain some insight into Prussian policy.

[731] The practice of intercepting correspondence increased significantly during this period. Rigby to Bedford, 16 Sept. 1762, Bedford MSS. Vol. 46, f. 2.

The King told Munichausen that the Duke of Cumberland knew every thing, things that he ought not to know, and he must be informed by some of his Council; that he found he knew all the Prussian affairs and Rodney's Instructions.[732] His Majesty thought himself safe, as he knew the Duke and Munichausen were ill together.

Viry had a letter from Count Canales,[733] their minister at Vienna, who had talked with Kawnitz, owned they disliked the Bourbon Treaty, that the danger was not at the present moment and might be prevented hereafter; thought the Court of Vienna better disposed.

April 5 1762: The Queen a great mind for a Court dress:[734] Lord Bute against it and stopped it. A.[735] said it would be some time or other, hinted that Lord Bute never saw the King but in a morning; that he grew uneasy and said he was only treated as a minister.

Justices for Denbighshire, which Lord Litchfield[737] had given to Lord Bute. His Lordship told the Duke of Newcastle that the King would turn him out if he did not make them. We went together from Lord Egremont's to the House of Lords. I represented to him that, if the King took such a step, I should think him very ill advised; that it would set the Whigs in a flame; that I was for abolishing parties but that it could only be done by taking the Tories in as individuals. For, if they stuck together as a party, the Whigs would do so too in order not to suffer themselves to be got the better of by a set of people who were not a third part so considerable as them; that I had proposed to Mr. Middleton by Lord Powis, that he should put them in the Commission, provided they would ask it of him. If he refused that I should not defend him. Lord Bute said: 'I will ask it as a favour of him.'

I told him that would not do because the Tories had given out in the country that they would not be obliged to him, but would force Mr. Middleton to make them; that such treatment was disrespectfull to the King's Lord Lieutenant and to a person of Mr. Middleton's fortune, whose family had spent immense sums to maintain the interest of this Royal Family against these gentlemen, who three or four years ago would have been angry if you had thought them anything but Jacobites. His Lordship said it was but reasonable: they should apply to Mr. Middleton and that he would endeavour to persuade them to do it.

[732] Cumberland's informant was Newcastle. Cumberland to Devonshire, 22 Feb., 15 Apr., Chatsworth MSS. 332/13,14.

[733] Count Canales, Sardinian Minister at Vienna, 1752–73.

[734] A regulation costume worn by those who attend Court.

[735] Probably Ashburnham.

[736] Richard Myddleton, M.P., Lord Lieutenant of Denbighshire since 1748.

[737] Earl of Lichfield.

Present at
Lord Egremont's—
Lord Chancellor
Lord Hardwicke
Lord Egremont
Lord Mansfield
Mr. Greenville
Duke of Newcastle
Duke of Devonshire
Lord Bute
Lord Legonier

April 10 [8][738] 1762: The Duke of Newcastle acquainted the Lords that he had desired this meeting to lay before them the state of the expence that would attend war in Portugal and to consider the method of laying it before Parliament.

A Minute was drawn up to advise the King that Monsieur Mello[739] should be informed that the King would send immediately to Portugal 6000 foot, 700 light horse, two companies of artillery men and a field train suitable to them; that provisions for maintaining men and horses should be sent from hence to such ports as the King of Portugal[740] should direct, and they to be at the expence of conducting them to the army. That some words should be added to the vote of credit[741] to comprehend this service more fully, though it was thought by most Lords, that the words of the last vote of credit would be sufficient.

The Duke of Newcastle threw out that he was afraid it could not be less than two millions. Mr. Greenville opposed it with great warmth, said there was no occasion for it, that the savings in other parts as Belleisle and in America would pay for the Portuguese service; that if two millions were to be voted, it would only be to increase the expence of Germany. The Duke of Newcastle replyed there was no intention of that sort, but in his opinion less would not do. Greenville answered him, attacked the commissariate, but as the sum was not now the question the Lords stopped the altercation. Lord Bute shewed indisposition to the German War, abused the King of Prussia and hinted at not giving him the subsidy.[742] Lord Mansfield gave in to everything he said and manifestly shewed a concert with him.

April 18 1762: [Bute] told me that the King had given the Duke of York leave to go abroad in a very kind manner, but had wrote a very strong rough letter to Prince William in answer to his application to

---

[738] April 10 in MS., but see Newcastle to Barrington, 8 Apr. 1762, Add. MSS. 32936, ff. 440–1. Egremont's Minutes of 8 Apr. 1762, P.R.O. 30/47/21.

[739] Martinho de Mello, Count of Galvas, Portuguese Ambassador in London, 1756–70.

[740] King Joseph I.

[741] An extraordinary subsidy of £200,000 was also granted. Newcastle's Minute, 8 Apr. 1762, Add. MSS. 33000, ff. 41–2.

[742] Frederick II gave no reassurance about his projects and, as Bute surmised, was angling for help from Russia against Maria Theresa in return for supporting Czar Peter III's interests in Schleswig-Holstein.

serve in Germany: an absolute refusal.[743] That the Queen had desired
the King to let her brother the Prince of Mecklenburg[744] [go] to
Portugal which H.M. hesitated about. Lord Bute undertook it and
succeeded. The Queen did not thank him[745] but said she supposed her
brother and Lord Bute were well together. The Tories had stopped
the Court dress. Lord Bute wanted me to object to it. I said I had
never been consulted upon it and should not meddle.

April 19: Viry[746] said that he had undoubted information that Lord
Hardwicke and the Attorney General[747] had frequent intercourse with
Mr. Pitt and Lord Temple, especially with the former; that it was
conjecture but he was sure of it.
not true.[748]

I gave him [Viry] an account of our proceeding at the meeting[749]
what passed between me and Lord Bute,[750] and my resolution if the
German war was put an end to, to retire from Council. As I could not
concur in measures that were the weakest and most dishonourable for
this country; weak because, [we were] after having supported the
King of Prussia through all his difficulties, we were going to quit him
when he was becoming powerfull and might be of service, and the
Empress Queen still strongly attached to France; dishonourable
because we were going to abandon our allies who had suffered so
much upon our account; that we should be left without a friend and
the scorn of all Europe. No nation would ever trust this country again.
That we were only going to transfer the Continent war to Portugal,
where the distance would make it as expensive if not more so than
Germany, and your troops not within call, and the climate as fatal to
them as the West Indies. He [Viry] very strong against the subsidy,
said if you gave it the King of Prussia you would enable him to carry
on the war and would have no peace. Viry in [this] spoke the language
of his Court who wish well to the House of Austria.[751]

Elliot of the Treasury told Mr. West[752] we shall fight our Portugal
[war] against your German war. Lord Bute told the Duke of Newcastle

[743] The Duke of York was given permission to join the fleet under Hawke. George III
to Bute, Apr. 1762, Sedgwick, 89-90.

[744] Ernest of Mecklenberg-Strelitz.

[745] The King did in her name. George III to Bute, Apr. 1762, ibid. 90-1.

[746] Viry to Devonshire, 18 Apr. 1762, Chatsworth MSS. 580/18.

[747] Charles Yorke.

[748] Devonshire was right to disbelieve Viry. Relations between Pitt and Temple on
the one hand and Hardwicke and Newcastle on the other were very cool.

[749] That of 8 Apr.

[750] During a conversation of 16 Apr., see Devonshire to Newcastle, 16 Apr. 1762,
Add. MSS. 32937, ff. 181-2.

[751] The Court of Sardinia depended upon Austrian goodwill to maintain their gains
under the Treaty of Aix-la-Chapelle.

[752] James West, M.P., joint secretary to the Treasury since July 1757.

that he had convinced Lord Hardwicke and reduced him to own we had nothing to depend upon but Providence. His Grace replyed he had received a letter[753] from his Lordship [Hardwicke] which said the contrary. Lord Bute started up in a passion and immediately went to tell the King.

Tuesday April 27 1762: at Lord Granville's:

9[754]

Lord President	Lord Chancellor
Duke of Devonshire	Duke of Newcastle
Lord Hardwick	Lord Egremont
Lord Legonier	Lord Mansfield
Lord Bute	

As to the 3 objects with Spain:

1. The King will not refuse nor never has justice on prizes.[755]

Treaty 1667, and Treaty of Munster, and 1670—[756]

2. As to evacuating the Establishment in the Bay of Honduras, the King will give satisfaction upon the territory of *the King of Spain,* when logwood is secured to us: that is, *couper, charger et remporter le bois.*

3. As to the Fishery upon the Banks of Newfoundland: what has passed with the Spanish Minister makes me flatter myself there will be no difficulty if the other point is once settled.

France:

The ultimatums the Basis:

Canada, we abide by the 1 Article of the French Memorial, and give 18 months for emigration.[757]

From what the Duc de Choiseul says there will be no difficulty about the cession of Canada and we give 18 months for emigration.

---

[753] Hardwicke to Newcastle, 18 Apr. 1762, Yorke, iii. 351–2.

[754] The number of Lords present. George Grenville was absent because of illness, *Grenville*, i. 442.

[755] See p. 134, n. 556.

[756] The Treaty of Madrid of 1667, the Treaty of Münster or Westphalia of 1648 and the Treaty of Madrid of 1670 were re-enacted under Article II of the Peace of Paris.

[757] See also p. 121. Originally, Britain had offered one year, which Choiseul rejected as too short.

As to the Fishery in [the Gulph of St. Laurance],[758] England adheres to her former offer of granting to France the liberty of fishing and drying their nets on the Banks of Newfoundland according to the Treaty of Utrecht and also that the French may fish on the coasts of St. Pierre and Miguelon and may fish in the Gulph of St. Laurence *provided they do not encroach* on the territory belonging to Great Britain.[760]

Pourvue qu'elle n'impie-toit pas sur les droit des coters de notre territoire.[759]

France last year having asked the Isle of Miguelon to be added to St. Pierre as an abri, we agree to it.[761]

Goree:[762]

France to give a plan for Asia.

Allow the cuvette,[763] if not a military work. Fortifications according to the Treaty Aix.[764]

The course of the Misisippi to be the boundary of the two nations.[766]

King of England does not desire that the King of France should break his faith with his allies and makes no doubt, but the King of France would [not][765] shew a reciprocity.

East Indies, as England is in possession France should propose a plan, the King will be ready to shew a good disposition as far as depends on him.

April 30: The same Lords[767] and Mr. George Greenville: revised the answer to the Duc de Choiseul's letter to Monsieur Solar[768] and agreed to it.

---

[758] Crossed out in MS. and restored by the editors.

[759] Marginal note by Devonshire.

[760] The terms put forward in the British Ultimatum of Sept. 1761.

[761] This concession, agreed by the Cabinet in late Aug. 1761, had been despatched to Choiseul on 1 Sept. Yorke, iii. 271-4.

[762] The restitution of Goree had been decided by the Cabinet on 18 Mar. 1762. Minute, 18 Mar. 1762, P.R.O. 30/47/21.

[763] The cunette or canal at Dunkirk was later inspected by a British engineer who advised on demolition before any treaty was signed.

[764] See p. 106, n. 395.

[765] Crossed out in MS. and restored by the editors.

[766] Marginal note by Devonshire.

[767] Those present were Henley, Granville, Devonshire, Newcastle, Hardwicke, Ligonier, Egremont and Grenville. Egremont Minute, P.R.O. 30/47/21.

[768] The French counter-proposal to Egremont's letter of Apr. 7, see p. 164, n. 725. Choiseul to Siolar, 15 Apr. 1762, Shelburne MSS. 9, ff. 118-27.

When that was over Lord Bute said he had not received the King's orders to take the advice of the Council in regard to the Prussian subsidy, but only mentioned it to know the opinion of Lords upon it: spoke strongly against it. Duke of Newcastle, Lord Hardwicke and myself for giving it, or at least not refusing it all. The rest against it except Lord Mansfield, who gave no opinion at all. He told me that these papers,[769] were never laid before him and therefore he had determined not to attend whenever this question should come on. I said as I was not acquainted with what passed on this subject, I could not pretend to give a thorough opinion on the point. So far I was very sorry to see we had lost the Czar and the King of Prussia, the cause I was ignorant of but that it was much to be lamented, for I was convinced if France saw that we had quarrelled with our allies, they would not come into the terms that they were now disposed to do, and we should never get so good a peace as we might have now, or even last year.

May 9 1762: (anecdotes) Mr. Hamilton, Lord Halifax's Secretary, said he believed he should soon be employed;[770] that it was over with the Duke of Newcastle; that Oswald and Elliot were persuading Lord Bute to set his Grace at defiance and be minister, but his Lordship hesitated and was afraid.[771]

Rigby said it was over with [the] Duke of Newcastle—that they should have all the speakers in the House of Commons, and Lord Bute would be strong enough to carry all before him.

My friend[772] told [the] Duke of Cumberland that they [the King and Bute] hated me now more than any body. They thought they could have done what they pleased with me, but finding I had an opinion of my own they were very angry, but were desirous of keeping me as they thought my name might be of service to them.

---

[769] The latest despatches from St. Petersburg and Berlin indicated that Czar Peter III and Frederick II were planning to extend the Continental war by an attack on Denmark. Mitchell to Bute, 2, 21 Apr. 1762, S.P.F. 90/80. Fear of subsidising such a venture decided the Cabinet against a renewal of the Prussian subsidy.

[770] William Gerard Hamilton, M.P., Chief Secretary to Halifax, the Lord Lieutenant of Ireland, was aiming at a rich sinecure.

[771] Elliot and Oswald, both lords of the Treasury, had supported Bute and Grenville against Newcastle over the vote of credit. Newcastle to Hardwicke, 2 May 1762, Add. MSS. 32938, ff. 20-1.

[772] Almost certainly Viry. Cumberland to Devonshire, 22 Feb. 1762; Viry to Devonshire, 20 May 1762, Chatsworth MSS. 332/14, 580/23.

The Queen came up as I was talking to Lady Augusta and asked who the King was speaking to. I told her Lord Dillon.[773]

Lady Augusta said: 'He speaks French better than anybody.'

I replied: 'He ought to speak well for he has lived [a] great part of his life in France and I believe has now a regiment in their service.'

The Queen said: 'Then probably he is a Jacobite.'

I answered: 'He was a Roman Catholick and when there *was any such* he most likely was one.'

The Queen said: 'I imagine Colonel Graham[774] that came to fetch me was one for he quarrelled one day at Strelitz with Madame ———[775] for abusing the Jacobites: pray, was he so or not?'

I answered that I did not know anything about him, for I had never heard there was such a man till he was sent to Strelitz. Lady Augusta said after the Queen was gone that she knew the history of his being turned out of the Dutch service and dismissed from among the contractors in Prince Ferdinand's army on suspicion of his being a spy, but she had never heard of his being a Jacobite.[776]

I told her it was reported he had been in the Rebellion, but I knew nothing of him.

July 23 1762:[777] The letters that gave notice abroad of the change in the ministry gave no assurances that there would be no change in the system.[778] It was expected there would have been either an immediate peace with France or a giving up the Continent. The first has not happened because France flattered herself to take advantage of our disunion and that our troops would be recalled from Germany.[779] Prince Ferdinand's success[780] and the difficulty of recalling the troops has prevented the other.

The alliance between the Heriditary Prince and Lady Augusta will take place. Finding that the demand of a separate establishment during the life of his father might be interpreted as an interested view, he leaves the whole to H.M., and only desired that he might shew

[773] 11th Viscount Dillon.

[774] Colonel David Graeme, M.P.

[775] Presumably a lady of the court at Strelitz.

[776] Graeme's parents were Jacobite, though he missed personal involvement in the '45. Contracts with Prince Ferdinand's army secured by Bute for him and Oswald were cancelled in 1760 for dishonesty. After George III's accession Bute had Graeme promoted full colonel in the British army and in June sent him to escort the future Queen from Strelitz. Namier and Brooke, ii. 523-4.

[777] Devonshire enters the events of 23 July after his entries for 29 July. The editors have transposed in the interests of chronology.

[778] The routine announcement sent to all ministries abroad, announcing Newcastle's resignation and Bute's appointment as First Lord of the Treasury, did not give the customary assurances that existing policies would continue. Grenville succeeded Bute as Secretary of State for the North.

[779] Yorke to Bute (most secret), 19 Jan. 1762, S.P.F. 84/495.

[780] On 24 June Prince Ferdinand had decisively defeated the French at Wilhelmsthal.

himself to the Princess and know she had no objection to him before the affair was absolutely fixed.[781] Prince Ferdinand's success has created great uneasiness in France and made the desire of peace still stronger. Spain is the great obstacle. The Court of Vienna is tired of the war, her [Maria Theresa's] pride and uneasiness at her disappointment[782] must have some time to subside, but she will soon wish to return to her old friends.[783] They don't approve of the war against Portugal.

July 23 1762: The French are so circumstanced that they must either fight or retire, not having a good communication with their magazines.

July 27 1762: The Duke of Bedford in extream good humour with the Duke of Newcastle, hopes they shall never break, and thinks Mr. Pitt the last man with whom his Grace should join.[784] The Duke of Bedford was unwilling to talk as to the negotiation but by what he dropped it now stands thus: he said he thought we were agreed with France, they consented to take Miguelon and St. Pierre, and France agreed to everything we asked but insisted to have St. Lucia restored to them, to which we consented;[785] that everything taken since the commencement of the last negotiation was to be restored, which would comprehend Newfoundland. It was asked if the Havanna was included in that: he answered no, that we had nothing to do with Spain in that negotiation, that our affairs with them did not go well. They talked high and had made some extravagant proposal about the logwood; that he believed the intention was to agree with France, and to insist that they should not any way assist Spain or enter into the war with Spain in consequence of the Family Treaty.[786] His Grace said the Duc de Choiseul had declared he would not conclude without Spain,[787] but hoped that when France saw what we were ready to do with them, they would not then stand out purely for the sake of Spain. If this is the true state of the case, the peace may be at some distance. (our

[781] The marriage between Charles, Hereditary Prince of Brunswick, the son of Duke Charles I, and the King's eldest sister Augusta was solemnized in 1764.

[782] At not recovering Silesia.

[783] Intelligence from Paris, Cressener to Grenville, 5 and 13 July 1762, S.P.F. 81/141. 12 [784] Various futile attempts were being made by friends common to Pitt and Newcastle to effect an alliance. H. Erskine to Bute, 14 June 1762, Bute MSS. (Cardiff) Bundle 5, No. 185; Namier, 331, 334, 341–2.

[785] The restitution of St. Lucia had been undertaken in a private letter from Bute and Egremont to Viry, with the knowledge of the King but without that of the Cabinet. The deception was kept up for a month, then stormy Cabinet meetings followed, Grenville and Egremont standing out for higher terms.

[786] Early in June Spain had made clear that she would treat only on the basis of the Spanish grievances, which was unacceptable. It was therefore decided to deal with France first and Spain separately. Shelburne MSS. 10, ff. 99–103.

[787] Choiseul to Egremont, 16 Apr. 1762, P.R.O. 30/47/1.

ministers) The Duke of Bedford said the ministers would not give over the hopes of it yet.

July 28 1762: Waited on the King, received very graciously. After talking of his health,[788] said he hoped still that we should have peace. He would tell me in great confidence that the French insisted on St. Lucia; that everybody was for letting them have it except one, who probably was *over ruled*; that there were difficulties
Mr. Grenville[789] about Spain. To be sure France would not say they would give them up, or not make their peace without them, though they might perhaps when they saw their own points given into, do it; that therefore he was against pressing them in a Memorial, but was for sending the Duke of Bedford[790] over with orders not to sign the Preliminaries, till he had assurances that they would not take part with Spain if our disputes could not be settled.

I agreed with the His Majesty and told him for one that I hoped he would if possible make peace, and that if it was not materially worse than what had been proposed before I left the Council,[791] that I would not only support it but endeavour to persuade other people to do the same.

He asked me what humour the Duke of Newcastle was in and what he would do. I replied that as far as I knew, he had not entered into any scheme of opposition, that some common friends of his and Mr. Pitt had proposed his joining with him, but that [he] had refused to listen to it. The King said: 'I am persuaded he will not enter into an opposition; he may find fault with measures but not go farther.' When he saw him he seemed to be in good humour.

I answered, that he could not be pleased in having been drove out of the ministry in the manner he was; that a person who had been a minister for so many years would find his time hang heavy upon his hands, consequently would grow uneasy, and in that case it would be impossible to say what part he might take. The King started when I named the junction of the Duke of Newcastle and Mr. Pitt.

The King said the terms would not be worse, but rather better than what had been proposed when we attended. I observed to him that making the Missisippy the boundary would make the peace better than what Mr. Pitt proposed. The King said France agreed to it, only desired to have New Orleans.

Viry called to: seemed much out of humour: said if we had been at

[788] The King had been ill the previous month.

[789] At the Cabinet of 28 July, Grenville agreed to surrender St. Lucia provided France withheld support from Spain. *Grenville*, i. 449 et seq.

[790] Bedford was appointed plenipotentiary to sign the peace preliminaries on 1 Sept. and Ambassador extraordinary on 12 Nov.

[791] Following Newcastle's resignation on 26 May.

Council the peace had been made long ago; that these people did not know how to make it and were above asking advice; that he had nothing to do with it; said George Greenville ruled the whole and that Lord Bute was a dupe to him.

July 29 1762: Count Viry came and shewed me the Preliminaries for the peace sent from France,[792] corresponding to what the King told me and the Duke of Bedford's account to the Duke of Newcastle.[793] I asked him about Spain and how those difficulties were to be got over. He said all that would end right; that the unreasonable propositions were Grimaldi's which Choiseul had got him to make in order to commence a negotiation. That he, Viry, had wrote to Monsieur Solar on the three points of dispute; that the Fishery should remain as it did by the Treaty of Utrecht; that we should evacuate our possessions on the method being settled of our cutting the logwood, and as to the prizes, that they should be determined in the same manner, as France settled theirs. That he had proposed[794] that the Duc de Choiseul should send that Paper to Spain as his own idea for settling their disputes with England, which he has done by a private messenger[795] with a letter to the King of Spain himself and another to Wall; Viry persuaded that if Spain was not reasonable, France would conclude without them. *That France had no engagements with Spain, but on those three points and consequently not obliged to go on with the war if a reasonable satisfaction was offered.*

He [Viry] then said that matters must be made up between the Duke of Newcastle and Lord Bute; that the latter wished to have him for his friend, and would give any honourable employment he should like.[796] I replied that was very idle language after he had turned him out; that they disagreed so much upon measures that they could never come together. He said when the peace was made there would then be no disagreement, for the Continent must not be abandoned, threw all the blame on George Greenville; said if he had forseen that we should have retired from Council, he [Viry] would have had nothing to do with the negotiation. *They [Bute and Egremont] were ignorant of business and above asking others to inform them.* That both Secretarys[797] had used him [Viry] very ill; that they were united and Lord Egremont thought if Lord Bute could not stand his ground that he [Grenville] should then be the first man. That he [Grenville] had

[792] Contained in Choiseul to Solar, 21 July 1762, Shelburne MSS. 10, ff. 361-75.

[793] Newcastle to Devonshire, 27 July 1762, Chatsworth MSS. 182/266.

[794] Viry to Solar, 22 May 1762, Shelburne MSS. 10, ff. 235-9.

[795] Choiseul to Solar, 28 May 1762, Shelburne MSS. 10, ff. 284-97.

[796] Hoping to involve Newcastle in responsibility for the impending peace treaty, Bute during July and Aug. tried to inveigle him into becoming Lord Privy Seal, which Hardwicke soundly vetoed.

[797] Egremont and Grenville.

been a constant enemy of the Duke of Newcastle, and encouraged Lord Bute to quarrell, intimated that if the agreement could not be made with the Duke of Newcastle, Lord Bute would be forced to come to Pitt, and that George Greenville would be for it.

July 30 1762: The Council met on the French Preliminaries[798] the 25th [26].[799] Lord Bute opened it by saying that he imagined the peace was made and that they should immediately send somebody over to France to sign it. Lord President[800] instantly objected; said he thought it very far from concluded; that nothing was done with Spain and till those disputes were accommodated, there could be no peace with France; for if you gave them up their seamen (prisoners), they might immediately join the Spaniards; that his Lordship might be duped by France but by God he would not. The whole Council were of Lord Granville's opinion against Lord Bute, so his Lordship was forced to yield. However they met on the 27th [28],[801] he talked to the different Lords and got them to come in to the proposition of the Duke of Bedford to go over to sign the Peace, provided France would give assurances of not assisting Spain if they would not hearken to peace.

I had a great deal of conversation with Mr. Fox, found him strong for Lord Bute.[802] He owned that the run against him both in Town and Country was very great; said if peace was not made it would be impossible for him to hold it.[803] If he could get the Peace he perhaps might: if not, he must come to the Duke of Newcastle, say he would give up business and return to Groom of the Stole. I replied if that was his scheme he must do it soon, for if once the riot began it would be too late, for what minister would venture to leave a man so near the King, who would have it in his power to ruin that minister whenever he had a mind? *Mr. Fox said if any set of people refused to let him [Bute] remain about the King's person, it would hurt them with the public.* I told Mr. Fox plainly that I was afraid he had contributed more than any man to persuade Lord Bute to take this rash and ambitious step, which in the end would undo him and create great vexation and uneasiness to the King, by holding a language that the power of the Crown could do everything. He acknowledged it was his opinion and that he had often in company held that discourse, but never to Lord Bute.

[798] Of 21 July, see p. 174, n. 792.

[799] 25th in MS. but see the minutes dated 26 July in Add. MSS. 34713, ff. 110-12. Bute to Egremont, 26 July, Add. MSS. 36797, ff. 6-7.

[800] Granville.

[801] 27th in MS. but in fact the meeting was on 28 July. Minute in Stowe MSS. S.T. 103a. George III to Bute, 28 July 1762, Sedgwick, 128-9.

[802] 'An Account of the Duke of Devonshire's Conversation', 31 July 1762, Add. MSS. 33000, ff. 95-100.

[803] For Bute to continue at the Treasury.

I then told him [Fox] I was sorry to see him attached so strongly there, that he was much abused for it, that he was going contrary to the opinion of those he had always acted with and to the person [Cumberland] to whom he had so great obligations. He said he did not apprehend that the Duke of Cumberland took it ill of him; that he differed with H.R.H. as to the German war but that he saw no alteration in the Duke's behaviour. I said he might not shew it to him, but that it was very visible to me that he was much hurt to see him quit him; that he had complained that he was gone over entirely to Lord Bute. I reminded him of the Duke's answer when he asked him if he might support the peace in the House of Commons; the answer was: '*Mr. Fox, I shall not be obliged to any friend of mine that supports this administration which I do not approve of.*'

Mr. Fox was much hurt with this conversation, said he had no engagements with Lord Bute, that he sometimes sent for him and asked him his opinion on particular points, but never consulted him as to any arrangements. That he should be against the German war, and support the Peace, and as to anything else he should act as he thought right. What had passed about the Duke dwelt upon his mind for he returned to it continually the whole evening.

July 31 1762: Dined at Claremont, the Duke of Newcastle said Lord Temple had desired Lord Lincoln to give him leave to come to Claremont; that it was to be sure with a view to find out what disposition he was in, and would in all probability make some proposition to unite with him. That therefore it was necessary to know the opinion of his friends, as he would take no part but what would be agreable to the Duke of Cumberland, Lord Hardwicke and myself.

I told him I thought it would be very wrong in him to make any agreement at present. That Mr. Pitt and Lord Temple would be for violent measures and nothing would satisfye them but forcing the King as they had done his grandfather,[804] by a thorough opposition, which as there were as yet no overt acts of the present ministry, must be looked upon as a factious measure to overturn the administration in order to succeed them. That my opinion was that his Grace should keep himself unengaged but give such an answer as should not make them despair; that he might say that he had retired upon measures; that therefore he would keep himself at liberty till he saw what turn things took and the sense of the nation and the Parliament when it met. That most probably questions would arise that would bring them together and then would be the time to talk; that his Grace should be cautious not to let them despair, lest he should throw them into Lord Bute's hands, and yet not to commit himself. Lord Hardwicke approved of this advice.

---

[804] Devonshire returns to his old theme in respect of events in 1756–7.

We then talked of what was to be done if Lord Bute should come to treat with his Grace. He said he would not go again into the Treasury. That if I would not take it, Lord Rockingham must go there,[805] with Mr. Legge for his Chancellor of the Exchequer, Lord Hardwicke President, Lord Sandwich Secretary of State and himself Privy Seal. If we agreed with Mr. Pitt, he the other Secretary and Lord Temple Ireland. Mr. Legge was there ready to do anything to destroy Lord Bute.

[   ][806] told me that Lord Bute was ill at present with the Queen. I take for granted it is for having made Lady Augusta's match[807] which disappoints her view for her brother.[808]

They [the King and Bute] did not know whether I was not come to resign.[809] They intended to be civil to me but not to trust me with anything.

I told the person[810] that I heard the King was much hurt with the papers,[811] and said I thought them infamous. They replied they had *not read them*, when they once knew a fact they had no curiosity; said the P[rince?][812] was out of spirits, pale and not well. Thought I was sorry a great friend[813] was too violent.

Sept 21 1762: Windsor Castle: The King said that Monsieur Nivernois[814] seemed to be a very fair, honest man and very desirous of peace, that he had made no objections to any material points but on trifles, such as asking that the clergy might have more time allowed them to retire from Canada than that granted to the other inhabitants. He made objections to what had been agreed about the Mobile but said it was not on their account but at the instigation of the Spaniards.[815] But that he had been told, it was impossible to recede; that then he said, pray write word to my Court, for I come only to sign, not to treat.

Lord Bute had told the Duke of Nivernois that if peace was made it must be done before the meeting of the Parliament for when they met

---

[805] A very early forecast that Rockingham might become Prime Minister, which he did in July 1765.

[806] Blank in MS.

[807] With the Prince of Brunswick.

[808] Prince Ernest of Mecklenburg-Strelitz.

[809] Devonshire's resignation was constantly expected.

[810] Unidentified.

[811] 'The battle of the weeklies', a journalistic contest between newspapers favourable or unfavourable to Bute and the proposed peace.

[812] Not identified but presumably a member of the royal family.

[813] Probably Fox, who was threatening the friends of Newcastle.

[814] Duke of Nivernois, French ambassador for signing the peace preliminaries.

[815] The Court of Madrid was indignant at not being informed of the arrangement made by Choiseul respecting the Mississippi boundary, which was drawn so as to include Mobile in British territory, thus affording access to the Gulf of Mexico.

and money was raised the people of England would have blood for their money and would not bear to hear of peace. The Duke of Nivernois had said that the Duke of Choiseul had full powers from Spain[816] and yet the only difficulty was on the part of that Court. I observed to the King that, that looked like chicane, and advised him if possible to have the whole settled before the meeting of Parliament,[817] for there would be Addresses and such variety of opinions as would throw everything into confusion. The morning the King left Windsor[818] he said there were letters come from the Duke of Bedford[819] which he had not seen, only a private one to Lord Bute[820] in which the Duke said he had sent over a most glorious peace and hoped there would be no objection made to it here.

Sept 24: Dined with the Duke of Cumberland at the Lodge,[821] told him of the warmth of Lord Temple and the disposition of our people to run into his measures; that I would concur in removing Lord Bute but would never run to the lengths that I was persuaded Mr. Pitt and his Lordship would be for to force the King; that it was much to be wished that Lord Bute would foresee his danger and retire in time; that he might be suffered to remain about the King's person. Whereas if the riot was once begun they would never rest till they drove him to the Isle of Bute. The Duke against violent measures; we agreed he should talk to Mr. Fox[822] and desire him to give Lord Bute notice.

Sept 30: Answer to the Duke of Cumberland: thoroughly satisfied with the reason that induced your R.H. to change your opinion; can easily imagine Lord Bute's eyes not yet sufficiently opened to see his danger and agree that there are not grounds sufficient to authorise a proposition in form; only afraid that if it is deferred the attack will come so strong that it will not be in the power of those who wish to avoid violence to prevent it.

Oct 1 1762: The Duke of Cumberland displeased with Mr. Fox for having gone farther in a conversation with Lord Bute than he was

[816] This was not strictly true. Spain had given her consent to an exchange of plenipotentiaries between Britain and France, and Grimaldi was authorised to participate. At the end of Sept. Charles III, chastened by news of the fall of Havana, agreed that France negotiate on his behalf.

[817] Due to meet in Nov.

[818] Of 26 Sept. Later that day he examined the despatches. George III to Bute, 26 Sept. 1762, Sedgwick, 137-8.

[819] Bedford's despatches of 15, 19 and 21 Sept. 1762 (all received on 24 Sept.), S.P.F. 78/252.

[820] Bedford to Bute, 20 Sept. 1762, Bute MSS. (Cardiff) Bundle 5, No. 160. Bute's reply of 28 Sept. Add. MSS. 36797, ff. 11-13.

[821] Windsor Lodge.

[822] On 28 Sept. Cumberland saw Fox and commissioned him to find out from Bute whether he had any intention of offering Newcastle office or of making an advance to Pitt. Fox saw Bute early in the afternoon of Thursday 29 Sept. Bute emphatically denied any intention of coalescing with Newcastle or Pitt.

directed, having told him that though H.R.H. wished for peace, he had rather any other person had been the author.[823] That Lord Bute had complained much that H.R.H. was his enemy, he did not know why. The Duke intends, if he has an opportunity, to explain to his Lordship that Mr. Fox had gone too far. But that he would own to him, that as long as his Lordship had confined himself to what might reasonably be expected by one who had the honour to be distinguished to so high a degree with H.M.'s favour, H.R.H. was desirous and did shew him all the marks of regard which were proper, and should have wished to have consulted or employed him in any business which he might have had [with] the King. But that he could not approve the sole power and direction of the affairs of this kingdom which his Lordship now exercised, *and that* by the exclusion of all those who had been old servants of his Family, and had shewed the most distinguished zeal and attachment to this government, and that H.R.H. did not think any administration proper for this country where those old friends and experienced ministers were excluded.

Mr. Fox had acquainted the Duke that the Duke of Bedford had transmitted a project of Preliminaries[824] which he hoped would be approved, and that in it the Havannah,[825] if taken, was to be given up without compensation.[826] Lord Bute was strongly for agreeing. Mr. Greenville insisted strongly that the Havannah would be taken, and that we should have some equivalent for it. Lord Bute doubted the taking of it and adhered to his opinion. Mr. Greenville likewise adhered and he and Lord Egremont declared they would not sign any treaty where there was not some compensation for the restitution of the Havannah.[827]

Mr. Grenville proposed to Lord Bute that the Dukes of Devonshire and Newcastle and Lord Hardwicke should be desired to attend the Cabinet Council on this occasion. Lord Bute rejected the proposal

[823] A reference to the following passage in Fox to Cumberland, 30 Sept. 1762: 'I told him [Bute] that your Royal Highness always was and would be very sensible of the King's civilities, for you loved him; and that I believed your Royal Highness had rather any minister made a good peace than his Lordship, but I was persuaded you had rather even his Lordship made it than that it should not be made at all.' Albemarle, *Memoirs of Rockingham*, i. 130-1.

[824] In his despatch of 24 Sept. 1762 (received 28 Sept), S.P.F. 78/253. George III to Bute, 28 Sept. 1762, Sedgwick, 138-40.

[825] News of the capture of Havana reached London on 28 Sept.

[826] A reference to Article XVIII, which provided for the return of Havana in the event of capture, and for the Spanish evacuation of Portugal.

[827] Bute would have accepted concessions over logwood but under pressure from Egremont and Grenville demanded either Florida or Puerto Rico. Left to themselves, Egremont and Grenville would have insisted on both. Shelburne to Fox, 1 Sept. 1762, Add. MSS. 51379, f. 211. Egremont to Bute, end of Sept. 1762, Bute MSS. (Cardiff) Bundle 7, No. 168.

with some seeming contempt, and said he could assure him that not one of them would come, and besides he had no right to summons two of them.[828] Lord Bute in mentioning Mr. Greenville's opposition said it was not ill intention, it was cowardice. What his Lordship's yielding to Mr. Greenville afterwards, (though very right), was, I won't pretend to say. Lord Bute found himself obliged to submit[829] and orders are sent to the Duke of Bedford to insist upon some equivalent,[830] and that thought of at present is that Spain should yield Florida and Fort St. Augustin[831] to Great Britain. That would certainly be a very valuable acquisition to this country, but whether a sufficient equivalent for the Havannah which makes us masters of all the Spanish West Indies I will not pretend to say. I remember in the last Spanish war it was much debated and greatly desired, and it was even thought by some that Florida and Fort St. Augustin would be a good exchange for Gibraltar.

Mr. Fox argued that is was impossible for Lord Bute to hold it [administration] when he could not govern his own people, and it was said that he had but one real friend in the Council which was my Lord Halifax. He [Fox] said that if Lord Bute had conducted himself wisely, had carried his collegues along with him, he might have supported it, that neither the Duke of Newcastle nor Mr. Pitt gained ground. On the contrary, many of the Duke of Newcastle's friends were gone over to Lord Bute. That his Lordship had great Levees at the beginning, and that he (Mr. Fox) frequently saw some of the Duke of Newcastle's friends at Lord Bute's house. He said that Touchet[832] and Linwood[833] said *they* had got *their* money.[834] However Mr. Fox is strongly of opinion that Lord Bute cannot hold it and I hear some of his Lordship's friends are of the same way of thinking, and it has been whispered that Lord Bute himself had said that he found it would not do, and that he should be glad to have his Gold Key again.[835] It is supposed that the Duke of Bedford will be extremely dissatisfyed with

[828] Newcastle and Hardwicke.

[829] Early in Oct., Grenville was pushed out of the Cabinet and relegated to First Lord of the Admiralty. Halifax succeeded him as Secretary of State whilst Fox became Leader of the Commons with a seat in the Cabinet. Notwithstanding at the Cabinet meetings of 22 and 25 Oct., it was decided that in return for Havana Spain must cede either Florida or Puerto Rico. Minute of Cabinet Council, St. James, 22 Oct. 1762, P.R.O. 30/47/21. Shelburne MSS. 12, ff. 139–40; Bute to Bedford, 24 Oct. 1762, *Bedford* iii. 137–8.

[830] Egremont to Bedford, 26 Oct. 1762 (counter project enclosed), Shelburne MSS. 12, ff. 105–32.

[831] On the east coast of Florida.

[832] Samuel Touchet, M.P.   [833] Nicholas Linwood, M.P.

[834] Touchet had been allowed to subscribe £200,000 of the new loan at profit of about 10%. Shelburne to Bute, 15 Sept. 17 Oct. 1762, Bute MSS. Nos. 44, 46.

[835] As Groom of the Stole.

Lord Bute for having given him up to Mr. Grenville,[836] as he may call it, and not supported his project[837] which he says he had brought about with great difficulty and values himself much upon.[838]

The Duke [Cumberland] was at Court on Thursday[839] to compliment the King upon the success of the Havannah. H.M. desired to see him in the Closet, expressed his satisfaction at the event,[840] but there did not appear any very great marks of real joy and satisfaction.[841] The King told the Duke he wanted to speak to him upon the present state of the peace and to have his advice upon it, and was very gracious throughout the whole conversation which lasted an hour. The King went through every Article of the Preliminaries.

Article 1   Limits of Canada: The King explained that part as we have heard it. The Duke said he thought that satisfactory.

Art. 2   Fishery in the Gulph of St. Laurence and the Banks of Newfoundland: The King stated it thus, that the French were to have liberty to fish in the *River*[842] St. Laurence and mentioned no provision that they should not come within a certain distance of our coasts;[843] that the French were to have the islands of St. Pierre and Miguelon; that it was to be stipulated in the Treaty that we should constantly have commissaries there to inspect them, and to see that they should not erect fortifications et cetera. But the French hoped or insisted that though this was so stipulated, His Majesty[844] would previously give his royal word that he would send no commissaries thither. H.R.H. objected very strongly to every part of this Article and told the King, (but in that I [Newcastle][845] was mistaken as I took the liberty of telling him), that he understood the French were

[836] Over compensation for Havana, which Bedford considered unnecessary.

[837] The preliminary peace treaty, which he had forwarded in his despatch of 24 Sept., see p. 179, n. 824.

[838] Bedford to Egremont, 24 Sept. 1762, S.P.F. 78/253, ff. 113-14.

[839] On 30 Sept., after the Drawing Room.

[840] The capture of Havana.

[841] See Newcastle's memorandum, 'most secret', of 3 Oct. 1762, Add. MSS. 32943, ff. 28 et seq.

[842] The concession to France did not include the right to fish in the St. Lawrence. Either Cumberland misunderstood the King or the King misunderstood the preliminaries.

[843] The limits within which French fishing was forbidden under the definitive Treaty were three leagues off the mainland and the islands of the Gulf of St. Lawrence and fifteen leagues off the coasts of Cape Breton Island.

[844] George III.

[845] Devonshire's account of the conversation between Cumberland and the King is drawn from Newcastle's memorandum of a subsequent conversation between himself and the Duke. The first person singular therefore is Newcastle referring to himself, a consideration which applies throughout these final pages of the Diary.

to have no farther liberty of fishing in those seas but what was granted them by the Treaty of Utrecht upon the Banks of Newfoundland.

I [Newcastle] told the Duke that we, (Mr. Pitt with us), had agreed to a certain liberty of fishing in the gulph provided they did not come so near as to infringe upon the rights of the coasts *attenant aux dites cotes*. But that I did not remember that we ever allowed expressly a liberty to fish in the River St. Lawrence. That being much narrower seems to me to be the most liable to objection, but of this I am not positive. H.R.H. then expressed to the King his disapprobation and indeed his indignation at the proposal, that His Majesty should give his royal word not to exercise a power given by Treaty for the security of the performance of it. He humbly beseeched the King in the strongest manner neither upon this nor any other occasion relating to this treaty to give his royal word. And urged it with this strong expression: 'Let the King of France give his word and break it if he pleases, but I hope your Majesty will never be induced to do it.' The Duke was afraid he had not made that impression he could wish upon this point, which makes me afraid it has been already promised by the ministers.[846]

Art. 3   Senegal and Goree stated as we know; the Duke no objection.

Art. 4   East Indies: The King did not explain the stipulations relating to them sufficiently to the Duke for him to form a judgement on them. I am told though the ministry give out that the East India Company are satisfied. The contrary of it is true; Sulivan[847] and the deputy chairman Dorrien,[848] friends of Lord Bute, say so. But the Chairman Mr. Rous[849] and the Company are very far from being pleased.[850]

Art. 5   Dunkirk, the Low Countries, and the renewal of the Treaty of Utrecht: The King seemed happy that they had

---

[846] Ultimately Bedford was allowed to give up the 'inspection raisonable' with regard to no fortifications on St. Pierre and Miquelon and accept Louis XV's *parole royale*.

[847] Laurence Sulivan, M.P., Chairman of the East India Company, 1758-9, 1760-2.

[848] John Dorrien.

[849] Thomas Rous, Chairman of the East India Company from Apr. 1762.

[850] For the differences between the Company and the government over the peace terms, see L.S. Sutherland, *The East India Company in Eighteenth-Century Politics* (Oxford, 1962), 89-100. It was agreed between Britain and France that the posts the French had held in 1749 be restored, with a 'no troops or fortifications' clause in respect of Chandernagore.

procured better terms with regard to Dunkirk than either were obtained by the Treaty of Aix la Chapelle, or than what we had agreed to accept.[851] For it was now to be put upon the Treaty of Utrecht *only* with this difference, that the cuvette should be allowed if the Engineers reported that no other consequence would arise from it but the preservation of the health of the town, for which the cuvette was necessary. The Duke then desired to know what security was to be given for the Low Countries. The King replied France engages not to retain Ostend and Nieuport. But what I can find [is] that engagement is only in general, that France shall evacuate Ostend, Nieuport, Wesel, Cleeves et cetera, and nothing more is said of the Low Countries. H.R.H. pressed the King upon the renewal of the Treaty of Utrecht, the only security England had for the guaranty of France of the Protestant succession. The King said that would be taken care of but nothing positive as to the renewal of that Treaty, and rather avoided giving a direct answer, which looks as if that was not done which appears to be so necessary.[852]

Art. 6   Relates to the King of Prussia, the evacuation of Wesel and Cleves, and the assistance that England and France are to give to their allies in Germany. As I understood the Duke, the French are to evacuate Wesel and Cleves[853] and to shew that the union subsists between France and the House of Austria in its full strength, France proposes that the King should give the same subsidy of £670,000[854] to the King of Prussia and they will continue their subsidy (the sum of which is not mentioned) to the House of Austria during the war between those two powers. The King said the whole had been communicated to the King of Prussia,[855] who was very well satisfied since the former Treaty had not been renewed, but the King himself made great objections, as it would oblige him to give the subsidy, which he was not engaged nor disposed to do. And this only because France was engaged to give their subsidy

---

[851] This point is unclear. According to the preliminaries, Dunkirk was to be restored to the state laid down by the Treaty of Aix-la-Chapelle, and a British engineer was to report upon how far the works, especially the new cunette (canal), conformed with that Treaty.

[852] Under Article II of the final Peace, the Treaty of Utrecht was renewed.

[853] The Prussian territories on the Rhine.

[854] Under the terms of the Treaty of Westminster of 1758, which had lapsed in Apr. 1762. The subsidy had been cancelled on Apr. 30. See p. 170.

[855] Grenville to Mitchell, 14 July 1762 (with enclosures), S.P.F. 90/80.

to the Empress Queen during the war, which was not his case.[856] The King said that the Duke of Brunswick and the Landgrave of Hesse had been acquainted with the whole and were very well satisfied.

Spain: As to the terms and conditions of the treaty with Spain, the King began upon the subject of the taking of [the] Havana and declared strongly that he was for some equivalent for it. [He] hinted at the difference of opinion among his ministers[857] but that he was for some compensation. [He] squinted at Mr. Grenville, not in a very respectful manner. The Duke applauded his resolution and shewed H.M. how necessary it was for his honour and good of the nation. The King hinted at Florida. The Duke gave no opinion as to the particular equivalent to be insisted upon. He begged to know of the King what was to be done as to the Family Compact. He could not find that there was to be any provision about it, but that there was to be an Article (which the King seemed satisfied with), to the following purpose: that all our Treaties with Spain were to be renewed, but that at the end of one year, either party should be at liberty to renew or not any one of the old Treaties, or to make any new one.[858]

I should imagine this must be a mistake, for such a barefaced imposition could not be accepted by any one English minister whatever, for it is no less than putting it in the power of Spain to dissolve all our Treaties of commerce and friendship with them, and leave the Family Compact in its full force. The Duke takes it as stated here, and expressed his high disapprobation of it to the King, and thought it the most monstrous proposal that ever was made, but made no impression.

It was either on this Article, or in relation to the subsidy to the King of Prussia or the evacuation of Wesel, that the King was again to make

---

[856] In the preliminaries, signed on 3 Nov., Bedford on his own responsibility accepted the payment by France of subsidy arrears to Austria. Unknown to Bedford, by the Convention of Fontainebleau of 5 Nov., French military supplies were to be left in Prussian towns for Austrian use whilst the old subsidy was to be maintained and new payments granted, disguised as 'arrear payments', if the war continued into 1763. By a peace agreement with Maria Theresa signed at Hubertusberg on 15 Feb. 1763, Frederick II retained Silesia and his territories on the Rhine were restored, which also rendered the subsidy issue academic.

[857] See p. 180.

[858] In the definitive Treaty concluded at Paris on 10 Feb. 1763, the commercial treaties between Britain and Spain were renewed unconditionally. Charles III of Spain greatly disliked these treaties, highly favourable as they were to Britain.

a promise or give his word.[859] The Duke took it up very high, and repeated his most earnest advice and request that H.M. would not give his word upon any occasion whatever relating to this Treaty. The Duke pleased with H.M.'s confidence and attention, but it did not alter his opinion upon any one point. He said he gave it according to his conscience without any personal considerations on any side, which he thought himself obliged to do when the King asked it of him. He [Cumberland] thinks there is an end of peace, for if our ministers insist upon Florida and St. Augustin as an equivalent, Spain will not agree but wait for the conquest of Portugal[860] to be exchanged against the Havannah.

He [Cumberland] said there must soon be an end of Lord Bute's administration and therefore it should be considered what should follow. He asked me whether I [Newcastle][861] could get the money for carrying on the war upon the extended plan. I told him I could not answer for it, but I was sure Lord Bute could not. I have since put the question to Mr. Walpole.[862] His answer was, that such a sum of money as would be necessary for the totality of the war could never be had, but where the moneyed men had a confidence in the stability and ability of the person to whom it would be lent, and that was not nor ever could be in Lord Bute. But if such persons[863] were at the head of the finances, and without screwing things up to the height perhaps that Mr. Pitt would have them, the administration were determined to break off for the present all negotiations and to resent the behaviour of France and Spain in this late negotiation and to insist upon more advantageous terms of peace in consideration of our late successes everywhere, that upon these considerations only, he thought the money might be had, taking advantage of the present general dislike to the terms of peace.

The Duke of Cumberland seems softened as to Mr. Pitt and Mr. Pitt has said to his creatures or intimates, that no one in this country is fit to be at the head of affairs but the Duke of Cumberland.[864] Duke of Newcastle of opinion that Mr. Pitt made that declaration more from dislike and contempt of others than any predilection for the Duke.

The Bedfords have said that the King told the Duke of Bedford that he intended to recall Sir Joseph Yorke from the Hague, for he was a

---

[859] Article XVI, under which George III gave his *parole royale* not to lend Prussia military assistance.

[860] The Spanish invasion of Portugal miscarried.

[861] A hint that Newcastle might return to head administration.

[862] Thomas Walpole, M.P.

[863] A reference to Newcastle and the old Whigs.

[864] Which occurred in July 1765, when Cumberland formed the first Rockingham administration which he managed until his death on the 31 Oct. following.

friend of the Duke of Newcastle's and informed him of everything.[865]
When Lord Bute was spoke to about it he said: 'No, he is a friend of
the Duke of Newcastle's. I won't begin with him. If the Duke of
Newcastle begins[866] he must take the consequences.'

I have reason to think that Lord Bute has said he was very glad of
our success at the Havannah, but that he wished it had not come so
soon by two or three days. That is, in other words, that we had
concluded a peace without taking the advantage of it. I believe such
a thing was never said before by an English minister but they copy the
Treaty of Utrecht throughout. Sir F. Gosling[867] of the City said that
orders were gone to the Duke of Bedford to propose to France to sign
immediately a separate peace with them, provided they would consent
to leave all our acquisitions made either upon France or Spain, and
all the French and Spanish seamen, in our hands till the general peace
is made with both: each in the meantime to withdraw their armies
from Germany except the French garrison of Wesel and Cleves.

[865] Yorke was not recalled but remained Ambassador at the Hague until 1780.

[866] To conduct a parliamentary opposition.

[867] Sir Francis Gosling was a partner in Gosling and Sharpe, bankers of Fleet St., who
handled much of the affairs of Robert Clive. Gosling was to be an ally to Clive in the
Court of Proprietors of the East India Company. L. S. Sutherland, op. cit., 102, 105,
117, 125.

INDEX